THE BLACK COW'S FOOTPRINT

Manufactured in the United States of America
♾This book is printed on acid-free paper.
C 5 4 3 2 1

Complete Cataloging-in-Publication data
is available from the Library of Congress.

ISBN 978-0-252-03116-8

The Black Cow's Footprint

Time, Space, and Music in the Lives of the Kotas of South India

RICHARD K. WOLF

UNIVERSITY OF ILLINOIS PRESS
URBANA AND CHICAGO

Contents

Place through the Senses / Place and "Pollution" / Music, Emotion, and *Kēṛ* / The Kota House / A Structuring Structure? / Other Sites of Importance / Summary and Conclusions

4 **Knowing When and Where** 103

Gaining Knowledge, Controlling Time / Spatiotemporal Factors Affecting Musical Learning / Learning from Recordings / How Kotas Analyze Their Music / Loudness, Extension, and Structural Nostalgia / Musical Evaluation / How a Performer Shapes a Piece in Time: Composing, Singing, and Rendering / Listening Guide and Musical Discussion of Mundan's *Bugīr* Rendition (Fig. 8) / Discussion and Textual Analysis of Cindamani's Rendition / Comparison of Two Renditions / Responding and the Metaphor of a "Gap" / Cultural Implications of Admixture / What Gets Transmitted with Music: The Shape of a God Tune Narrative / Conclusion: The Where and When of Knowing

5 **Points of Anchor** 133

Anchoring Places of a Kota Culture Hero / Holidays / Tempo, Convergence, and Closure / Anchoring in Ceremonies / Anchoring of Larger Performance Units / Music and Eclipses / Metvāy's Version / The Temporality of Irregularity

6 **Affect and Subject** 162

Open Forms of Spacetime / Closed Forms of Spacetime / Ceremonies and Travel / Spatiotemporal Parameters of Status / Remembrance / Emotional Contour and Texture / Musical Emotion / Food / Shifting Sands / Affect and Subject

7 **Ceremonializing the Self** 186

Devr: The Kota God Ceremony / Music and Spacetime in the God Ceremony / Pac Tāv and Varldāv: The Green and Dry Funerals / The *Pac Tāv* / Bovine Sacrifices / At the Cremation Ground / The *Varldāv* / Bond-breaking / Conclusion: Models, Objects, and Mutability

Tables, Maps, Figures, and Photographs

Tables

Maps

Figures

Photographs
(16 pages, between pp. 64 and 65)

1 Panoramic view of Kolmēl village from the north

2 Dance day of Kolmēl god ceremony: men dancing on *ākēr pacāl* (both photos)

3 Naming ceremony. Elders and ritualist lined up according to rank
Two visitors kneel in deference to K. Puccan

4 Kota van with Kota bow and arrow insignia and god's name: Śrī Kambaṭṭarāyar
Kota fancy dance dress (*āṭ kupāc*)

5 Women dancing in *gagvāl*
Enlarged gagvāl

6 S. Cindamani in 2004

7 K. Mundan in 2004

8 Replacing the skins on a *par*

9 Making and playing the *pījl*

10 Women washing clothes by *ākēr* water tap, Kolmēl (2004)
Widow crouches in front of her husband's dry-funeral bier, surrounded by family

11 The millet-pouring tune plays thunderingly and the women begin to cry. Dry funeral, Kurgōj village, November 1997
The *mel pac mog* is instructed to touch the *koṭanm* millet to his forehead

12 The dry funeral procession commences
Procession to dry funeral ground: umbrella height and pole thickness proportional to age of deceased

13 Women dancing on the *ākēr pacāl* on the dance day of the god ceremony

14 Kaṇṇan (2004) wears headphones as he rehearses for the god ceremony
Musicians tighten the skins of their drums by the fire in the *gagvāl*

Guide to Abbreviations and Pronunciation

Abbreviations

Ko.	Kota
Ir.	Irula
Ta.	Tamil
S.	Sanskrit
EVS	Slips of paper upon which the linguist Murray B. Emeneau recorded lexical information during his Kota fieldwork. These contain etymological notes, usage contexts, and cross-references with the narratives eventually published in *Kota Texts*
CD #	Track number on Compact Disc (included in the American edition)
(Mandelbaum, Month Day, Year p.)	Dated page number reference in David G. Mandelbaum's fieldnotes
DEDR	*A Dravidian etymological dictionary*, 2nd ed.
DBIA	*Dravidian borrowings from Indo-Aryan*
OED	Oxford English Dictionary, online edition, *c*. 2002
TL	Tamil Lexicon
verb-	The stem for Kota verbs listed first in an entry in DEDR
x < y	Word "x" derives from language "y"
inc.	Dravidian verbal form of first person plural which includes the speaker and the listener

Pronunciation

Kota short vowels contrast with long vowels, which are indicated by a macron. Dental consonants contrast with retroflex consonants, which are indicated by an underdot. Retroflexes, which are stronger in Kota than in Hindi, for example, are pronounced with the tip of the tongue curled back on the roof of the mouth. Alveolar consonants, indicated by underscores, are pronounced with the tongue pressed against the bony ridge behind the teeth. "T" and "d" in American English are usually pronounced as alveolars. Nasals are pronounced in the same position as the consonant that follows, unless otherwise indicated. Aspiration is common but not phonemic in Kota.

Rough equivalents of Kota sounds, provided below, are based on American pronunciations of English words. Words from others languages, such as Tamil, are transliterated according to the Library of Congress system, except for spoken Tamil, which is indicated as such.

a "a" in "a lot"

ā "a" in "car"

i "i" in "pickle"; see also, note for "y"

ī "i" in "Tina"; see also, note for "y"

u "oo" in wood, but sometimes a cross between "i" in pickle and "oo" in wood.

ū "u" in "rude"

e "e" in "fetch"; in initial position, "ye" as in "yellow"

ē "a" in "gale" (pronounced without a dipthong); in initial position, "ya" as in Yale

o very short "o," roughly as in "open"; in initial position "wo" as in "swollen"

ō long "o" as in "tone" (without a dipthong); in initial position, "wo" as in "woeful" (without the dipthong)

k "k" in kite

g "g" in "go"

c varies between "c" in "cello" and "c" in "cell"

j varies between "j" in "jelly" and "dz" as in "red zipper"

ñ "n" in "sponge"; for Kota words, this letter appears only in conjunction with "c" or "j" ṭ roughly, the "t" in "curtain" (pronounce the "t" with the tongue further back)

ḍ roughly, "d" in "curd" (pronounce the "d" with the tongue further back)

ṛ roughly, "d" in "curdle"; this is a retroflex flap, very similar to ḍ, but shorter

r "r" in "roll" (sometimes rolled)

ṇ roughly, "n" in "urn" (pronounce the "n" with the tongue further back)

ṯ "t" in "put"

ḏ "d" in "thud"

ṉ "n" in "gun"

t "t" in "sit there!"

d first "d" in "bead thread"

n "n" in "gun" or with tongue placed according to the consonant that follows

p "p" in "peter"

b "b" in "but"

m "m" as in "many"

ḻ (Tamil only): pronounce the French "j" while smiling and saying "l" at the same time

ḷ roughly "l" in "curl" (pronounce the "l" much further back in the mouth)

l "l" in "let"

y "y" in "buy. Note: "y," "i," or "ī" appearing before or after a final stop tends to exert an effect on the opposite side of the consonant. So, for example, the pronunciation for the term *kuyt* (family) could range from *kuyte* to *kuti*. The name "Mathi" (whose spelling I retain in Anglicized form) could be pronounced Māyde or Mādi. The common Indian name Pārvatī is pronounced Pārvayt in Kota

ṣ (in words of Sanskrit origin) "sh" in "shoe"

ś (in words of Sanskrit origin) "s" in "Christian"

v "v" in "very" or "w" in "wall"

Acknowledgments

I benefitted from the assistance, advice, wisdom, and kindness of persons too many to name. My first debt is to the Kota community and in particular to my most generous Kota guides, teachers and hosts: R. Mathi, S. Raman, S. Cindamani, K. Puccan, Pa. Mathi, V. Mathi, Dr P. Varadharajan, R. Lakshmanan, L. Gunasekaran, T. Bellan, K. Mundan, and K.K. Bellan. R. Kamatn (a.k.a. Duryodhana) has been not only an unflagging research assistant, but also like a brother. Duryodhana journeyed to Chennai to review, refine, and critique the entire manuscript, which I summarized for him, section by section, in Tamil. Many friends and colleagues read drafts or sections of the book and provided helpful criticisms: Amy C. Bard, Stephen Blum, Mauro Calcagno, Charles Capwell, Martin Clayton, Joan Erdman, Michael Herzfeld, Paul Hockings, James Kippen, Frank Korom, David Lewin, Nancy Munn, Bruno Nettl, Kay Kaufman Shelemay, and several anonymous reviewers.

I owe much to David G. Mandelbaum, whom I never met, but whose fieldnotes, journals, recordings, and films taught me a great deal. The Bancroft Library, Michael Mandelbaum, and Ruth Mandelbaum all provided me access to parts of his collection. The Madras Government Museum, the Indiana University Archives of Traditional Music, the British Library Sound Archive, and the Archives and Research Centre for Ethnomusicology of the American Institute of Indian Studies permitted me to consult their collections, which contain historical recordings of Kota music.

Murray B. Emeneau has been immeasurably helpful with Dravidian linguistic matters and shared his original Kota fieldnotes with me. Judy McCulloh at the University of Illinois Press skillfully helped me negotiate the hurdles of the publishing process and Rukun Advani of Permanent Black quickly took on the project and efficiently saw the manuscript through production. Claire Krantz provided assistance with illustrations, William Noble shared his fine Nilgiri map, and Nazir Jairazbhoy and Amy Catlin gave me access to their Nilgiri fieldwork; Nazir allowed me to include his recording on the CD available in the American edition of this book. Deepak Albert assisted me in my initial fieldwork. A.C. Soundarrajan and Vatsala kindly hosted me for my first months in the Nilgiris and Ganapati helped me a great deal. A. Rajaram and Meena sustained me physically and intellectually. To all these friends, colleagues, and family I wish to express heartfelt thanks.

I gratefully acknowledge research funding from a US Department of Education Fulbright-Hays grant, and a grant from the American Institute of Indian Studies. The President and Fellows of Harvard University generously provided me leave for writing this book. I also benefitted from a fellowship year at the Radcliffe Institute for Advanced Study, an ACLS/SSRC/NEH International and Area Studies Fellowship made possible by funding from the National Endowment for the Humanities, and a summer stipend from the National Endowment for the Humanities.

Finally, I thrived on the love and support of my family, Amy C. Bard, Oliver Isaac Wolf, my parents, and my grandparents.

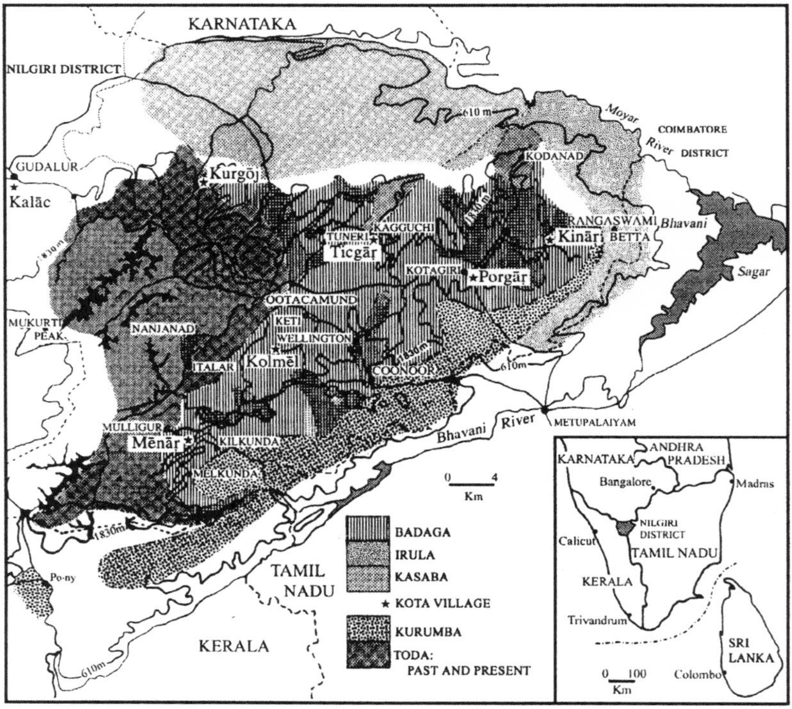

Map 1: Areas Related to Nilgiri Groups
(courtesy William Noble)

CHAPTER 1

Introduction: Of Kotas and Cows

"The first step to knowing who we are, is knowing *where* we are, and *when* we are." John Cleese, playing a school headmaster in the 1985 film *Clockwise*, admonished a recurrently tardy school organist with these stern words, which raise a general question: how *do* particular aspects of negotiating "where one is and when one is" contribute to the ways in which humans constitute themselves as individuals or groups? This book is an inquiry into the ways in which the Kotas, a South Indian minority community, make and remake aspects of themselves and their world through music, dance, and other activities. My approach is guided by themes in Kota worship and mortuary ceremonies and motivated by an interest in how aspects of space, place, and time are socially deployed or constructed.

The Kotas live in the Nilgiri Hills, a region bordering the South Indian states of Tamilnadu, Kerala, and Karnataka. Distributed in seven villages and numbering less than 2000 at the time of writing, the Kotas are dwarfed by the population of surrounding indigenous and immigrant peoples. Long known for their participation as artisans in a system of inter-community exchange, the Kotas now balance their involvement in village matters of ritual, craft, and music with their needs to make good in a modern urban economy. They avail themselves of opportunities afforded them by way of education as well as by employment in nearby towns and cities as far away as Delhi and Bombay. They speak multiple languages: Kota (*kō mānt*), which is their own Dravidian language; Tamil; a number of other regional languages, notably Badaga; and a few speak English and Hindi as well. This complex interplay of local "traditional" concerns and modern socio-economic ones gives rise to perennial anxieties over "who" the Kotas are and should be.

The musical and ritual activities considered here occupy a common spatial and temporal world. Analyzing this world—seeing how Kotas organize and execute their actions in time and space and how they attribute meaning to their activities—yields subtle insights into Kota creations of self and group. In Kota dance, for instance, the order and location of male and female dancers differentiate Kota performances from those of others in the region while upholding more general principles of Kota socio-cultural organization. Kota men, who always dance first, separate themselves from women, just as in virtually all arenas men are supposed to act before and be physically higher than women. In contrast, men and women of one of the other local "tribal" communities, the Paniyas, dance in separate circles, but simultaneously; and those of a third, the Irulas, dance at times separately, at times intermingled in the same circles, and sometimes even concentrically. Hence, Kota dance style spatiotemporally maps one aspect of Kota social organization while differentiating Kota dances from those of Paniyas and Irulas.

The organization of Kota instrumental music also bears on distinguishing individuals and groups. I was initially struck by the apparent looseness with which some melodies performed by double-reed players in several Nilgiri Hill communities fitted their accompanying drum patterns (CD 1). I wondered how Kota musicians coordinated some of their more free-floating melodies with the accompanying drums, for at times they didn't seem coordinated at all. Most experienced performers, I learned, orient their melodies around structural drum beats, what I call "anchor points," and more or less fit the rest of the melody in the intervening spaces. Less experienced or talented performers are less able to keep melody and percussion in phase, thus giving the impression that the melodies and drum patterns are not connected. The melody and the percussion ostinato represent two ways of getting from Point A to Point B in time, one through the fluid, inconsistently metered presentation of pitches in sequence, the other through the somewhat more regimented flow of metrical drum strokes.

The problem of combining melody and percussion ostinato leads a musician to multiple possible solutions—choosing different points as A and B—as he attempts to keep the melody in phase with the drums. Each solution constrains how the repetition of the melody in the next cycle will coincide with the drums. These solutions ground intersubjective bonding as teams of two *koḷ* (shawm) players strive for the musical and cultural ideal of perfect unison. What it means to be united and divided is an issue of debate among the Kotas and serves as a principle theme of this book as well. The musical solutions for playing "as one" come to define sets of individuals or groups in terms of their musical styles over time, as one generation succeeds another. Musical style also congeals according to residential patterns: villages or sets of nearby villages tend to play the same melodies in the same ways.

One of my aims in this work is to refine the study of what is, sometimes too causally, termed "identity." Musical activities contribute to a sense of individual and social belonging at many analytic levels. I also wish to push the limits of a musical disciplinary perspective by giving substantial analytic weight to non-musical activities. In considering matters of order, for instance, it is important to note not only how a Kota musical piece is located within a sequence of possible pieces, but also how it relates to a sequence of other more complex events that may or may not include music: cooking, processing, consulting a diviner, or cleaning a house.

The term "spacetime," which I have adapted from the work of anthropologist Nancy Munn, conveys some of the linkages between these domains of experience. A "form of spacetime," a "spatiotemporal form," or simply "a spacetime," will henceforth refer to some definable pattern with respect to both time and space within which a set of related events is performed or, in the case of natural events, perceived to occur.[1] I consider "pattern" in the broadest sense. Unpredictability is a pattern, for instance, which pertains to the sequence of funerals performed over the course of a year; the spacetime of funerals thus differs from those of events that can be planned. The events that constitute a pattern may vary in number or magnitude; the length of time and expanse through space may similarly vary. A form of spacetime may also involve the patterning of a related set of virtual events, that is, events which are remembered, evoked, described, or metaphysically accomplished through ritual. The landscapes marked out by processionals; the range of extramusical events to which musical performances refer; and the phenomenological shape of music's intended effects, such as transformations of the spirit (*āvy*), are all forms of spacetime in my usage.

Four spatiotemporal forms are particularly important because they appropriately describe salient aspects of my Kota data, usually corrrespond with Kota ideas of (if not terms for) what they are doing, and help me specify particular aspects of Kota subjectivity and identity. These are: (1) "anchoring," latching on to and organizing events around selected moments and places; (2) "centripetence," moving physically and morally to the center, de-emphasizing differences and, in Kota terms, "making god" (*devr gicd*); (3) "centrifugality," moving outward from the village during a funeral and drawing attention to the identity of the individual; and (4) "interlocking," formally joining complementary components—village, kinship, affinal, or households units; and musically, drum parts.[2]

These forms (which are also processes) are interrelated. So, for example, the individuation of identities/subjectivities in (3) is the basis for bringing people together in (4). Though they exhibit some cross-cultural validity, the four forms do not operate autonomously in any one cultural context; nor are they, obviously, the only processes that observers or social actors may discern. I have attempted to lay out these processes simply in Table 1. It is the task of this book to show the myriad ways in which these forms act in combination and convey some of the subjective subtleties they would seem to produce for the actors involved.

Table 1: Spatiotemporal Forms of Identity (Skeletal Version)

Spatiotemporal Form	Ceremonial Association	Aspect of identity
anchoring	—	sense of grounding
centripetence	god ceremony	wholeness and sameness
centrifugality	mortuary ceremonies	individuation
interlocking	mortuary ceremonies	wholeness and difference

We may take it as axiomatic that agents always have at their disposal multiple, often competing, ways of organizing themselves in space and time, among which they must choose. Choosing is an act of staking claim, differentiating one person or group from another, creating a sense of order for a particular purpose. What differ from culture to culture and analytic domain to analytic domain are the possible models, systems, or points of reference available to actors and the socio-historical or, in the musical case, aesthetic conditions under which they make choices. Points of reference, or "anchor points," then, need not be short term and perceptual, as they sometimes are in Kota instrumental music. They may also include longer-term destinations in processions or even pilgrimages, and dates or events in the calendar year.

Members of many religious communities have engaged in heated disputes over matters of which calendar to use and how to calibrate the dates (see Duncan 1998) because they have recognized the ways in which control over the calendar is linked to vital aspects of "who they are," to hark back to the phrase of Cleese's character. The Kotas, too, recognize this connection and have made strategic use of their choices—most remarkably by shifting the ritual constitution of the "new year" from the first sowing ceremony (in the 1930s) to the god ceremony, the major annual ceremony for the Kota gods. The reasons for this are complex and must be treated in detail elsewhere. Kotas were able to manipulate their cycle of activities over the course of the year, giving less weight to one moment in the cycle and more weight to another.

These musical and calendrical examples of "anchoring" suggest that identity and subjectivity are to be found in continuous processes of dislocation and relocation. A musician strays from the metric cycle, only to return to it in certain places. Kotas appear to have changed their minds about where the year begins, but they have not given up the idea that the calendrical cycle has a beginning.

The reader may have guessed at this point that I am using "anchoring" as an enabling metaphor, one that provides windows of insight into those aspects of group identity or individual subjectivity that can be described in spatiotemporal terms (cf. Tambiah 1985a). It is not my task to catalog all the kinds of musical and social anchoring there could possibly be, nor is it my aim to align the examples in order to search for cultural essences in their homologies. Rather, I wish to explore the implications, for the Kotas, of this and other spatiotemporal forms, which are, I believe, part of much human experience.

Anchoring implies arriving somewhere at some time. The tales of Kota arrivals in their seven villages provide a qualitative perspective on the process of anchoring. In a prominent story, from which this book's title is drawn, a divine black cow of ancient times indicated with its hoof where each Kota village (*kōkāl*) should be founded. On the sites of these "black cow's footprints," the ancestral village founders built their dwellings. The founders' descendants continue to reside in each village's respective "house of the erected post" (*kab iṭ pay*) built on that original spot, which constitutes a center of moral gravity. People treat the area and those who live within it with special respect. Ceremonies often begin or end there.

The Kota story of the black cow's footprint cements a relationship between a people and their land by using an ancient pan-Indic sign of divinity, the cow. Two common folk etymologies for the word *kōkāl*, "cow leg" and "Kota place," further reinforce this relationship and give voice to two formal kinds of identity claim. One claim is individuating: Kotas assert themselves as a unique indigenous "tribal" community given divine mandate to inhabit seven villages in the Nilgiri Hills. The other is integrative: the bovine theme invites Kota membership in a "sacred" world that encompasses many communities across the subcontinent, especially those who call themselves Hindus.

Permutations among the paired processes of integration and differentiation, and centripetence and centrifugality, contribute to the ways in which Kotas constitute multiple kinds of subjectivity, social units, and identification as a whole community. The processes of organizing dances, setting a ceremonial date, and founding the village all exemplify the point that people in some sense find themselves when they latch on to, or anchor themselves in, specific times and places. The Kotas became fully Kota when they arrived in their villages.

The Major Ceremonies

Centripetence and centrifugality are broad ways to describe physical and moral modes of orientation in the two major ceremonial complexes, the "god" (*devr*) complex epitomized by the god ceremony, and the "death" (*tāv*) complex consisting of a cremation and a secondary mortuary ceremony. Collectively, these take up somewhere between three and six weeks of the year; they cost the most money, involve the most detailed ritual activity among the largest number of villagers, require the greatest degree of behavior modification, and involve the most significant music of all the year's observances. The ceremonies are compelling and crucial to understanding much of Kota culture and society. "Ceremony" here refers to a performance unit that encompasses smaller units of discrete actions, which I shall call "rituals" and which Kotas term *cātrms*—which are prescribed by rule.[3] By "ceremonial complex" I mean the set of all ceremonies and rituals that Kotas understand as belonging under a particular rubric.

The god ceremony takes place over 10–12 days in Kolmēl village, my main field site. At this time Kotas constitute the presence of their three main gods through moral, unified behavior and attractive music and dance. The ceremony's date is finalized after elders witness the first waxing crescent of the new moon in December–January. But well before this, a spirit of anticipation fills the air as villagers gather wood in preparation for the all-night dancing around bonfires and purchase provisions for special meals. They prepare their ceremonial dresses and dance costumes, buy new street clothes for the final days, and rehearse some of the more rare or difficult pieces of "god" repertoire by singing, whistling, or playing softly on the bamboo clarinet (*pulāng*). As the season approaches, members of the village gradually begin to conduct themselves within the village boundaries with heightened care and respect, entailing vegetarianism, less drinking and feuding, more wearing of "traditional" Kota clothes, and remaining barefoot within the village. Ritual officiants and then the rest of the villagers clean and purify their houses using special plants. This process of anticipation and ritual lead-up over the course of weeks and days is a form of "anchoring."

In the initial rituals, certain individuals create and transfer a series of special fires, some of which are conduits for divinity. The first significant musical performance begins immediately after several of the fires have been lit and transported from one place to another in the village. The "house of the erected post" plays a key role here, for in front of it, in the *gagvāl*, musicians anchor the first part of the ceremony in the domestic part of the village. They play a series of cascading blasts on their brass trumpets (*kob*), forcefully beat their frame and cylinder drums (*tabaṭk* and *par*), and blow their shawms (*koḷs*). The special term for this powerful act of commencement, *ōmayṉ*, "sounding as one," embodies key social values which resonate throughout Kota culture in rituals, moral tales, and everyday practices. The musical sounds not only alert the surrounding communities of the ceremony's onset, they are also believed to extend into the heavens, where god hears the forceful blasts as invitations to enter the village. Kotas project their music centrifugally; those who hear it respond by moving (from the Kota village perspective) centripetally.

That night, and on subsequent days, villagers attempt to read signs from the father god (*ayṉōr*) through the words of the diviner, or *tērkārn*.[4] Kotas express their joy, unity, and respect for god, as well as entertain him by performing instrumental music, dancing, and singing (CD 2). A number of instrumental pieces are linked with particular ritual actions such as food-offering and bathing; others index shared tales of moral value which remind villagers of the link between community integrity and divine power. Temporal implications of musical performance that extend beyond the configuration of musical elements, then, include the momentary appropriateness of a piece in its ritual context and the time in the past to which that performance refers.

As the days progress, activity shifts from the domestic area to the temple area in the center of the village. This is another example of centripetence; here the agents are members of a Kota village. As villagers come together in the center, so too do the three gods enter the three temples in the center of the village. The three main Kota gods in Kolmēl village are Doḍaynōr ("big" father deity), Kunayṇōr ("little" father deity), and Amnōr (mother deity). (Kotas have also incorporated additional deities into their pantheon, both within and beyond the confines of their villages, and they travel to temples and festivals of others to participate in worship as well.) Kotas use the phrase "making god" (*devr gicd*) to refer to the performance of the god ceremony for the three gods. Part of this "making" once consisted of re-thatching the temples. In the case of the modern cement temples, Kotas perform emotionally charged commemorative rituals that culminate in the throwing of thatching materials on the roof of each temple. At such moments, the upward motion is highlighted by the *koḷ* players, who interrupt their "temple-opening tune" with a piercing tremolo on the highest note of the instrument (CD 3). Kotas give repeated emphasis to certain such aspects of orientation and motion, both horizontal and vertical, in their rituals.

Along with the instrumental pieces which refer to narratives, and the ritual of re-thatching, Kotas use many god ceremonial activities to gain experiential access to a virtual, if lost, utopia. The acts index aspects of what Kotas view as their traditional past. Throughout the ceremony, Kotas articulate structural sections of the ceremony with pieces of musical repertoire and dance. The commencement of the ceremony's final segment is demarcated with a women's dance, which accompanies the process of removing precious metal offerings from the face of the temple. Kotas feel dispirited at this juncture, for their return to everyday affairs and the departure of their gods is imminent. Transitioning to the quotidian is centrifugal in this case. Kotas spend the last days of the god ceremony in their domestic areas once again, where they dance, sing, and play games.

"Death" ceremonies are of two kinds: the "green" funeral (*pac tāv*) in which the corpse is cremated, and the "dry" funeral (*varldāv*) in which relics of all those deceased over a period are recremated. This latter ceremony, which may last up to twelve days, serves as the formal end of death in a village: the souls of the deceased are made to reach the land of the dead; the widows and widowers are given license to remarry; and the villagers are free to celebrate the god ceremony again.

As in the god ceremony, instrumental pieces in both kinds of mortuary observance demarcate and contribute affective and indexical meaning to structural sections of ritual. The green funeral begins with the sounding of drums and a horn (*kob*) to announce the death. As the corpse is washed and ritually prepared for transport to the cremation ground, musicians perform a selection of lachrymose melodies at will, occasionally inserting a ritually specific one to correspond with the ongoing action. Special pieces are associated with the motions of mourners carrying the corpse. Musicians play as others carry the corpse through the threshold of the house, out of the front yard, into an intermediate zone beyond the village, and finally to the cremation ground, where musicians play the "bier lighting tune" (CD 4) more or less at the right moment. No music follows the cremation. Music, then, adds substance primarily to centrifugal ritual action during the funeral. Villagers return home quietly, then purify themselves appropriately, and eat a special meal.

The dry funeral begins with a ritual of pouring millet on the ground in front of the houses of each of the bereaved. The action of pouring, the ritual accompanying it, and the special melody played at this time, are intended to bring the spirit of the dead person into the memorial millet. The millet is subsequently processed and incinerated along with bone remnants that were preserved from the initial cremation. A second class of melodies is used near the peak of the ceremony to call all the spirits of the dead to the dry funeral ground in order to welcome the recently deceased into their midst. The fact that constituting the spirit in millet and sending it off to the land of the ancestors are related rituals is phenomenologically reinforced by a similarity in the two rituals' melodies that Kotas themselves recognize (CD 5, 6). One aspect of what we could call funerary musical spacetime consists in this process of calling the spirit forth and then sending it thither.

Just as in the green funeral, during which a bier is set up in front of the deceased's home, in the dry funeral "biers" (actually chairs) are erected and decorated with all manner of colored ribbons, umbrellas, photographs of the dead person, colored cloths, and, most importantly, ritual objects that signify the deceased's gender, status, and personal habits or preferences. Many if not all of these items are cremated with the "bier," relics, and millet at the ceremony's climax. In this sense, through funerals Kotas symbolically individuate the deceased and emphasize the separation of the individual from the living, while at the same time enhancing the transition of that individual to the community of ancestors who are believed to live on in the land of the dead, or "that land" (*ānāṛ*). Songs sung at dry funerals are the same as those of god ceremonies, for through the funeral the soul of the deceased is being "entrusted" (*opicd*) to god. The funerary complex thus provides a formal structure through which Kotas progress spatiotemporally from mourning to celebration, with a great deal of subtle mixing in between. Kota understandings of their melodic genres and rituals composing the ceremonies also reinforce the complexity of this affective contour. The spatiotemporal progress in the god ceremony is somewhat the reverse; after proceeding from the everyday to the blissful, the turning point (when metal offerings are removed from the temple) is one of mild dejection. Yet the dancers and musicians are carried forward by the momentum of the occasion for several more days of rituals and music before the ceremony finally ends.

In contrast to the abstemiousness of participants in the god ceremony, those at the dry funeral are free to eat meat and (especially men) to consume alcohol. Various rituals of what I call "interlocking" emphasize the interconnectedness of the whole Kota community. After the rituals at the dry funeral ground are completed, for instance, all return to the village grounds for a concluding set of dances in which a male representative from each of the seven villages dons a costume and joins in a special "community costume [dance ritual]." This *jādykupāc* is defined by representational participation and the interlocking of villages and, thereby, kin groups, rather than by particular steps or accompanying melodies.

The dry funeral has been the subject of ambivalence and debate in a number of villages since the 1930s. The activities at stake have been of a sort with those that Hindu reformers since the late nineteenth century have attacked, partially as a response to challenges presented by complex interactions with the West, with missionaries, and particularly with the British. These have included the slaughter of cows and buffaloes, public consumption of alcohol, engagement in unruly activity, and amorous adventures which were, it seems, loosely concealed. The solution taken up in one village, Porgāṛ (New Kotagiri), was to discontinue the ceremony entirely.

In brief, then, ceremonies in the "god" complex are physically and theologically centripetal affairs that serve to consolidate villages into wholes and assert continuity of the community; through the god ceremony Kotas articulate unities of communal sameness. Funerals, in contrast, are centrifugal and embody social principles of difference and change on many levels. But unity is not absent from funerals. An emphasis on differences defined by such things as kinship, gender, and residence makes it possible to define community relationships through forms of "interlocking." In ever-changing ways Kotas constitute themselves in relation to both divinities and spirits of the dead—the metaphysical foci of these two kinds of ceremonial complexes. The oscillation between stressing identity among individuals in one ritual complex, the god ceremony, and differences among them in another, funerals, does not create a contradiction. Rather, it defines the shape of an important aspect of Kota temporal experience, one that is reinforced by the sequential form in which Kotas perform musical pieces, and the "meanings" of these pieces (i.e. well-known specific references or intended functions) as they are apprehended in time.

* * *

The Kotas belong to a discrete and highly reified social category in India, the "tribe;" in Hindi and Tamil *ādivāsī* (original inhabitant); or Tamil, *paḻankuṭi makkaḷ* (ancient-race people)—Kotas comfortably use the terms from all three languages.

The Kotas as a Tribe

"Scheduled Tribe" is a census category applied by the Indian government to communities such as the Kota who are regarded as autochthonous to a region, and who many believe preserve an ancient way of life. No definitive criterion determines who does or does not warrant the tribal designation. Tribal status is a matter of political and cultural debate in which distinctions may turn on matters of cultural knowledge involving musicianship, artisanship, and premodern technologies.

The term tribe now used in India is partially colonial in origin. Historically rooted in colonial social classifications in Africa (Cohn 1987a, 201–23), "tribalism" initially meant the maintenance of a way of life based on ethnicity and membership in a kin-based community (a *tribe*). Later it came to mean "obnoxious modes of behavior in multiethnic circumstances that threaten and endanger normal coexistence among persons from different ethnic groups" (Ekeh 1990, 688).

This idea of tribe, born from the inability of the British to control their "frontier" populations, has become less salient in some parts of post-independence India, where tribe has come to signify the indigenous or authentic. Unlike in Africa, where the term has been abandoned by many as politically incorrect, the tribal designation is assumed with pride in India by communities that use it to court special treatment. The line of distinction between tribes and castes has been historically difficult to draw and frequently remains a bone of contention as local communities struggle for access to resources, education, and jobs.

The relevance of the tribal concept for this book extends beyond mere contextualization, for it exemplifies the way in which identities are founded on particular sorts of spatiotemporal claims. In asserting themselves to be tribal, Kotas affirm special historical rights to the lands they inhabit. Since the ancient places of tribal peoples were supposed to be pristine forest lands, expressions of tribal identity frequently involve the manipulation of forest imagery. Modern tribal peoples such as the Kotas have domesticated the pejorative connotation of "wildness," transforming it into a form of cultural knowledge: how to survive, how to be "natural."

Kotas are accustomed to deploying representations of tribals for non-Kotas. One Kota ritual specialist from Mēnāṛ village, named Angarn, exaggerated when he said, "You can discern an *ādivāsī* because he will be roaming the forest collecting honey and things." Unlike the "modern" person, who shoots with a gun, the *ādivāsī*, Angarn explained, uses a bow and arrow. While Kotas in fact use rifles and not bow and arrows, they remain self-reliant in many other areas and make most of their musical instruments.

The framers of the Indian constitution realized that modern life was going to impinge increasingly upon tribal people, their physical environments, and their customs. They entrusted the nation with the responsibility of seeing to tribal welfare and "uplift" by providing educational opportunities, jobs, and medical attention (see Mehta 1991, 172). The Kota community acutely feels the effects of swelling populations around them. Industry has expanded, land and resources are scarce, and tourism is intensive. The administrative center of the Nilgiri District, Ootacamund (also known as Ooty), is a resort town. Squeezed and threatened, the Kotas lament, at times, the small size of their own population—which was about 1,500 in 1990—and frequently debate the future of their community. Maintaining their villages as primordial Kota places, ideologically anchoring themselves in a premodern time, and emphasizing the distinctiveness of their "culture" (Ta. *kalāccāram*) through such forms as music have been essential to the Kotas as they constitute themselves as a viable, moral community in twenty-first-century India.

Tribal Status, Kota Music, and Power

Aboriginal status, in the view of many Kotas, imbues both gods and music with a significant measure of potency. Not only do Kota gods prefer the music of their tribal devotees, even some deities in temples erected by immigrant plains-dwellers favor tribal music over the music of their Tamil patrons (see Wolf 2000/2001a). Perhaps this is because, as one Mr Rajan—known as "Dancing-ground Rajan" for the location of his home in the village of Mēnāṛ—believes, all *ādivāsī* music shares an intense emotional quality. Some even hold the view that animals partake of this aboriginal potency. The Kotas' own "country cows," for instance, are likened to *ādivāsī*s and praised for their "power" even though they produce less milk than larger, cross-bred, foreign cows. Rajan linked the "power" of *ādivāsī*s to matters of character: "They will not be proud; they will be 'open.' They are always 'frank.' They will not express excessive rage. They will eat and sit quietly. *Ādivāsī*s will observe new events carefully, they will not leave old ways behind, they will be self-restrained (*kaṭṭuppāṭu*)." Rajan implies that "tribalness" involves a form of morality, a respect for the past, an acute sensitivity to activities in the world. Angarn raises similar points aligning several etymologies of the Kota ethnonym, *kōv*.[5] "In Tamil, *kō* means king. Another meaning of *kō* is cow. Among us, *kōv* means 'behaving properly.' If a Kota person is not acting justly, we will ask, 'Are you a *kōv*?' The *ādivāsī*s used to live in the forest, so they know the proper way to conduct themselves. The others don't. This is the difference."[6] As the anthropologist Michael Herzfeld has observed in another context, such "verbal iconicities . . . provide compact instances of the differentiating character of origin myths . . . and legitimate the moral boundaries of culture" (Herzfeld 1997, 69).

Kotas embrace positive tribal images and reject negative ones. According to the respected musician K. Puccan, Kotas stopped playing music for their Toda tribal neighbors after they were alerted to a Toda claim—allegedly made when Queen Victoria summoned groups of *ādivāsīs* to Madras during a late-nineteenth-century visit (which she never made)—that the Kotas were hired workers whom they brought to the Nilgiris from the plains. Puccan recalls becoming aware of this disinformation in 1952, when his village mates were trying to gain admission for their children in a special tribal school. They found a record of the claim in an Ooty library, revealing what they perceived as a Toda stratagem to portray the Kotas as plains people rather than tribals, and thus exclude them from the school. As Puccan explained subsequent events (in Tamil):

> In 1956, Jawaharlal Nehru came here. As many *ādivāsī* things there were, we took and showed to him. We asked, "before we came, what were they [Todas] doing? Where was the churning staff for the milk? Without knives how did they cut the bamboo?"[7]
>
> He [Nehru] saw everything: the fire starting [i.e. by friction using tree roots], our 'dress,' 'dance' [using the English words]. One person helped us file a suit against the Todas. In the Sessions court there was a judicial enquiry.
>
> He passed a judgement. Who? Nehruji, "you [Todas] are not *ādivāsīs*, you only are the immigrants. They [Kotas] are the *ādivāsīs*."

Puccan went on to say that the Todas do not know music and did not learn from the Kotas: "They're simple forest dwellers, where would they learn?" Puccan here strategically deployed several locally relevant ideas of tribe as proof of indigenous status in the region. Kota "tribalness" is encoded in items of indigenous manufacture and in the performance of music and dance. Embraced are the nobler characteristics of tribal identity: self-sufficiency as evidenced by tool making; artistic prowess and creativity as proven by the ability to play unique music and perform dances. Puccan projects negative, primitive stereotypes of the tribal onto the Toda, in this case (as Puccan portrays them here) the Nilgiri equivalent of the country bumpkin.

India's tribes are Janus-faced, signifying both the organic, natural rootedness of the nation in a diversity of indigenous people, and disconcerting images of the backward, the primitive. When social actors deploy reified ethnic (and national) definitions to their advantage in one context (perhaps to gain political recognition), these definitions may return to haunt them in another, leading to "embarrassment" or "rueful self-recognition." Such sentiments lie at the heart of what Herzfeld calls "cultural intimacy" (Herzfeld 1997, 6). So, while Kotas eagerly embrace primordiality for the "power" they think it confers, they dissociate themselves from "traditional" behavior that appears promiscuous and do not openly sacrifice animals—especially cows—in their villages because these behaviors are signs of tribal primitiveness (Kuper 1988, 60; 80–1; Tylor 1866; McLennan 1865). By stimulating processes of embracement and dissociation, "cultural intimacy" becomes deeply generative of diachronic processes. For the Kotas, cultural intimacy hinges on what it means to be a tribe.

Dubbed "sons" of the proverbial "soil," tribals have played a special role in Indian nationalist conceptions. At least since the time of Independence, Indians have celebrated the local arrival of a national figure with the music and dance of nearby inhabitants. "Tribal" arts are particularly favored not only because tribals anchor national identity in the local, and not only because they are aesthetically moving (as Rajan suggested), but also because the performance of such arts by different communities articulates a kind of organic solidarity and serves to enact India's credo, "Unity in Diversity." Although tribals are popularly represented in stereotypically simple ways, most tribal peoples themselves interact with the modern nation state in complex ways—they vote, listen to the radio, watch television or movies, and agitate for rights. They also consume local versions of commodities that are found widespread throughout the world—cassettes, Western clothing and shoes, and so forth. The Kotas see themselves as part of multiple communities: as Indians, as Indian tribals, as world indigenous peoples ("do you have tribals in your country?" they ask), and oddly, as people who have some natural kinship to Americans—both are "frank," as Rajan put it. Kotas see themselves as fundamentally integrated: ideologically and morally linked to multiple communities.

At the same time, Kotas enact strict practices of differentiation from others: kinship and marriage, for example, bind Kotas tightly and exclusively to one another. Movements in India and throughout the world to break free of provincial, racial or religion-based constraints on alliances have not (yet at least) affected the ways Kotas operationalize their kinship. The spatial and temporal aspects of Kota kinship and marriage today tell us much about their contemporary self-conceptions.

Kota Kinship and Spatial Organization

Kinship in the Dravidian Kota language follows what Lewis Henry Morgan called the Iroquois-Dravidian system, which is classificatory and does not distinguish between lineal and collateral kin. The entire community is so compact and interconnected that all men of the same generation are terminologically either older/younger brothers (*aṇ-karāḷ*), or they are brothers-in-law/affines (*ayḷbāvan*). Similarly, all women of the same generation are related to men as sisters or as wives/affines (*peḍ*).

Rows of houses, called *kērs*, correspond with patrilines in the ideal system. Adjacent houses articulate brother relationships in a single generation. Houses further apart in a row, and to a greater exent on "upper" and "lower" rows of a gentle slope, map relationships of brotherhood further back in time. For the purposes of establishing who can be married to whom, each village has three *kērs* and marriage is *kēr* exogamous. That is to say, "brothers" live in a row (or two) of houses, women whom they can marry live in a separate set of rows or in different villages.

No terminological distinction is made between men and women as couples who have actually undergone marriage rituals and those who are only potential marriage partners. The difference is recognized in practice, however, particularly now because the bourgeois Hindu ideal of one-husband one-wife is dominant. Nevertheless, the terminological system does relate to ritual practice in the diffuse ways in which affinity is articulated: some of these articulations are more marriage-like than others, and, historically, Kota marriage has never been a single, elaborate, binding ceremony, but rather a series of simple, easily reversible rituals performed over a course of days, months, or even years.

One aspect of the ritual simplicity of weddings is the lack of special musical repertoire. This stands in strong contrast with worship and death ceremonies, associated with which are highly specialized and internally differentiated repertoires. The lack of ritual elaboration for weddings corresponds with the more general lack of emphasis on the marriage

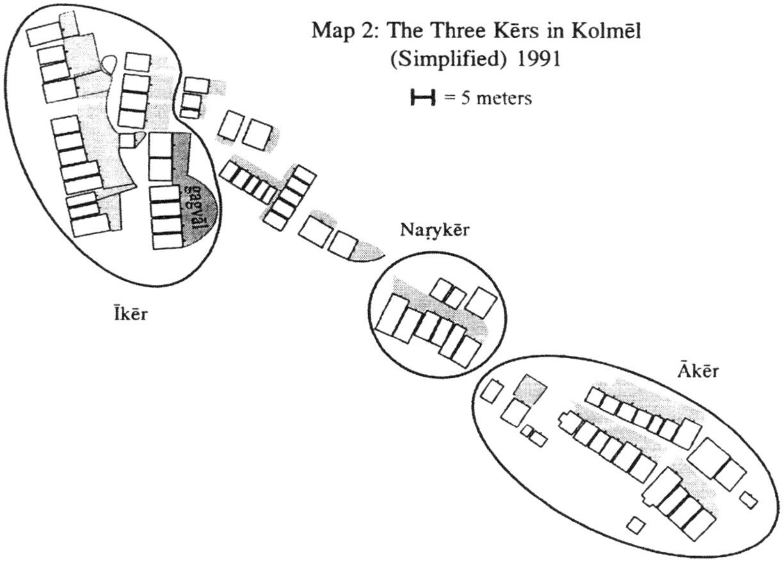

Map 2: The Three Kērs in Kolmēl (Simplified) 1991

bond: Kotas self-consciously cite their freedom to marry and divorce at will as a distinctively tribal practice.

The nature of "alliance" is a major issue in the construction of identity in South Asia. Each Hindu caste follows its own rules for whom one may marry, although some version of the Dravidian preference for cross-cousin marriage is characteristic of South Indian and not of North Indian Hindus. (Muslims follow their own traditions.) The strength of the marriage bond is closely tied to status in high-caste and upwardly-mobile Hindu households. In contrast, Tribes and Scheduled Castes (Untouchables) are caricatured as lowly, uncouth creatures who cannot control their libidinous desires.

Tribal societies in India probably do accommodate a greater array of possible relationships between young men and women than do most conservative Brahman communities, to draw one of the starkest possible contrasts. The sheer diversity of local marriage practices among all the populations of the subcontinent, however, would militate against drawing meaningful distinctions between tribe and non-tribe solely on such bases.

"Tribal" Living

Tribals also live in a variety of physical circumstances. Some have distinctive foods, forms of clothing, plastic arts, and music; others do not. Some continue to live in relatively isolated tribal regions and lack many modern amenities. But many of them, such as those found in the Nilgiris, live as peasants, virtually indistinguishable in the bazaar from their caste Hindu, Muslim, and Christian neighbors—unless they choose to dress specially. Although tribals may engage in distinctive religious or economic practices—the Toda dairy complex in the Nilgiris is a famous anthropological example—many work alongside members of other Indian communities, often in tenured government posts (allotted by quota to tribals), which include the postal service, banks, and factories.

While most Kotas in the early 1990s lived in wattle and daub houses with ceramic tile roofs, many have modified their houses considerably or are building new ones now (in 2005). Some live in the flat-roofed cement constructions which are common on the Tamil plains and increasingly popular in Nilgiri towns, where householders may like to add additional stories to their houses in future. All Kotas have a home in one of seven exclusively Kota villages—even though some of them live close to their jobs, away from the village. Many Kota village houses have electricity, a few have telephones, and mountain stream water is available in a few common taps. Buses run near these villages, and a major town is never more than one hour away. Next to Kolmēl village, where I conducted most of my fieldwork, are teashops, provision shops, a tailor's shop, and agricultural lands owned by neighboring communities.

A wide variety of interests and economies intersect in Kota villages. While the inner workings of Kota rituals have little direct involvement with world events, the physical environment through which Kotas move on a daily basis—whether in ritual or casually—is thoroughly implicated in this wider sphere. One year I noticed that the local bus shelter was inscribed with a fictive bus-stop name in Malayalam: a film crew from Madras had taken advantage of the low site cost to make a commercial film in Kolmēl. Other modern structures had changed their functions: a disused solar power station became a young men's clubhouse.

Performance semiotics in public spaces have become more complex in light of political events that extend beyond the Indian nation's borders. In May of 1992, the Kotas were called to perform for the visit to

Ooty of the chief minister of Tamilnadu, M. Jayalalitha. On this occasion, one group leader wanted to ensure the excellence of the performance and proposed that the group assemble in Ooty beforehand to practice (this call to practice was a first in my experience). The group felt well prepared after a single day. A call was then issued from the chief minister's staff: the Kotas were to return and "practice" for two more days. "Practice," it turned out, meant that they would watch out for Sri Lankan Tamil militants, who might make an attempt on the chief minister's life (Rajiv Gandhi had been assassinated earlier that year). So the Nilgiri tribal folk are no mere isolates: they are very much "connected" with their immediate surroundings and implicated in far-reaching political circumstances.

Kota Music at Home

Kotas have been complexly "connected" with surrounding societies for a long time, but the nature of this connection has undergone mutation. In the copious ethnographic literature on South India's Nilgiri Hills, Kotas are renowned for their roles as musicians and craftspeople in a system of economic and ritual exchange which was already in decline during the 1930s and is now for the most part defunct. Nilgiri societies, once viewed as relatively discrete, each "exploit[ing] its particular ecological niche," are now better viewed as part of one larger Nilgiri society, like ethnic groups in the United States (Hockings 1997, 2). Kotas occasionally play music for the neighboring Badagas, with whom they once had hereditary, reciprocal relations; but they are now more likely to play for inter-tribal gatherings, political functions, Hindu temples, or the most important connoisseurs—themselves.

Since anthropologists once emphasized this system of exchange, they inadvertently created the impression that Kota music's primary importance was its part in a complex intercommunal transactional system. On the contrary, the moral focus of Kota music, for Kotas, appears long to have been a small number of ceremonies internal to the community—and many of the musical components of these ceremonies did not involve transactions with non-Kotas. So, despite the demise of the classic exchange system, the musical culture that Kotas value the most—which stays in their villages—remains vital, continuing to interpenetrate and give meaning to their rituals and everyday life.

This is not to say that indigenous music, as important as it might be in some contexts, is central to all areas of Kota life. Music's cultural meaning may sometimes be best explained by using phenomena other than music as points of departure. Kotas pride themselves on their multiple talents, their artisanship, and their ability to take up new jobs and excel at them against all odds. School, agricultural work, carpentry and blacksmithing, and day jobs leave little time for the kind of music-making Kotas regard as significant. Intensive, community-defining musical activities are fitted into the cracks, concentrated only during the god ceremony and during funerals. Musical performance is but one of many constitutive forms of action in these complex events. This is one reason for my focus on the spatiotemporal processes by which actions are carried out.

Kotas may have the opportunity to sing songs, to go to movies, or to listen to the tape recorder; men and women occasionally worship at Tamil temples, where they sing *bhajan*s and/or listen to recorded devotional music. But these forms of making and encountering music can hardly be combined with the making of music at god ceremonies and funerals to compose a single meaningful category—what ethnomusicologists sometimes call "musical life." One may sensibly study the "musical life" of professional musicians, as in Daniel Neuman's *The Life of Music in North India*, or of a subculture of self-proclaimed musicians. It doesn't make much sense to speak of the "musical life" of the Kotas because music-making is so diffuse.

Musical Spacetimes, Concepts, and Theories

Kota music-making can be described in relation to a number of spatiotemporal forms, some of which musicians may register their impact upon as they mature. Take for instance the sum total of all the places and times in which an individual finds it appropriate to perform particular pieces. As actors move through this structure—performing or listening to music in the proper times and places—they are both following culturally prescribed scripts and imprinting their actions on the memories of others, who will then either continue to follow or choose to depart from the models they have observed. Actors may establish new models for contextualizing musical performance by, for example, shifting the ritual deployment of a specific melody from one part of a ceremony to another, as has happened in Kurgōj village with an important dry funeral melody.

A more limited form of musical spacetime is created from the sequence of articulations (notes, drum strokes) in any musical performance. Movements of the musicians provide some of the spatial dimensions of such a spacetime, as do, in different ways, the breadth and distance listeners perceive when they hear musical elements projected from different locations. Musical qualities of pitch and timbre may differentiate one articulation from the next. Anchor points and first beats in percussion ostinatos hierarchically differentiate articulations as well.

In talking about musical processes, scholars, musicians, and other social actors frequently invoke larger spatiotemporal conceptions. In the Kota case, these conceptions are closely linked with bodily orientation and movement. When Kotas refer to a melody's upper register (*mēl dāk*), for instance, they use a metaphor that "mediates connections within [the] experience[s]" (see Jackson 1996, 9) of physically playing a melody and hearing it as a sequence in space. When a player performs in the upper register, he does so literally on the highest part of the slightly downward-pointed instrument. In similarly embodied terms, Kota dances and melodies both consist of sequences of "steps" (*meṭ*). Extending this imagery of stepwise increments, K. Puccan used the common South Asian simile of a melody as a "path" (Ta. *vaḻi*): one can traverse the village directly or via a circuitous route. Melodies as several series of note-articulations and paths as several series of temporary destinations are both flexible relative to fixed endpoints; these linked musical-spatial concepts reinforce the idea that Kotas think of some melodies as flexible, fluid, or malleable in an abstract spatiotemporal sense—at least in comparison with drummed ostinatos.

The question before us is how to relate these musically implied concepts to broader notions of time and space articulated in different ways in music, other action, or verbal discourse. Fig. 1 presents a model of Kota music situated at the center of four concentric layers. The first, or inner, layer is the immediate musical environment, the Nilgiri Hills. The music of the Kotas shares with that of other Nilgiri tribes a number of similarities, including but not limited to the phenomenon of the shawm melody "floating" over the percussion pattern. The second encompassing layer is the wider Indic musical environment in which, to use the same example, musical interest often derives from the interplay of a "free-rhythmic" melody with a more regular, "metered," accompaniment on the drums. The third layer can be viewed from two perspectives, geographical and theoretical, as suggested by the arrows.

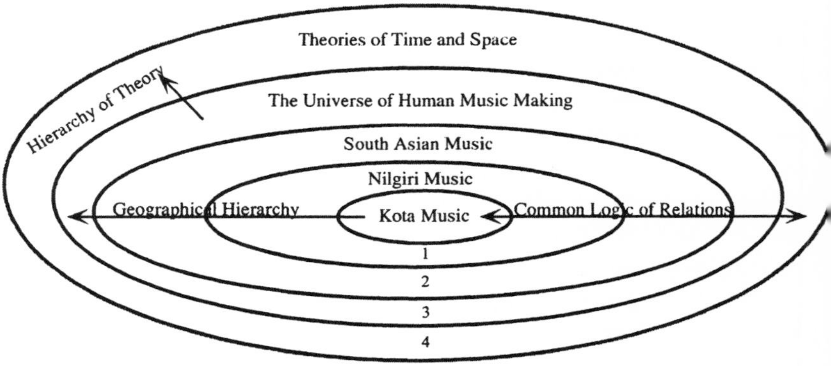

Fig. 1: Nested Hierarchies of Kota Music

Extending the geographical hierarchy we may free ourselves from the Indian subcontinent and consider Kota music simply as a kind of music in the world. In music theoretical terms, we may find that procedures in Kota music-making are encompassed within a larger universe of what many humans do when they make music. Abstracting our "floating" melody example further, for example, we find that throughout the world musicians often must coordinate among multiple rhythms that have more or less ambiguous or flexible rates of change (see Blum 2004, 240).

In what ways do Kotas recognize differences between melodic and percussive articulations of rhythm in their music? Obviously they must recognize some degree of difference or the issue of "anchoring" melodies to their percussion ostinatos would never arise. "Melody" and "percussion" can be rehearsed separately from one another as well, as when individuals practice a melodic instrument without accompaniment. The metrical underpinnings of some melodies, when the players are not guided by drum beats, are difficult to discern. The piece played on the bamboo trumpet, *bugīr* in CD 9, and Puccan's vocalization of the "temple-opening tune" (CD 10) both share an underlying ten-pulse metrical framework that is not easily recognizable when listening to either melody alone. Such solo melodies may lack obvious markers of meter because the musicians who perform them seem to be more preoccupied with matters of melodic contour and relative pitch durations than large-scale metric structures. *Koḷ* players orient some melodies to framing patterns of drum beats only when those beats are actually present. Puccan could not, for example, indicate the main beats with his foot while playing the "temple-opening tune." The internal flexibility of melodies such as the temple-opening tune requires some external point of reference for that flexibility to make sense. Though dance tunes and simpler ritual tunes are, by and large, straightforwardly metric, some dance tunes also depart artfully from the main beat (CD 11).

The fourth layer in Fig. 1 moves beyond music to encompass concepts of spatial and temporal relations in other arenas of human activity. In Layer Four, our contrast between floating melody and relatively rigid percussion ostinato is reproduced analogically in the verbal concepts of Kotas, anthropologists, or theorists of time and space. Tantalizing comparisons can be made between our exemplary contrast and some of the anxieties Henri Bergson and others have expressed in their positing of essential differences between pure, undifferentiated "duration" experienced by a person internally, and time as segmented in the world around.[8]

In Layer Four, the hierarchy shifts from one of geography to one of theory. This is justifiable because the parameters of discussion in all four layers involve the logic of temporal and sometimes spatial relations. For example, the notion of a "path" links musical processes in Layer Three with the broader spatiotemporal conceptions of Layer Four. Terms for path are common in Kota and Tamil discussions of music and in languages associated with many musical traditions cross-culturally (e.g. Robertson 1979). In India, various words for "path" are used metaphorically for spiritual journeys or ways of accomplishing a goal. Another linking concept can be found in the English word "rhythm." In musical terms, rhythm has been described as a multidimensional phenomenon of "independent variables" such as duration, pulse, and meter (Powers 1986). But "rhythm" is also used by English speakers to describe both spatial and temporal relations in non-musical domains, from the simple "rhythms" of life to the "regularity in the way something is repeated in space" (OED s.v. "rhythm" 8).

In similar respects, aspects of temporal contrast in Kota melody and drumming—fluidity, flexibility, plasticity *versus* segmentariness, measuredness, regularity and rigidity—belong with the more general categories—conceptual, philosophical, or practical—that people use to talk about or organize their world. The larger point is that musical processes in time and space deserve consideration in the wider arena of discourses about action and events more generally. What Kotas actually do, including how they use their categories and concepts, should be considered on par with Kota verbal explanations of what they do. For explanations are not "transcendent views that somehow escape the impress of social interests, cultural habits, and personal persuasions" (Jackson 1996, 1). If any area of human activity deserves such phenomenological consideration it is music-making.[9] We cannot expect any language to map adequately the territory of musical action, nor should we expect music-makers to index verbally everything important about what they do.

Human beings constantly juggle, choose among, or attempt to reconcile the many spatiotemporal representations which they form when perceiving and creating the rhythms of events in the world. Melodies, patterns of discrete drum, calendrical articulations, the flow of "everyday life," agriculture, or a ceremony, are all willful orderings of events or actions set against other possible orderings. These orderings are themselves situated in time and space and therefore subject to manipulation and change (see Munn 1992, 116).

The Village Council

In the context of this study, some willful orderings of events emerge from negotiations among individual agents in the Kota village council or *kūṭm* (from a verbal root meaning "to join or come together"). *Kūṭms*, composed of men, are scheduled on fixed or ad hoc bases; they may be small or large, and include representatives of one village or all seven. In a god ceremonial *kūṭm*, Kotas actively listen to and interpret the words of the possessed diviner. Ordinarily, the *kūṭm* will entail a great deal of shouting and apparent chaos, especially if many men are present. Those known for their eloquent speech and fair sense of judgement may sway the others with their opinions. In the end, a group of elders will briefly separate themselves from the group to render judgement.

The subject of *kūṭms* include choosing a date for a ceremony, punishing those who have violated custom, reconfiguring custom, resolving property disputes, deciding issues related to communal property or space (building, repairing, allowing the presence of outsiders), dividing costs or responsibilities for rituals or other village duties, and choosing village representatives (such as musicians) for a variety of public or government-related affairs. Kotas believe that faithfulness to the ways of the past will yield success and fecundity in the future. They decide what constitutes such faithfulness through the *kūṭm* and share the widespread Indic belief that righteous action confers a sort of enabling power on individual and community. Kotas use the word *catym*—roughly, truth, genuineness, or virtuousness—to refer both to mode of behavior and its favorable result.[10] When Kotas use the term *catym*, they are always enacting a time-sense, invoking a form of morality whose value lies in its status as historically prior to any emerging present.

More than by people, *catym* is possessed by the Kota gods (*devrgūḷ*) and the ancestors (*ānāṭōr*): they are powerful, truthful, and ideationally rooted in the past. Kotas share with Hindus and followers of many religions a belief in a primordial period when men and gods were closer. During the god ceremony, Kotas strive for unified action through ritual, music, and dance, and for a oneness of mind, a state of agreement called *oḏop*. For they believe there has been a decline in righteousness and unity since the period of original union, at which time Kotas would also have possessed maximal *catym*. The god ceremony gives Kotas the opportunity to temporarily counteract what they perceive as a negative historical trajectory, and thus to make themselves whole and vital once again.

Catym is closely linked with a system of rules or customs called *kaṭs*. Kotas use these rules to define themselves as members of a moral community. Literally meaning "knot," *kaṭs* do "bind" Kota behavior; but, in *kūṭms*, Kotas also negotiate and recreate their *kaṭs*. Music may be indirectly involved in this process as well, for in some villages (not Kolmēl) musicians play instrumental melodies to help induce possession in the diviner whom they will occasionally consult in village matters.

Kaṭs, which permeate everyday ways in which Kotas comport themselves, are spatiotemporally contingent. For example, one should not cross one knee over the other directly in front of elders or important ritual specialists.[11] During a god ceremony, a former Kota postman gesticulated at my wagging leg: my crossed knee was supporting my arm as I trained my video camera in the direction of the principal ritualists. I was sitting perhaps fifty feet away from the tent, within a broader area cordoned off at all other times of the year. Because of the ritual importance of the place and time—the center of the village during the god ceremony—and the personages involved, the "rules" became somewhat magnified, extending out in space. Although I was fifty feet away, it was as though I sat directly in front of the honored men. Similar rules contribute to the structure of respect in Kota society, and their force is place- and time-dependent.

Ethnographic and Historical Issues

Ethnic Relations in "Traditional" Nilgiri Society

A nostalgia for things removed in time and space is partially responsible for an enduring Western fascination with the "native" inhabitants of the Nilgiris. This began with Father Giacomo Fenicio's visit to "Toda mountain" in 1603, where he found his first Toda, "a huge man, well proportioned, with a long beard and hair like a Nazarene falling on his shoulders" (Fenicio 1906 [1603], 724). The Todas appeared, "in accordance with the rumour, to be of those who were driven from the territory of S. Thome by the many wars in former times and scattered through these parts . . . a race of men descended from the ancient Christians of St. Thomas" (Fenicio 1906 [1603], 719). The promise of finding long-lost peoples who had escaped the passage of time captured the imagination of observers and, later, scholars.

The system of ritualized exchange also caught the attention of these observers. Todas were given pride of place in many early accounts. This must have bolstered their sense of ritual superiority, which they had already gained in the subcontinental context by adhering to vegetarianism. Even their musical behavior, characterized by their performing poetically elaborate songs (Emeneau 1971) and hiring Kotas for instrumental music, conferred high rank in the Indic context, where performing vocal music and acting as patron are both signifiers of status. Both Todas and Badagas paid Kota musicians, in part with sacrificial buffaloes, for performing at their funerals. As clients, instrumentalists, and consumers of cattle flesh, Kotas were constructed as inferior in the Indic code. It would be a mistake to assume that Kotas accepted inferior ranking, however.

Badagas, the other major Kota patrons of the recent past, are an immigrant cluster of castes who began arriving in the Nilgiris after Muslim invaders defeated the Vijayanagar rulers of the Mysore area in 1565. These "northerners" (the literal meaning of Badaga), fleeing south, quickly assimilated themselves with the local inter-tribal system, sometimes learned Toda or Kota languages (fluently), and eventually absorbed features into their own Kannaḍa dialect that could "only have

[been] acquired from the Nilgiri languages" (Emeneau 1989, 137). They now share a great deal culturally with the Kotas and Todas, including ritual practices such as the secondary mortuary ceremony (Hockings 2001, 62).

Interaction among Todas, Kotas, and Badagas has long been fostered by their spatial configuration: they are all concentrated in settlements on the Nilgiri plateau. The seven (largely endogamous) Kurumba tribes of gardeners and hunter-gatherers have been less directly interactive: they live on the edges of the plateau, on the steep slopes of the Nilgiris, and along the foothills in the Wynad area of Kerala just to the west (they also extend into Kerala and Karnataka states). Irula agriculturalist and gatherer subgroups are also distributed along the edges of the plateau and have been in structural positions similar to those of the Kurumbas *vis-à-vis* the plateau communities: they are regarded with fear as sorcerers. In the Wynad region of the Nilgiri foothills and to the west in Kerala live the Paniya tribe, who remain in abject poverty as "agrestic serfs" for landowning Badagas and the Chetti trader community. They have little interaction with Kotas, except perhaps those of Kalāc village near Gudalur town, and are musically quite different. The Kotas, Irulas, and most Kurumba groups share a great deal musically and employ cognate sets of musical instruments.

Two ritual-economic systems were in operation, one set on the plateau, another in the Nilgiri foothills and the Wynad region of Kerala (Bird-David 1997). The system on the plateau, at least, is represented by Nilgiri inhabitants as having been ideal and fair, only later becoming corrupted by selfish, avaricious, or status-seeking groups. The remembrance of the idealized inter-tribal system has generated what Michael Herzfeld calls "structural nostalgia," the "rhetorical longing," replicated in every generation, for a lost "reciprocity" (Herzfeld 1997, 111). This "system" now signifies traditional Nilgiri society, just as *jajmānī* in Hindu villages has come to symbolize "traditional India" (Fuller 1989). Kotas themselves maintain nostalgia for perfect reciprocity in the distant past, while many of them simultaneously feel they have been mistreated in more recent times.

In the "traditional system," families of Kotas called *muṭgārn* provided goods and services to the other communities. In exchange they received grain from the economically dominant food producers, the Badagas; clarified butter, sacrificial buffaloes, and sometimes raw foods from the pastoral Todas; and forest produce and services as watchmen from

Kurumbas. To Badagas, Kotas were essential providers of funeral and festival music, pottery, carpentry, thatching, leather and metal goods. Kota music, along with a number of ceremonial items, was also indispensable at Toda funerals. Although Todas considered Kotas ritually defiling, they accepted from them pottery (for use in the home and the less-pure Toda dairies), and depended upon them for axes, knives, and jewelry.

Kurumbas were feared as sorcerers but were nevertheless needed to provide Kotas with ritually important objects, which could only be obtained from the forest areas they inhabited. Kotas see Kurumbas as true jungle people, tribals' tribals. In contrast to the tall, somewhat light-skinned, reddish-complexioned Kotas and Todas, the Kurumbas are diminutive, dark-skinned, with curly hair and almost negroid features. These physical features of "forest people" appear again and again in Sanskritic writings over the centuries (Thapar 2001), which suggests that the broad pattern of spatial/social othering was deeply embedded in a shared subcontinental classification scheme and was not merely the result of later reifications (such as the census; see Cohn 1987b)—although these no doubt register in the more complex notions of "tribe" today.

Although Kurumbas were, and continue to be, feared, Badagas and Todas ranked them above Kotas, largely because Kotas were observed to consume the meat of cows (some have given this up), and at times, carrion (Kotas now deny this ever having been the case). Kotas in the 1930s began refusing to provide services to Todas and Badagas because they were discriminated against: the Nilgiris was increasingly modernizing, but Kotas were being denied admission to schools and even barred from tea stalls frequented by Badagas. Economic and demographic changes, combined with the increased availability of goods for purchase in the bazaar, rendered Kota services less essential. Kotas fought back by withholding their services as musicians. As the Badaga population grew out of proportion with that of the other communities of the hills, it was also no longer possible to maintain traditional relationships of exchange based on hereditary agreements between pairs of families.

The Nilgiris' physical environment most certainly influenced the ways that early writers represented Nilgiri tribals. Under British colonialism, many expatriates wrote letters describing the climate and countryside, which reminded them of England (e.g. Harkness 1832). The region still retains now some of the beauty extolled in nineteenth-century accounts, but the landscape has also been transformed through the influx of significant populations from other parts of India and Sri Lanka, as well as by the cultivation and processing of tea, the introduction of non-native plant species, tourist development, and local industry—in particular, Hindustan Photo Films, the major national producer of photographic and x-ray films. Natural beauty played an important role in the construction of what Marie-Claude Mahias appropriately calls a "tribal sanctuary" in the Nilgiris. The beauty of the place drew people in. "The more the region opened up geographically, socially, and economically, the more the aboriginal peoples were seen as being different, primitive, associated with the jungle (or savage), and consequently the epitome of a tribe" (Mahias 1997, 326).

Aside from its "tribal inhabitants," one of the remarkable features of the Nilgiri district, given the quantity of literature written about it, is its small size, a mere 958 square miles. Triangular in shape, this hilly region, located in the state of Tamil Nadu, borders Kerala and Karnataka states to the west and north and lies at the juncture of the Western and Eastern Ghats, the two most prominent mountain ranges of South India. While forty per cent of this region lies above 5,900 feet, the elevation reaches its climactic 8,640 feet above mean sea level at Doḍḍabeṭṭa (lit. "great peak"), the second highest peak of Peninsular India (Lengerke and Blasco 1989). The Nilgiri district as a whole is populated by endemic animal and plant species that benefit from fertile soil, and until recently, abundant rainfall. The plateau surmounting the Nilgiri massif is blanketed with savannah grasslands said to be some 3,000 years old (Blasco and Thanikaimoni 1974); sporadic wooded areas, locally called *sholas*, are spread throughout the grasslands in hollows and ravines. The southern and western slopes of the Nilgiris, which were once covered with dense evergreen forests, have also been subject to transformation: many have now been leveled and converted into tea plantations.

The Nilgiri Hills are one of the favorite tourist spots in India, their importance for newlyweds comparable to that of Niagara Falls. (Each year, a few young brides tragically plunge to their deaths posing for honeymoon pictures at the edge of a precipice.) Since "tribes" of the Nilgiris remain important tourist attractions, the idea that the Nilgiri tribals continue their customs from time immemorial continues to be propagated. Several Toda hamlets are quite close to Ooty and frequently attract curious visitors; a center for Toda handicrafts, housed in a cement, reverse-parabolic-shaped reproduction of a Toda house, similarly draws tourists interested in buying the characteristic Toda-embroidered cloth—now available as tote-bags and table runners. Kota villages receive less traffic, but still find a place on some tourist circuits. While living in Kolmēl I observed vans stop at the edge of the village, with lavishly dressed North Indian women emerging with their husbands for a timid glimpse of the natives. I felt like something of a zoo-keeper—or the wrong person for that cage—and most certainly spoiled the scene from the perspective of the tour guide.

Emerging Populations and Shifting Demographics

The British founded Ootacamund in 1827 as the headquarters of the Nilgiri part of Coimbatore district and later the summer residence of the Madras government. The Nilgiri district had come into the possession of the East India Company following the defeat of the Muslim ruler Tipu Sultan in 1799. Shortly after the first road to Ootacamund—already under construction in 1820 (Price 1908, 23)—was built, the demographics began rapidly to change: those who had inhabited the region for centuries quickly became a minority.

By the time of the 1881 census, the ethnic groups most closely associated with the Nilgiri Hills, the Kotas, Todas, Badagas, Kurumbas and Irulas, composed only 37 per cent of the total population of the Nilgiri district (Hunter 1886, 10: 308–9); in ten years the population had increased by 41,533 persons to 91,034—mostly consisting of new laborers who were attracted to the area for jobs on coffee and tea plantations (Hunter, 309). Badaga agriculturalists and cattle herders of this district have increased most dramatically in population, from an estimated 24,130 in 1881 (Hunter 1886, 309) to between 171,000 and 300,000 in 1997 (Ethnologue.com). By 2001, the total district population had reached an alarming 764,826. The Kota and Toda populations, in contrast, have not changed significantly: Kotas were counted at 1,065 in 1971 and were estimated to be 1,500 in 1990 by Dr P. Varadharajan.[12] This, if nothing else, would account for the intense degree of cultural concern within the Kota community over what it means to be Kota, what compromises need to be struck to succeed in the modern world (as a Kota), and the extent to which sharing of land, language, music, gods, and the purported realm of the dead might threaten or bolster the viability of the community.

The emergence of distinctive Nilgiri communities may be framed in terms of two broad spatiotemporal processes: populations coming (or remaining) together and moving (or staying) apart. Reconstructing the histories of these populations is, in part, a matter of aligning these shifts with other significant events inscribed in stone, described in cave paintings, or retold in oral forms.

One method of reconstruction is through language: The Kota and Toda languages form a subgroup of the South Dravidian group of languages in South India, generally thought to have separated from pre-Tamil before the earliest Tamil literature, some 2,000 years ago.[13] Kotas and Todas may have migrated to the hills at least this long ago and remained sufficiently cut off from the mainstream population on the plains to develop their own languages independently (Emeneau 1989).[14]

The hills have never been entirely cut off from the plains, but neither have they been as integrally a part of a state network as they became after roads began to be built and transportation improved. It has long been accepted that the Nilgiris have been touched by warfare, traversed and populated by plains populations, and affected by state policies or taxes. Despite these interventions, there are few records of major upheavals, and the Nilgiri Hill communities remained stable enough to develop and maintain their own cultural characteristics.

Scholarship and Knowledge

The Nilgiri Hills are an excellent site for investigating the relationship between the history of scholarship and the emergence of particular forms of knowledge. The focus of earlier Nilgiri ethnography on the ritual and economic relationships among indigenes derived both from an abiding interest in India as a place whose principal defining feature for the West was "caste" and anthropology's heritage as a discipline searching for human universals—as well as cultural differences—in societies believed to be untainted by westernization or industrialization (thus the focus on tribes rather than on, say, Anglo-Indians). If these interests served as the engine for some Nilgiri scholarship—reinforcing such categories as "tribe" that continue to be used by local actors themselves—the scholarship thus produced also reflected back and influenced the course of research on South Asia generally. Nowhere is this better exemplified than in the work of the anthropologist David G. Mandelbaum (1911–87), the first American cultural anthropologist to conduct fieldwork in India, and the Canadian linguist Murray B. Emeneau

(b. 1904), the first philologically trained North American scholar to take an anthropological interest in Indian culture, and to apply philological methods to unwritten Indian languages.

Emeneau used his three years' fieldwork on Kota, Toda, and Kodagu to lay the scientific groundwork for Dravidian historical linguistics. He is known for, among other things, his concept of India as a "linguistic area": the idea that the languages of the subcontinent, through mutual influence, attained distinctive areal features despite their origins in distinct language families. Aside from his numerous publications of a technical linguistic nature, his most substantial Kota work was a four-volume collection, *Kota Texts*, dictated in the Kota language by his principal informant, K. Sulli. Dravidian linguists continue to plumb the depths of these meticulously collected texts—and the accompanying grammar and phonology of Kota—for further understandings of the Kota language.

After completing his initial research on the Kotas (1937–8) and publishing a number of important articles on aspects of Kota culture and society, Mandelbaum deferred completion of his Kota book manuscript in favor of learning about the society and culture of India more generally. Although he never completed the Kota book, his field materials (copious notes, recordings, film footage) are so important to the historical framing of the present work that they, and he, merit additional consideration.

A student of Melville Herskovits and later of Edward Sapir, Mandelbaum arrived in the Nilgiris in April of 1937 after a brief stint in Kerala among the tribes of Travancore and the Jews of Cochin (Mandelbaum March 21, 1937; Mandelbaum 1939a; 1939b). He was drawn to the Nilgiris by his old colleague Emeneau and worked with Emeneau's English-speaking informant, Sulli. Sulli would come to the room of Emeneau, and later to that of Mandelbaum in Ooty, and provide information for a rupee a day. This allowed Sulli to take leave of his teaching job.

Mandelbaum's reliance on Sulli, whom he found largely accurate, was tempered by two traits, the tendency for "his recollection . . . to be neater and more integrated than was the historical actuality," and to portray himself "much larger in his account than he may have [actually been] in the event." Sulli's information was more reliable when he gave "an impersonal account of, say, ceremonies, [in which] these traits . . . [did] not prevail." Sulli's work with the scholars gave him the courage to fight against some of the prevailing customs in his community (Mandelbaum 1960, 307). His first critical move was to cut his hair, for adult Kota men were expected to wear their hair long.

The 1930s was a time of stress for the Kotas of Kolmēl village: a decade after a lice-borne disease had decimated the village, there were still no ritual specialists to conduct ceremonies in the traditional fashion. Partly in response to this devastating event (which was believed to be evidence that the Kotas were committing some terrible wrong), and partly to improve their social status in relation to their Hindu and tribal neighbors, a movement arose to advocate worshiping a new set of Hindu deities while another movement arose attempting to modernize Kota ways—particularly in regard to the slaughtering of bovines, the seclusion of women during menstruation, and the male style of wearing the hair long. Sulli led in some of these reforms and was subsequently barred from joining in communal worship. Sometime during this period, Sulli composed a song decrying cow sacrifice that was recorded both by Mandelbaum and by the Dutch musicologist Arnold Bake. Three other men and boys joined Sulli in his separation from the village, one of whom, the late A.K. Rangan (who was about five years old when Sulli cut his hair) became one of the most popular and innovative Kota song composers, but, like his uncle, remained estranged from the village until his death (1997).

Fieldwork Background and Dramatis Personae

Having previously spent two years (1982–3, 1984–6) in South India studying the *vīṇā,* a classical stringed instrument, I returned there in September of 1990 seeking a different experience and the opportunity to use different analytic tools. My first four months of fieldwork were spent seeking a field site and attempting to gain a broad sense of local music-making in the villages of Kotas, Todas, Irulas, and Kurumbas. Traveling from village to village, I felt most welcomed in the seven Kota villages and was invited warmly to participate in activities related to both everyday life and death. The personal connections I was able to establish gave me confidence that I could conduct research effectively, and the richness of instrumental ritual repertoire in Kolmēl village struck me as unparalleled in all the Nilgiri tribal repertoires.

After my initial period of field research (September 1990–November 1992) I returned to the Indian subcontinent to take up a new project from November 1996 to February 1999, and spent an intermittent four months of this time in the Nilgiris, pursuing questions raised by my earlier research. Other brief visits and email correspondences after I began to write the present book allowed me to investigate matters relating to the calendar and agriculture that had eluded me on earlier visits.

During most of my field visits I resided in Kolmēl (Tamil: Kollimalai), a Kota village of about fifty households. In order to be productive and personally comfortable, I rented my own room in the largest house of the village, known as *banglo* (Bungalow), where I had a bed, desk, and shelves for books. A television and VCR allowed me to use "feedback" techniques, and eventually to create collaboratively a seventy-minute documentary of the Kota "god ceremony" (*devr*), with Kota-language narration.

While living in Kolmēl I participated in and observed all the major Kota ceremonies, learned to dance men's dances, and to perform on all their three types of drum (*dobar, tabaṭk, kiṇvar*). Since I was less successful in learning to play the wind instruments, *koḷ*, *pulāng*, and least of all the *bugīr*, I did not attempt to participate by playing these instruments in public. Working out the fingering of some pieces on these instruments helped me enormously in understanding and notating the melodies, however. In the course of my research I became familiar with a great number of songs and learned to sing them as well. No public venue as such existed in which it was appropriate for me to sing, but among friends, and in the context of clarifying a word or musical phrase, I had ample opportunities to sing with, for, and sometimes against, Kotas.

I was able to balance my privacy needs with my wish to take advantage of intimate village living by accepting the hospitality of the family of my friend, field assistant, and consultant, R. Kamaṭn (a.k.a. Duryodhana), who lived in a small, shingled, wattle and daub dwelling on the side of the village opposite the Bungalow. Duryodhana's mother, R. Mathi, cooked for us and I, in turn, returned the affection as a fictive second son, helping out with day-to-day grocery expenses and errands in town. Food is a medium through which Kotas articulate degrees of social/familial closeness. Every morsel of food Mathi cooked was suffused with the affection (*gav*) she felt for me—and she let me know it.

Food production embodies temporal continuity, whether through the bit of yesterday's bean stew (*udk*) thrown into the fresh food made today, or through the lingering heat in the hearth (*elkāl*)—a locus of domestic divinity—stoked with fresh wood at each mealtime. As I sat in the *gaṇcatī* (man's place) next to the hearth at every meal, the family's generous hospitality, binding time (cf. Fernandez 1966, 69; 1986a, 45) and space, slowly integrated me into the household. Mathi died suddenly in June, 2001, at the age of about sixty; not a day passes without my thinking of her or feeling for her family and friends.

I had the opportunity to experience both the hardships and social pleasures of fieldwork with many Kotas in all seven villages. The chapters of this book are filled with anecdotes, life-historical details, songs, and traditional stories provided by the most important of my consultants. The most prominent of these dramatis personae are listed below for convenient reference (those resident in Kolmēl are listed with a house number. {#} corresponds with houses shown on Map 3):

Dramatis Personae

1. Duryodhana: my field assistant, *koḷ* player, aged twenty-three in 1990 {1}
2. R. Mathi (deceased): Duryodhana's mother, composer of a few mourning songs {1}
3. S. Raman: Duryodhana's father, player of all instruments, singer, carpenter, and blacksmith. Aged sixty-five in 1990 {1}
4. K. Puccan (deceased): most respected *koḷ* player of all seven villages; elder, storyteller; classificatory elder brother of Raman. Aged seventy-eight in 1990 {2}
5. P. Varadharajan: Puccan's son; doctor; *dobar* (drum) player {3}
6. S. Cindamani: female singer, dancer, storyteller; originally from Kurgōj village. Daughter Meena married to late grandson of K. Sulli {4 and 5}
7. Caḷn (deceased): elder brother of Cindamani; former *mundkānōn* of Kurgōj village
8. A.K. Rangan (deceased): disenfranchized Kota man whose innovative songs were being sung by Kotas in many villages in the early 1990s. Nephew of K. Sulli {6}

Map 3: House Locations of Dramatis Personae, Kolmēl Village, 1991

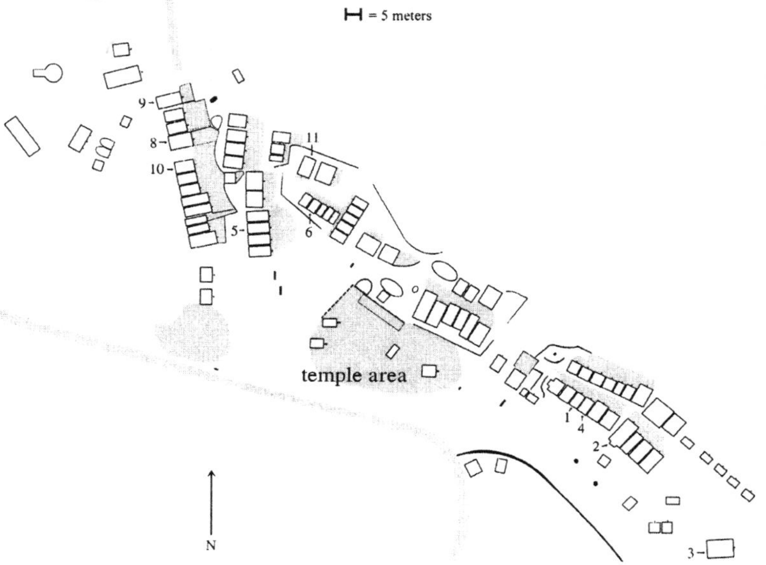

The white rectangles in this map represent buildings, which are for the most part houses. Their fronts are indicated with a small knob on one end, usually facing north-east. The two leftmost and one rightmost building in the temple area are temples; the other rectangle is a structure on which Toda clarified butter offerings were once burned. The light shadow in front of most of the house rows are *kavāls*, or mud-packed yards.

9. K. Jayachandran: banker from Porgāṛ village, married to Puccan's daughter. Learned important pieces of repertoire from tape recordings of Puccan
10. Sakole: dancer, *dobar* player, my landlord. Aged ninety + in 1990 {7}
11. Va. Kamaṭn (deceased): former *mundkānōn*, childhood friend of Puccan, protagonist in construction of Tamil-style temple; reformer of rituals and customs, wealthy landowner {8}
12. Sridharan (deceased): *Mundkānōn* (~1990–2000) who left his post at the age of about thirty-three in 2000 and later committed suicide.

Sulli was his mother's paternal grandfather {9 is the *doḍvay* or *mund-kānōn*'s house}

13. Pa. Mathi: elderly female singer, dancer, ex-*tērkārc* (wife of *tērkārn*) {10}
14. V. Mathi (deceased): singer, lived in Ticgāṛ, used to visit daughter in Kolmēl regularly {11}
15. Richard K. Wolf: ethnomusicologist {7}

Kota Villages

Kota name (Tamil name): approximate locations with respect to Ootacamund

Kolmēl (Kollimalai): seven kilometers south

Mēnāṛ (Kundah Kotagiri): thirty kilometers south-southwest

Kurgōj (Sholur Kokal): twenty-five kilometers northwest

Kalāc (Gudalur Kokal): fifty kilometers northwest (nestled within Gudalur town)

Ticgāṛ (Trichygady): fifteen kilometers northeast

Porgāṛ (New Kotagiri): thirty kilometers east (just outside the town borders of Kotagiri)

Kināṛ (Kil Kotagiri): fifty-five kilometers east-northeast

* * *

This book proceeds theoretically from "stasis" to "motion," focusing first on "place" (Chapter 3), then "time" (Chapter 5), and then "spacetime" (Chapter 6). The structure is not rigid, however, for place, time, and spacetime are woven together throughout. Each chapter also lays groundwork for the next. My integrative approach also focuses on interconnections among different kinds of data—musical, ethnographic, historical, textual—rather than compartmentalizing them. I have presented both the data and the arguments in increments, revisiting themes, enriching models, and filling in details as the book progresses. Some may find the arguments and the evidence for these arguments technical at times, now and again engaging the specialties of the musicologist, the anthropologist, the South Asianist; but I have tried to lay bare the basic ideas of each chapter for all readers to understand. For those who wish to read the fuller ritual context for my discussion of the god ceremony and mortuary ceremonies earlier on, I recommend making a brief detour to Chapter 7 right now. For others, the detailed treatment of these rituals might make better sense after having been introduced to the themes of these rituals gradually over the course of this book. The poetics of the book's organization lie in the simple fact that social life is learned as an amalgam, a network of relations, whose significance becomes clear only as one moves through the spaces and times of one's own life.

CHAPTER 2

Shawms and Songs

In this chapter, I explicate the structure of Kota music, explore its affinities with the larger musical environment, and consider the ways in which Kotas construct their unique musical tradition. The tribal communities of the Nilgiri Hills maintain a distinctive musical profile with respect to their plains-dwelling neighbors. Members of Kota, Irula, and most Kurumba tribes of the Nilgiris share cognate ensembles of shawms, cylinder drums, and frame drums.[1] The specific melodies and timbral features of the instruments vary from community to community, sometimes from village to village. Such differences articulate subtle aesthetic sensibilities at the most local level.

Several of the percussion ostinatos are virtually identical for all these communities, making it possible for a Kota to drum along with an Irula group, or for Kurumba musicians to accompany Badaga dances. Some melodies played by all of these tribal communities (e.g. Beṭṭa Kurumba, CD 12) share a style of drifting loosely across their percussion ostinatos. All of these communities share the practice of assigning particular melodies to rituals and other actions, especially starting out, "crossing" thresholds (Ko. *kaṛtd*), and processing along paths (Ir. *dāṛi koḷal*).

The Kota *koḷ*, about twenty inches long with double-reed attached, has a conical bore and six holes. The *vag* tree (*Salix tetrasperma*), from which wood the bell is carved, grows in coomb forests near some Kota villages. Members of other tribes use different local materials for their instruments, which obviously contributes to the timbral variety of each community's ensemble.[2]

Kota instrument-makers usually determine finger-hole positions on their wind instruments by comparing new instruments with existing ones and by feeling where the holes should naturally fall. Many *koḷ* makers

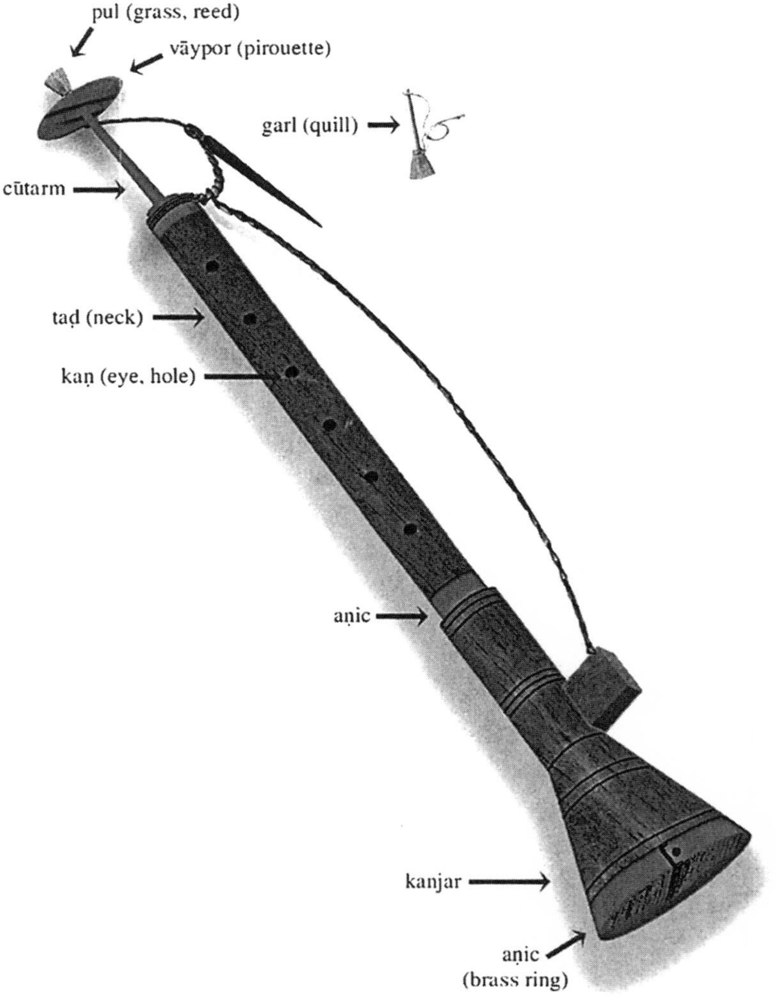

Fig. 2: Parts of a *Koḷ*

play the instrument themselves. *Koḷ* melodies (also called *koḷ*) are somewhat constrained by the physical characteristics of the instrument, but players more than compensate for the slight differences between instruments and the irregularity of the reeds by manipulating embouchure and air pressure. Pairs of *koḷ* players need to make periodic adjustments to remain in unison.

Some *koḷ* melodies are organized in balanced segments which converge around particular scale degrees; the instrumentalist articulates these scale positions by touching on adjacent holes and inserting ornamental flourishes. No Kota term for "scale" or "mode" as such exists. Kotas do use the classical Indian musical term, *rāgam*, by which they mean melody. Melodic contour rather than precise intonation defines melodies. The "same" pitches in analogous phrase positions, or in repetitions of a melody, vary in intonation by as much as a quarter tone.

Instrumentalists play many of the same melodies on all three wind instruments, *koḷ, pulāng* (bamboo clarinet), and *bugīr* (bamboo trumpet), by using the same fingering patterns. Since contour is more important than pitch or timbre, variations in these instruments' tonal and timbral profiles are not important for distinguishing pieces from one another. On all three instruments, players produce melodies with intervals that fall in between standard Western intervals: microtonal variations and tremolos on single tones are characteristic and intervals of approximately three-quarters of a tone are not uncommon. Melodies on all three also share the tendency to be punctuated by what I call a "*gag*" tone.[3] This pedal tone is set off from the main melody by an interval of between a minor third and a perfect fourth (sometimes displaced by one octave). Some vocal melodies gravitate toward wind-instrument intonations, others operate within a limited range of whole and half tones, and still others belong to the world of mellifluous Indian film melodies. This plurality of melodic possibilities is not problematic for Kotas, who have been interacting with a variety of others in multiple realms of activity for generations.

Accompanying the *koḷ* players, drummers maintain an ostinato, usually consisting of three layers: a frame drum (Ko. *tabaṭk*), which leads the percussion and sets the basic pattern, a deep-sounding and sometimes larger cylinder drum (*dobar* or *gumbar*), and a higher-pitched cylinder drum (*kiṇvar*) interlocking with it (CD 13; Fig. 3). The general Kota term for cylinder drum, *par*, is cognate with other Dravidian terms for drums (DEDR 4032). The modifying prefixes in Kota that distinguish bass from treble are onomatopoeic: the bass drum sounds "*do do*" or "*gum gum*;" the higher-pitched one sounds "*kiṇ kiṇ*." The drum shells, once fashioned of wood, are now metal, often used containers obtained

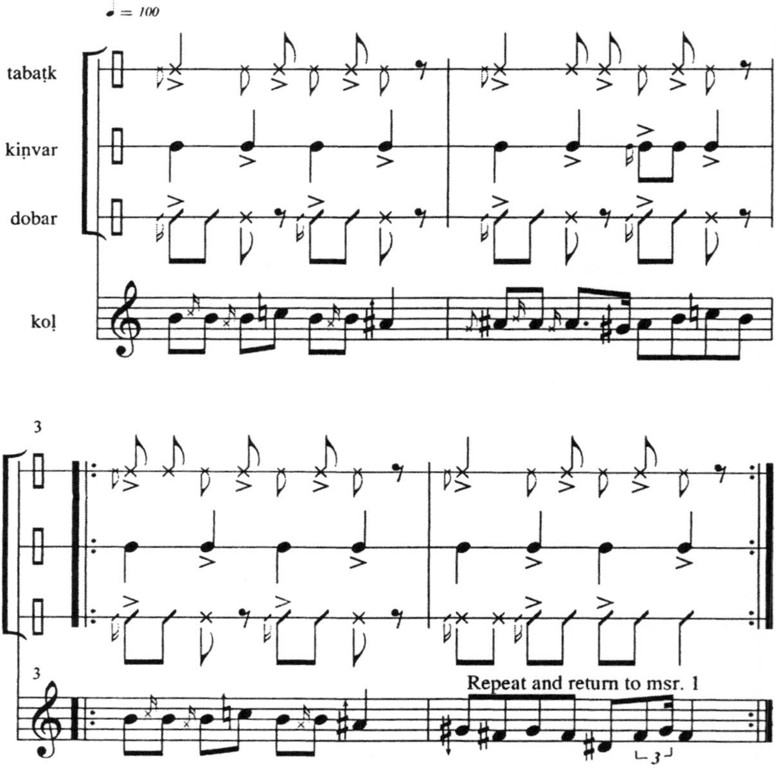

Fig. 3: Kota Women's Dance
in *Tiruganāṭ Dāk*

from the bazaar. *Tabaṭk* frames, fashioned by Kotas in their blacksmith shops, are affixed with goatskin heads; *par* heads are generally deer-skin, oxen, or cow hide. Cymbals (*jālrāv*) may also accompany the ensemble as additional time-keeping devices, but they are optional. (See photo section: Steps in drum preparation.)

The Kota term for percussion ostinato, *dāk*, means "type" or "section" and applies to either rhythmic or melodic patterns. Percussion *dāk*s are named according to a variety of criteria. Even though the total number of structurally distinct patterns is very small (as few as four, depending on how one counts), the names of patterns, and even the proclivity to name or conceptualize patterns under group rubrics, varies among the seven Kota villages. Fig. 3 (CD 13) shows the *tiruganāṭ* or "turning dance" pattern which accompanies both dance and non-dance melodies and which can range considerably in tempo. Patterns used for accompanying men's dances are played more rapidly (e.g. mm 184) than those for women's dances (e.g. mm 100) or for ritual melodies that do not involve dance. One women's dance melody is provided here as a convenient index to the percussion pattern. The melody is internally more regular than either the first Kota example or the comparative example from the Beṭṭa Kurumba tribe. The degree of internal flexibility ranges across the repertoires. In the Kota case, melodies accompanied by rapid percussion ostinatos appear to be more regular and metric than those accompanied by lugubrious ones.

Dancing and Drumming

Male dancers usually articulate *tiruganāṭ* with steady, alternating footsteps, four counts per drummed cycle. In men's dances, which are simpler than those of women, dancers emphasize counts one and three by rising up on the toes slightly and straightening the knees just prior to landing. Men spin to the right, to the left, to the right, and to the left again; each dancer crouches and keeps his arms out, fingers somewhat splayed for the first three spins. For the final left spin, they all straighten up, raise their hands and move them about above their heads while calling to god "*ō. . . ḷy.*" A common *tiruganāṭ* men's dance tune consists of four balanced phrases, each one percussion-pattern-cycle long. One cycle of the dance equals two melody repetitions and eight repetitions of the percussion ostinato. Not all melodies are so symmetrical, however, in relation to the dance. Within a given men's dance, the relationship between the number of foot counts in one spin and the next is not always consistent. Some dancers take care to coordinate their spins with musical phrases; others are more casual about their rates of turning and when they change direction. These laggards have to spin quickly to synchronize their position with that of the other dancers at some anchor point (such as the beginning of the melody) to avoid total chaos.

Women align their dance movements with the internal articulations of the dance melodies more assiduously. Style of anchoring in the dance, then, is gendered, and turns on its head the common association of men with structure, logic, and linearity, and of women with intuition, feeling, and uncontrolled agency. Musicians cannot impose this highly structured approach to dance on women merely by playing. Kotas do expect women to dance precisely, however, and as a consequence men take care to be especially exact in their drumming for women's dances.

Women revolve by stepping slowly when they dance; they also turn by pivoting their feet, heels close, toes pointed out at nearly right angles. Unlike men, who dance with their palms open, female dancers hold their hands open or precisely close them in time with the music. Open- and closed-hand positions do not alternate simply, but rather in units of OC (open-closed) and OOC (open-open-closed). Meanwhile, the female dancers either stand erect and hold their arms at shoulder level, or bend over and hold them closer to waist high (elbows remain bent). In combination, these dance moves provide complex counterpoints to the positions articulated on the drums and in the melody. Women refer to their dances with such names as "one turn dance," (*oḏ mar āṭ*), "two turn dance," and "four turn dance," which are more descriptive and specific than the names of men's dances.

The "one turn dance," which has twelve counts of a half-note each, is danced to the melody in Fig. 3. The formal structure of the melody, ABB (= 4 + 4 + 4 counts), keeps each melodic cycle in phase with the dance. However, women also perform the same dance to another melody in *tiruganāṭ dāk*, which is only eight half-note counts long and does not feature internal repetition. For every two repetitions of this dance, *koḷ* players must repeat their melody three times. Instrumentalists don't pay attention to the relationship between dance and melody cycles to the extent of waiting for women to complete a full cycle of dance before they stop playing the melody; more important is how much time remains in a given time period (e.g. before sunset), and which other tunes they plan to perform. Musicians also make errors. If the B Section of the melody in Fig. 3 is not repeated, the dance gets aligned differently with the melody; the dancers might re-anchor their moves at the beginning, or they might just continue repeating the dance with the new alignment.

Performers on each drum may vary their patterns independently of the others, within the small range of options for a given drum. Neither the order, number of repetitions, nor any particular combination of variants are prescribed. Individuals develop habitual ways of responding to one another that are not verbalized—a subtle elaboration by one drummer might serve as an invitation for a second drummer on the same drum to join in on that variant, or stimulate a different drummer to produce a variation on his pattern.

The *tabaṭk* pattern provided in Measure One, a common denominator to all variations, is generally the first one Kotas learn. The main *tabaṭk* variations on the recording (CD 13) are represented in Measures Two and Three. The *tabaṭk* player's left hand holds a small stick and softly taps the drum (indicated by smaller, downward pointing stemmed notes) in between the strong right-hand strokes (indicated by notes with stems up). Tension might be created by leaving out a stroke in one cycle. The contrast between the very deep open stroke on the *dobar*, indicated by a notehead, and the muffled stroke, indicated by an "x," is important. Whereas the *tabaṭk* player may alternate among a number of equally weighed variants, the *dobar* player should provide a firm foundation with a basic pattern in *tiruganāṭ dāk* and only occasionally insert contrasting patterns, such as that in Measure Four.

The *kiṇvar* player has fewer opportunities for variation. The significant *kiṇvar* contrast is between a resonating tone created by hitting the drum head near the edge with the fingers together (stem down), and a higher-pitched ringing tone created by slapping the head with fingers splayed (stem up). Although the *kiṇvar* part is rhythmically simple and repetitive, only a few excellent players can produce the ringing *kiṇvar* stroke well. The sound is denoted by a special verb, *ēkaḷc-*, meaning to shout out to someone without using his or her name, as in the English "hey!"[4] A characteristic interlocking effect is produced by pairing the ringing *kiṇvar* sound with the muffled *dobar* sound (in the predominant pattern); both are offset from the principal strokes of the *tabaṭk*. The deeper strokes of both cylinder drums coincide with the *tabaṭk* only on the first beat of the cycle. Kota drumming can be thus described as a multilayered, minimally varied ostinato pattern that is used to help *koḷ* players maintain tempo and, more generally, rein in their melodies.

These features of Kota drumming invite broader South Asian musical comparisons. Harold S. Powers notes affinities between South Asian and West Asian musical traditions in terms of their shared use of stringed instruments and the prevalence of conjunct melodic movement; he also points out a shared musical process in South Asian and South-East Asian traditions: the use of idiophones to delineate temporal cycles. What distinguishes the music of South Asia from that of its neighbors, according to Powers, is a particular emphasis on drumming (1980, 72): "As in South-East Asia, [drummers] are released from having to keep time. . . .

In South Asia hand-clapping and hand-waving, cymbals and even cyclically repeating melodic phrases are also available to control the metric cycles. At the same time the South Asian drummer, like his western Asian counterpart, is associated with only one melodic line at a time, so that he is not inhibited by being merely one part of several in a multilayered, complexly articulated instrumental ensemble as is, for example, his Javanese counterpart" (1980, 72).

The association of South Asian drummers with "only one melodic line at a time" does not prevent them from participating in the layered, multi-part drumming ensembles of some folk and ritual traditions, including those of Kota and other Nilgiri Hill tribal communities. Elsewhere, *ḍhol-tāshā* drum ensembles are composed of as many as three independent parts: two ostinati and one improvised part, plus cymbals.[5] The drumming ensembles of South India's Scheduled Castes, Cakkiliyar and Paraiyar, also tend to have more than two layers. In none of these, however, is the ensemble texture as complexly articulated as that of the Javanese gamelan.

Tribal Music in South Asian Contexts

It is more difficult to situate Kota music in relation to other kinds of "tribal music" because the concept of a "tribal culture" is problematic and because so-called tribal populations participate in multiple musical worlds. A search for what is musically "tribal" risks deteriorating into a forage for what is most exotic. One could treat the concept of tribe as merely a reification, whereby any similarity in music among "tribes" is merely coincidental. Or one might consider how local actors construct tribal music discursively in specific settings. It is also possible to synthesize what is available from existing musicological descriptions of tribal musical practices. These three perspectives can provide mutual critiques. The third approach, in particular, challenges us to incorporate so-called "tribal" musical processes into our larger understandings of South Asian music. In writing on "tribal" traditions of music, scholars have drawn attention to asynchronous rhythmic components, parallel harmonies, bitonality, and large interval skips.[6] One way of systematizing some of these observations and combining them with some of my observations on Nilgiri tribal music is to note that "melodic patterns, patterns of stressed and unstressed beats, numbers of beats in a cycle (either percussively or melodically articulated), and patterns of movement" appear to operate semi-independently. Performance, composition, and improvisation in such tribal musics become "matters of negotiating the conjuncture of these entities."[7] This process, in the Kota case, involves anchoring.

This synthesis will tell us neither what all tribal music will sound like, nor what any community values musically. It would be hard to imagine musical traditions that lack any principle for coordinating elements of a performance. But it may prove useful to ask, in any musical tradition, what the temporal regulating principles are, how tightly they regulate, and whether the principles themselves change over time.

Specific kinds of cyclical coordination seem to be at issue in the South Asian context. Today's two systems of *tāla* in North and South Indian classical music evolved to enable musicians to coordinate multiple time structures—drum patterns and melodies—in particular ways. Even the common drone could be seen as a solution to the problem of coordinating melodic segments in tonal space, horizontally or vertically.[8] The question of whether such forms of coordination were seen historically as "problems" in the South Asian region remains open, but, as the music theorist Lewis Rowell pointed out, "the words 'regulate' and 'control' occur more frequently in Indian music literature than in any other theoretical literature, raising the speculation that there was something there that threatened to get out of control" (pers. com. April 30, 2002; see also Rowell 1982, 33).

One such process of regulation can be observed in the "slow *khyāl* genre of Hindustani vocal music" in which the "singer's durationally irrational *ālāpa* phrases float and drift over the surface of pulse and meter." At the end of each cycle, "the vocalist pulses his melody for a few seconds. The pulsed fragment is timed so as to reach the main note of a little fixed motive . . . precisely at count number 1, together with the drummer" (Powers 1986, 701–2). Martin Clayton contrasts this "melismatic style" with a "syllabic style," in which melodic articulations more closely match the regular subdivisions of beat and pulse (Clayton 2000, 50–2). The contrast applies to Kota melodies as well (compare CD 1 with CD 13). In the Kota case, the metric cycles marked out by the drums last only 3–4 seconds—much shorter than those of most classical *tāla* performances. The *koḷ* melody, which also repeats, is generally no longer than a minute and often lasts only five seconds. Structurally comparable, even the most "melismatic" Kota melodies seem "metric" at particular points where a note corresponds with a drum beat; unlike the Hindustani example, the locations of these Kota anchor points vary according to the melody. Although the potentials for change are not explicitly presented in the Hindustani example, the points of convergence, or anchor points, in Kota music can vary somewhat among performers and over time.

All Kota instrumental pieces are defined individually, by melody, as either "god tunes" (*devr koḷ*), "funeral tunes" (*tāv koḷ*), or "dance tunes" (*āṭ koḷ*). As "genres," each of these three categories of melody is "polythetic" (Needham 1975) in that they are not reducible to a specific melodic or rhythmic profile—except that men's dance tunes tend to be faster than the others. Rather, a tune's membership in a genre is defined by convention, by ad hoc similarities between one tune and another, by association with particular kinds of ritual, or by the perceived ability to generate an affective profile of varying complexity (Wolf 2001). Each of these basic genres is subdivided according to particular ritual function, or class of functions, some of which overlap.

Ambiguous musical genre boundaries are found in special ritual circumstances (Wolf 1997a, 290).[9] When musicians play the "buffalo calling tune" during the dry funeral in Kurgōj village, they recall the period when this music was literally used to entice buffaloes and to egg on men who would wrestle these sacrificial buffaloes to the ground. Out of embarrassment and "rueful self-recognition" (Herzfeld 1997), Kotas continue to sacrifice buffaloes, silently, in secret and secluded places, if at all. The buffalo-calling tune continues, however, to enliven the dance funeral participants perform in honor of the collective deceased. It is a funeral tune, but not a sad one; a dance tune, but not so named and not played in the context of other dance tunes; and it is a ritual-sacrifice tune, in connection with which no sacrifice is any longer performed. The borderline generic status of this musical piece draws attention to ambivalences in Kota interpretations of sacrifice, dancing, and celebration in mortuary contexts.

Classification of Percussion Patterns

The identification of percussion patterns (*dāks*) by name and category presents a different set of problems. In Kolmēl village, Kotas use three names for all their patterns: *tiruganāṭ dāk* ("turning dance type"), *cādā dāk* ("plain type"), and *koḷāḷ dāk*. *Koḷāḷ* is the Kota ethnonym for the Cakkiliyars, a Telugu-speaking Scheduled Caste whose members are renowned as drummers and who have, on occasion, been known to play along in Kota ensembles. Kotas say they borrowed this rhythmic pattern from the Cakkiliyars. The otherness in origin is extended to usage context: Kotas play *koḷāḷ dāk* with melodies for non-Kota deities, such as Māriyamman (CD 14).

Slow and fast versions of *tiruganāṭ dāk* as notated in Fig. 3 are recognized as the same rhythmic pattern in Kolmēl village, but not always in other villages. A slower version would accompany a funeral tune, a faster version a men's dance. As for the other major patterns, Kotas in Kolmēl use the term *cādā dāk* to denote patterns of not only different speeds, but also, from one analytic perspective, different numbers of pulses. In the version of *cādā dāk* performed for god and death rituals, the pattern can be heard as ten pulses, divided 3 + 2 + 2 + 3 (structurally not unlike the Turkish *usul, Aksak Semai*). For dance, the pulses are articulated much faster, and the rhythm sounds either like $\frac{3+3}{16}$ or $\frac{3+4}{16}$ depending on whether or not the second half of the duple structure appears longer than the first half. In *cādā dāk*, dancers give each half of the duple structure one foot count. Some of the dances danced to *cādā dāk* are virtually identical with those danced to *tiruganāṭ dāk*. I cannot explain why the latter is called the "turning dance" and not the former. Kolmēl Kotas might understand these sets of pulse patterns, $\frac{10}{8}$, $\frac{6}{16}$, and $\frac{7}{16}$, to be versions of the "same" pattern because they perceive them as gestalts (see Wolf 2000/2001a), with structural beats falling in the pattern of L-S + L-L (Long-Short plus Long-Long), and because they share a common *kiṇvar* pattern:

	1			4		6		8	
L	R	.	L	R	.	L	.	**R**	.

The left (L) and right (R) strokes are resonant ones which players produce on the *kiṇvar* with their fingers together. The right stroke in bold (**R**) is the "ringing" stroke. Numbers indicate stressed strokes on the *tabaṭk*.

The versions of 6- or 7-pulses, really too quick to count out as discrete pulses, use the same *kiṇvar* pattern, molded or deformed to fit around the structure of *tabaṭk* strokes:

	x			x			
7	**1**	2	**3**	**4**	5	**6**	7
	1R		1R	L		**R**	

Strokes marked "l" do not exactly line up with the beat or pulse. These internal subdivisions are organized relationally with, or "anchored" to the principle *tabaṭk* strokes (bolded). The *tabaṭk* emphasizes first the (unequal) binary division indicated by the x's and secondarily the bold pulses 3 and 6. Additional strokes are added in variations as well. The point is that the relative durations of strokes at counts 1, 3, 4, and 6, fall into the pattern L-S + L-L, as do the important strokes of the 3 + 2 + 2 + 3 pattern. The isomorphic *kiṇvar* pattern is imposed upon (anchored to) the important strokes of each accordingly. This may explain why some Kotas said that both patterns are different speeds of the same *dāk*.

The problems of notating Kota percussion rhythm recall Constantin Brăiloiu's discussion of *aksak* (Turkish, "limping") rhythms, "irregular *bichronal*" rhythms (1984, 136) which are based on two units of duration—short and long. Using Brăiloiu's system, one might represent two versions of *cādā dāk* not precisely as $\frac{6}{16}$ or $\frac{7}{16}$ but as "double compound measures" of 3 + 3 (1984, 140: Fig. II.d.2), with the second set of three, when accompanying some melodies, consisting of a slightly longer beat, here indicated by a dot:

The dot is not exactly an additional half-unit, but merely an indication of extra length. This helps circumvent having to quantify a very fast pulse that is not counted as such by Kota musicians. The slower form of *cādā dāk*, in similar fashion, could be represented as a form of double compound measure with asymmetrical long beats (1984: Fig. II.a.10). Here the dot does indicate half a unit:

This representation of meters reflects something of their perceptual and gross forms. All three *cādā dāk*s are made to sound "binary" by the places Kota emphasize, or "anchor," their primary drum strokes.[10] The first beat is particularly important. When a *koḷ* player "pulls" or "drags" (*iḷv-*) a note extensively he should hear and see the *tabaṭk* player emphasize the main beats so he can resume the melody at the correct point in the cycle. The *koḷ* player may ask the *tabaṭk* player to "*kaṭṭicṭ iḍ*" (roughly, "hit hard").

Other Instruments

Outdoor contexts call for two instruments in addition to the *koḷ*, three drums, and cymbals. Kotas play *kob*s (curved, brass, valveless trumpets) loudly in cascading pairs to add excitement to the dance, to call god, or to announce a death. The *ērdabaṭk*, a kettle drum used to announce the beginning of important events, is not considered to be part of the *koḷ*'s instrumental ensemble. Kotas strike it "for ritual's sake" (*cātrtk*) without regard to meter or melody, the drum's sound being insufficient to carry an announcement very far.

Kotas avoid all these instruments indoors because they are too loud, and there is no reason to play the *ērdabaṭk* indoors. For practicing *koḷ*s (*koḷ* melodies), Kotas use the *pulāng*, an idioglottal, bamboo clarinet. It has six finger holes, like the *koḷ*, but its intonation is different, even considering that players can manipulate pitch by varying embouchure and air pressure.[11] The same *koḷ* melodies can be played (though with difficulty) on the *bugīr*, a bamboo trumpet that usually has five holes (CD 9).[12] The bamboo jew's harp, *pījl*, is now rare (CD 17). Traditionally-minded Kotas, especially in Kurgōj, keep an instrument on hand in case a female family member dies, for which it is ritually needed.

Like other unusual sound-producing instruments, such as the mirliton and bull roarer, the jew's harp is associated cross-culturally with disembodied voices, possession, and the spirit world. In the Kota case, the *pījl* is said to be played by the spirits of deceased women as they depart the world of the village and travel to the land of the dead; the same is the case with the unusual-sounding *bugīr*, said to be played by men as they make this spiritual journey. In both cases, the instrument is ideally cremated with the corpse. Both instruments have been part and parcel of the domestic realm, associated with music-making among friends. These instruments may have fallen into disuse because their dynamics are so limited. The sheer volume of everyday activities, a sound-world of radios, televisions, cassette recorders, and electric blenders ("mixies"), would drown out their subtleties. In homes without electronic gadgets, the volume of loudspeaker music blaring from temple festivals, weddings miles away, and political speeches broadcast from vehicles, reverberates throughout the hills and insinuates itself into the home.

Genres, Contexts, Songs, and Composers

All Kota instrumental pieces played outdoors have ritual associations. Singing is less contextually delimited, but its moral and aesthetic qualities are relevant to their ritual contexts. Women collectively perform *devr pāṭ* ("god songs") while dancing in a circle and clapping their hands (CD 2, 18, 21, 37). This is said to create auspiciousness at the ends of structural sections of *devr* and the *varldāv*. *Āṭḷs*—songs of grief, mourning, or fear—in contrast, are not associated with rituals and may be sung at almost any time (usually by women) for personal enjoyment or reflection (CD 7, 20, 23, 27, 31).

Men and women also compose a variety of songs in the Kota or Tamil languages, sometimes based on film songs. This proclivity toward drawing on musical forms and styles from the surrounding sound world is extremely common in India, even among members of genealogically closed communities such as the Kota. Kotas do not consider the music of outsiders to be defiling. Less borrowing takes place in the realm of instrumental music, owing largely to the physical constraints of the *koḷ*. It is easier to adopt a shawm tune from a neighboring tribe, whose instruments have similar tonal profiles, than from songs in mass circulation, which tend to be built on sequences of whole and half steps. Such popular songs would be hard to recognize on the *koḷ*, or would require more effort than musicians are evidently willing to make in order to convincingly reproduce them.

The cultural constraints on who can compose and on what topics they can compose are best represented in the negative: no culturally recognized "type" of person composes; no explicit restrictions exist for song content—although the ribald, sexual content of folk songs elsewhere in India is notably absent. One woman from Ticgāṛ village composed a song about her clever cat, using the melodic lilt of Tamil *kummi*-style songs. Another, from Kolmēl, sang about her wonderful husband and how he climbs up and down the hill to Gandhipet to catch the bus each day; some, I should add, find this a rather bland topic for a song. One man sings about god, another about fire, a third about his beloved. Residual taxonomies for songs include lullabies (*tālāṭ*) and "fun" songs (*tamāc*).

I find it useful to characterize Kota song composers in terms of their repertoire—its extent, popularity, innovativeness, and complexity—as well as in terms of their sometimes idiosyncratic personalities. Some individuals are known for only one or two songs, even though they may have composed many. Some singers compose many songs, but their compositions are not sung by anyone else—perhaps because the songs are personal or private, the singer is reserved, or the song is too complicated to be learned by casual listening. The compositions of popular composers, such as A.K. Rangan, catch on and last. In keeping with the observation that songs do not carry defilement, Rangan's estrangement from the village appears to have had no impact on the ascribed musical value of his songs. Other social practices, such as the degree to which an individual interacts with others by sharing songs, or participating in singing or dancing, do have an impact on musical transmission. Such interaction is constrained by gender roles: women have a common venue for singing together. Men do to a lesser extent; they may playfully sing along with women during the god ceremony, or they may sing *bhajans* (devotional songs) in Hindu temples and Kota temples for Hindu deities (e.g. the Kōjkāl temple for Rangayṇōr). But personality and personal history are at least as important as institutionalized roles. The few songs that Duryodhana's mother, R. Mathi, composed were so personal that even Duryodhana did not know of them until she sang one for me. Her songs are not sung by others. R. Mathi's hesitancy to share her songs had as much to do with the personal nature of the content as it did her more general bashfulness about dancing and singing in public. Not all Kota women share this personality trait.

Women are only accorded limited recognition for their musicianship as singers and composers, because singing is considered less specialized than playing instruments—especially the *koḷ*—all of which are played by men. Since very few Kotas maintain knowledge of *pījl* playing, the question of female musicianship on instruments does not arise at all. In collecting genealogies, I found that women and men tended to mention (or perhaps remember) less about the singing capacities of women than they did the *koḷ*-playing of men (see Appendix). But the mother of K. Puccan is remembered for her musicianship because of the *āṭḷ* she composed, which, some eighty years later, is still sung.

Despite the ad hoc nature of song content, Kotas continue to recognize the two genres, god songs (*devr pāṭ*) and mourning songs (*āṭḷ* or *dukt pāṭ*), as the "traditional" ones—clearly a reflection of more general cultural values that are registered in ritual. To understand what Kotas mean when they label songs in this way, we should analyze a few songs.

A God Song by S. Raman

I spent much time in the home of S. Raman, the father of my close companion and assistant Duryodhana (R. Kamaṭn). Raman occasionally made instruments and worked on other carpentry projects. I often heard him singing, playing, and composing recreationally; and frequently found myself eating dinner to the sound of Raman's radio, under the flickering shadow of his oil lamp's wick.

As of this writing, Raman remains adept in playing and singing all forms of Kota music and also evinces a talent for singing Hindi and Tamil film-song melodies. His singing voice, like his speaking voice, is thick and a bit nasal—certainly not beautiful in the manner of mellifluous "filmy" voices. Raman's skill lies in his control over pitch and his ability to swing rhythms and ornament melodies. His mastery of the *koḷ* was second only to that of Puccan in 1992. In the assessment of some villagers in 2001, younger men were rising to Raman's level and Puccan had become too old to play. Raman is personally regarded as a bit of an oddball, much relied-upon for his musical and carpentry skills, and well known for composing one song.

Raman's song in 1992 was popularly known outside the village as a "Kolmēl *pāṭ*," a song of Kolmēl village. Most Kota songs are identified with particular villages, either through the identity of the composer or through topographical features mentioned in the lyrics. Songs do not remain in their home villages, however. Women transmit them when they dance together in other villages, which they visit or move to after marriage.

Raman's composition, a god song (*devr pāṭ*), didactically describes normative behavior during the god festival (CD 18).

Analysis and Exegesis

This text is held together by almost rhyming phrases, correspondences between parallel endings such as "-umē," "let us . . ." (do, the verb), emphatic endings, "ē," and polite imperatives, "-īmē," or "-umē." The melody, too, tends to resolve at points where each rhyming segment ends. The relationship between melody and text is somewhat unpredictable. Most of the piece is a single melody whose phrases are divided up and rearranged in verses or the refrain, "Father, older brother . . ." Like much Indian folk and classical music, this version of the song features contrasting melodic sections, one centering on the lower octave, another on the upper. Lines 1–3 are usually used as the refrain, but in this version only Lines 1 and 2 actually return in the sections marked as "refrain."

"Father, older brother, younger brother, listen!"
as Sung by S. Raman, August 8, 1992

1. ayo aṇe karāḷē oriḍumē	1. Father, older brother, younger brother, listen!
2. aṛcāyḷ uḷē orgādīmē	2. Under the ceremonial tent don't sleep!
3. ōḷy ōḷy id̠irē aṭē āṛmē	3. Saying [the holy syllables] "ōḷy ōḷy" Dance!
(Refrain repeats)	
4. ōmayṇ acā jāyt elme kay tacirē cōyme id̠uge	4. Communities who don't know the sound of Kota instrumental music all clap their hands saying "god"
5. amede jāydk eytre ivorke vadegā	5. From where does this sleep come to our community?
1–2	(Refrain)
6. ācde āṭalme amke alāge	6. The dances which are danced are not for us
7. aṭd ūṭmale amkāyṛe alā	7. The feasts which are cooked are not for our sake
8. āṭ āc āciṯe kāl ēṭmēle	8. In the process of dancing while their legs are hurting
9. ācōrkāyṛe jōṛ māṭme	9. For the sake of the dancers Change the melody
1–2	(Refrain)
10. kulilā jāytāyṛe kukayrādīme	10. In the manner of senseless types Please don't sit!
11. ayṇōre amnōre oriṭuge	11. Amnor and Aynor are listening
12. kōv jāyd ām id̠ire koṇḍāṛumē	12. Saying "we are the Kota community," Let's celebrate!
1–2	(Refrain)

Line 2 admonishes men and boys not to sleep under the ceremonial tent, *arcāyḷ*. During the central days of *devr*, the god ceremony, men and women stay separate from one another at night, men under the tent, women in the home. This gendering of place reduces the opportunity for men and women to have sexual relations, which are forbidden throughout the ceremony. Each night, before women retire to their homes, groups of men and women alternately dance in circles around a bonfire to the accompaniment of *koḷ* music. The charge that men not sleep has two implications: a few men, including at least one *mundkānōn*, must remain awake twenty-four hours a day, keeping vigil in the *guṛyvāl*, or temple area, out of respect for god. Second, participating in music and dance on this occasion is a way to entertain, and thus, honor, god. The timing is important. Kotas believe that god's presence in the center of the village, by the temple, is fuller, more intense, during the god ceremony. Proper behavior toward the divine—and toward one another, as in my crossed-knees anecdote—must be observed more rigorously than usual.

While the men dance, they intone a long, almost eerie syllable that sounds like "oh," stretched out over the course of a full breath of air ("*ōḷy*" in Line 3). The syllable is significant purely as sound, a call to god. The significance of sound is also invoked with the word *ōmayṇ* (Line 4), "sounding at once," which is a proper term referring to the way in which instrumental music is initiated, fanfare-like, on each day of the god ceremony. When all the men have assembled, the instrumentalists play together as loudly as possible, making the sound extend, they believe, not only far around them in the Nilgiris but also into the realm of the gods (*devr lōgm*). The term is also synecdochic for Kota instrumental music in general. "Ō," the first syllable of *ōmayṇ*, is related to Dravidian terms for singleness, uniqueness, or unity (DEDR 990); through word and sound, then, *ōmayṇ* indicates a valued spatiotemporal form. Raman uses *ōmayṇ* in this song to negatively modify the word for community, caste, or type (*jāyt*), "all castes who don't know *ōmayṇ*," in this case, non-Kota South Indian women who clap their hands, dance, utter their gods' names, and sing *kummi* songs. The rhetorical meaning of Lines 4 and 5 is, "if non-Kota people can energetically sing and clap their hands even though their music is inferior to ours, why are we allowing sleep to overcome us?"

Lines 6 and 7 express the idea that dancing and eating ritual food is not merely for the joy of celebrating, but for the "making" of god. Lines 8 and 9 bring the singers into the context of performance once again, describing how the exhaustion of all-night dancing affects the dancers' legs, and ordering the instrumentalists to change the melody to maintain the dancers' interest. The word used for tune here is not *koḷ*, the usual technical term, but rather *jōṛ*, the term for the entire ensemble. The usage is metonymic.

Raman uses alliteration and assonance in Lines 6 and 7, drawing attention to the central phrases "all the dances danced" (ācde āṭalme) and "the entire ritual meal which was prepared" (aṭd ūṭmale), featuring contrasts between long and short vowels [ā] and [a], the two long vowels, [ā] and [ū], and a reversal of the phonemes [m] and [l]. In Lines 8 and 9, "When [their] legs hurt" is subtly rhymed with "change the tune." Alliterating in Lines 10 and 11, Raman draws attention to the [k] sounds in "who have no sense" and "don't sit." Line 11 contrasts the vapid personae of Line 10 with those of the gods, *ayṇōr* (father god) and *amnōr* (mother goddess), and ends the line with the verb "to listen," which begins with the same syllable as the suffix of respect *-ōr*, in the names of the gods.

Kotas, including Raman, appear to have modeled their techniques of prosody on those of A.K. Rangan. Alliteration and assonance have no bearing on the status of a song as a god song (*devr pāṭ*) or mourning song (*āṭḷ*) but did, in the 1990s at least, contribute to a song's aesthetic merits. It is worth taking a brief detour to examine a masterful example of prosodic manipulation in Line 3 of Rangan's song, "You, daughters of Kotas, stop crying!" (CD 19). "*Pate*," "*patīme*," and "*pace*" create an alliterative effect with the repeating [p] sound. The two halves of the phrase are balanced by the resemblance between the words "*digle*" and "*mogne*" and the long [ā] vowels in "*kātiṭe*" and "*āciyo*." The next line is also clever in reversing the order of the sounds [k], [a], and [t] for words that provide parallel functions in the sentence: the firewood "in the wood pile" (*katle*) and the baby "in the lap" (*takuḷḷe*).

3. pate digle patīme kātiṯe pace mogne āciyo	3. Having deprived yourself for ten months you gave birth to a newborn
4. katle vergme takuḷḷe mogme tāv nāṭke kēypiyo	4. You've sent the firewood in the heap, and the child in your lap, to the funeral ground

These techniques of verbal construction have long been used in folk music and classical poetry of the Tamil region.

Returning to Raman's song, the conclusion consists of a reflexive call to all *Kōv*. Since few non-Kotas can follow the language, this call is not directed outward, but rather reaffirms for the Kotas themselves this sense of collective difference from outsiders. Reflexivity and self-awareness in songs through lyrics of the type, "we are doing x," or "we should do x," are common in god songs. Songs may also embed the organization of performance in the text with particles such as "gō," which marks the end of a line as the speech of one woman calling to another. This reflective aspect of Kota god songs highlights a second aspect of "cultural intimacy." Communities engage in processes of self-representation not only in the public sphere, but also in the intimacy of their own environment, using culturally coded means of language, music, and dance.[13]

Not all the codes are exclusive: this song shares a pervading compound-duple/triple cross rhythm with much vernacular and mass-mediated music of the subcontinent, where it is often articulated in percussion accompaniment or melodic hemiola. The more localized environment for the underlying meter, which could be analyzed in $\frac{6}{16}$ with passages in $\frac{3}{8}$, is that of South Indian women's circle dances, *kummi* in Tamil. Raman draws attention to such dances performed by outsiders, women who "don't know the sound of *ōmayṇ*." Kotas belong to this musical environment; Raman symbolically distinguishes the song as rhythmically "Kota" by classifying it in *cādā dāk*—much as an Indian classical musician would identify a piece in a particular *tāla*, or a European musician in a particular meter. Raman takes a musical interest in the rhythmic intricacies of songs and percussion patterns and enjoys toying with classificatory ambiguities. Although not all Kota pieces, new or old, are strictly metrical, Raman has attempted, on occasion, to "correct" other Kotas' compositions which do not conform to one of the Kota instrumental rhythmic patterns. God songs need to be metrical if women are to be able to clap their hands and dance to them.

Though the meters of god songs call for some degree of precision, the particular textual means for organizing rhythm are flexible. Since even composers who write down their texts do not necessarily sing them as written, we should expect quite a bit of textual variation among Kota singers in general. My landlady, the late Mangiammal, in her rendition of Raman's song, substituted *jōṛ etmege*, "play the band," for "change the tune;" and concretized implicit ideas, singing "*ayṇōr* and *amnōr* are watching, they have come in order to watch dancing," and "dance for *ayṇōr-amnōr*!" She concluded not with "we are the Kotas," but with "those who are there should dance happily and beautifully." Keeping the tune in her mind, she sang the topically appropriate words and fitted them as well as she could. This is another kind of anchoring: making textual variations, even ones that make one stray from the beat, eventually return to a stable rhythmic framework.

Each performance of a song comprises a pool of key phrases or motivating concepts, a narrative basis for ordering these textual elements, a melodic idea, and a metrical framework. Each of these elements is potentially flexible. In god songs, though, metrical handclapping must rein in the other components—much as should the percussion *dāk* in the instrumental realm. In some songs (CD 20), the singer articulates the melodic shape and metrical pattern of a song through a series of vocalizations, usually on the syllables "la," "le," "li," or "lo," and on vowels. These may be smoothly connected or separated by glottal articulations, and they may vary in the course of the song.

Songs of Grief (*Āṭḷ*)

In songs of grief or sorrow, called *dukt pāṭs* or *āṭḷs*, meter is less consistent than in other kinds of Kota songs. Some *āṭḷ* singers articulate these songs with long pauses of uneven duration. This resembles the style of funeral laments upon which some singers model their songs. Still relatively spontaneous in origin, such tearful lamentation, or "crying," *agl*, is still inchoate as song. Though tuneful and containing affectionate words to the deceased, these expressions tend to be interspersed with sobs and halted breathing. "Crying" is rhythmically and melodically less musical, to Kotas, than "songs" (*pāṭs*) such as *āṭḷs*.

Perhaps as an extension of the genre's association with crying, intervals in *āṭḷ* melodies are more flexible than those of god songs, which tend toward whole and half-tone combinations. Owing to this intonational flexibility, which embraces intervals in the three-quarter-tone territory, *āṭḷ* singers can be accompanied by *bugīr* players. *Koḷ* players are likewise able to fashion new funeral melodies from *āṭḷs* they have heard. The tonal characteristics of *āṭḷs* may also come across as more subtle and variable than those of god songs because mourning songs are meant to be sung solo. Without a group singing together, an individual has fewer points of reference. A singer can thus more easily take liberties with rhythm and ornamentation.

Women are the primary carriers of the *āṭḷ* tradition, though men do compose and sing these songs as well. Unlike for god songs, no ritual setting exists for *āṭḷ*s that would tend to perpetuate the association of this genre with women. One explanation for the gendering might be sought in the structure of funerary grieving, where women more copiously shed tears; another might be found in the domestic context where these songs are casually sung. The prototypical performance situation (from the point of view of Kotas in the 1990s) is that of a grandmother visiting her married daughter or son, hanging about the kitchen, socializing, telling stories, and singing. Girls learn these songs from their mothers and grandmothers. Boys tend to be less present and less mindful. Even K. Puccan, a great musician on the *koḷ*, could not remember the words to the song his own mother composed on the death of his father.

An *Āṭḷ* to Puccan's Father

Puccan remembered little of his father, Kavdn, who died unexpectedly during a journey to Ooty. But he did remember the pitiful story of his mother, K. Mangi, who was left to return home for help retrieving her husband's corpse. Puccan alluded to this song once when he was demonstrating other funeral tunes for me, for the melody of this *āṭḷ* is also suitable as a *koḷ*. Duryodhana's mother, Mathi, had learned the song from Puccan's elder sister, Boylac Nic, and sang the version reproduced below in 1992 (CD 20).

This example illustrates characteristic features of the genre: individualization of the subject; addressing of the deceased with kinship terms of endearment (rather than of literal relationships); use of formulaic phrases, especially those that foreground a tone of emptiness, negation, and inability; specification of place names along a path; and intonation of the vowel [a], often with a glottal stop, before each phrase whose first word begins with a consonant. In this case, the vowel is always on the tonic pitch.

Suffering from exhaustion, Kavdn paused for a rest. Sleep, in the

Āṭḷ: "Kavdayo" as Sung by R. Mathi

*denotes departures from melodic pattern established in the initial vocalization

	la la la, la la la . . . la la la, la a la . . .		(vocalizations inserted between verses 3–4, and 6–7; second half of phrase varies between "la a la" and "la la la"; melodic fragment different between verses 12–13)
1.	enīṇā kavdayō enekōma kavdayō	1.	my father Kavdn father what shall we say, Kavdn father?
2.	bajārme ōbōd̲ī enīṇā enīṇā kavdayō	2.	you said, "let's go to town" my father, my father, Kavdn father
3.	vagvāṛme pacāle kukarci kavdayō	3.	in a grassy area near a vag tree you say, Kavdn father
4.	orkēne id̲iya māntekēḷōne kavdayō	4.	you said, "I'll sleep" one who doesn't listen, Kavdn
5.	mēkaṛce kavdayō māntāṛāde oyrgiya enīṇā kavdayō	5.	get up Kavdn father! you slept without speaking my father, Kavdn my father
6.	ucire īlāde oyrgiya kavdayō	6.	without life you slept, Kavdn father
7.	oj āce ānēna enkōma enaṇe kavdayō*	7.	I have become a lone woman what shall we say, my older brother Kavdn father
8.	āgācārē vadēna enīṇā kavdayō	8.	I come along the Āgāc route my father, Kavdn, my father
9.	gurkāne kāvile gurkāne kāvile enne veyntāra kavdayō	9.	the Gurkha policeman the Gurkha policeman asked me, Kavdn father
10.	oyrgūd̲re aṛydēna* enīṇa kavdayō	10.	I said "he is sleeping" my father, Kavdn my father
11.	oj āḷe vaciṯe ōṛōyṛd̲re ōcēna enīṇa kavdayō	11.	leaving (you) one man (alone) I ran my father, Kavdn my father
12.	toḍbāle cēydēna enīṇa kavdayō	12.	I reached tobāl my father Kavdn father
13.	kōkāleke vadiṯe pacire ōnēna enīṇā kavdayō*	13.	I came to the village and took someone and went and took someone and went Kavdn father

āṭḷ, is usually polysemic, referring either to death or to an unconscious state in which gods or the spirits of the dead may communicate with the subject. The sleep–death ambiguity is played upon in several ways. First Kavdn announces that he will sleep. (Let us for the moment overlook the scene in which Mangi tries to wake her husband up.) Next, a Gurkha policeman asked her why Kavdn was lying down; she responded that he was sleeping, knowing full well that he was dead.[14] Mangi's refusal to identify "sleep" as "death" can be read as a form of resistance to government authority. "That sleep which is not sleep" is an epithet for death in *āṭḷs*. Mangi was afraid the body would be taken away.

After Kavdn went to sleep, Mangi addresses Kavdn as *māntkēḷōn*, "one who does not listen to words/advice (*mānt*)." This formulaic phrase, virtually meaningless here and included in many *āṭḷs*, is a marker of the genre, a signifier of otherness. The deceased is gently reprimanded as one who doesn't listen to advice, to words of good sense, which may have saved him from his unfortunate fate. Neither can the dead person listen any longer to the words of the living.

Mangi calls to Kavdn, "get up," but being one who doesn't listen, and now can't listen, he does not respond. The negative constructions that follow are stylistically typical of the genre, "you slept without speaking." The expression for speaking, "*mānt āṛd*," means literally to "move" or "agitate" words (*mānt*). "You slept without life," moves from the image of silence to the explicitness of death as absence of life.

In two places, the song refers to the loneliness of the individual. This common stylistic trait is important for understanding the *āṭḷ* in its social articulation with death rituals: these rituals emphasize and elaborate upon the individuality of the human subject. First Mangi refers to the state of herself as "one woman," left as a widow in her husband's absence, and also left alone in a possibly frightening forest area without anyone she could trust. Later, out of pity for her poor dead spouse, she refers to her husband as "one man," left alone in the wild as she set off to obtain help from someone in the village. This image of Mangi alone in the forest with her dead husband is poignant, and perhaps one of the reasons the story of this death has survived several generations. Another reason for the song's survival may be its melodic simplicity. Knowing a bit of the melody, the story, and the formulae of the *āṭḷ* make it easy to construct this piece in performance.

At the song's end, Mangi summons help after running back to the village, her arrival home signaled by the name of a god's place, *toḍbāl*.

A focus of rituals and stories, this is a place of prayer whenever a Kota leaves from or arrives in the village along the *āgāc* route.

The melodic range of this *āṭḷ*, like that of many others, is limited to a fifth. The pitches approximate a minor pentachord with a slightly sharp "third." The melodic framework Mathi establishes in her initial vocalization remains fairly consistent until she approaches the line about the Gurkha (Line 9). The fact that Mathi repeats the antecedent phrase here, and then breaks the melodic pattern shortly afterward, suggests that she was uncertain of the text. Perhaps she was attempting to insert a fragment from the story into the song for the first time, or in a new way. Shortly before this, Mathi makes her first slight departure from the melodic pattern with the insertion of Kavdn's name; in several of the lines following, reiteration of Kavdn's name appears as an appendage to the main melody. Pushing to the end of her breath in several of these extended lines (and with a vocalization between Lines 12 and 13), Mathi's voice evinces a hint of the strain and emotionality that emerges even stronger during some other *āṭḷ* performances. When Mathi reaches the end of her breath in Line 10, she articulates a clear stop (rather than fading out) and then begins the next line. While subtle in this performance, this form of articulation is idiomatic—more common and distinctive in *āṭḷ* renditions by older people who did not develop their early musical tastes listening to smooth-edged musical models of film songs.

Having now taken stock of a few distinctions between god and death songs, we may ask what "difference" they make for Kotas. Or more pointedly, what do Kotas "make" the differences between their genres to mean?[15] Musical distinctions raise issues of more than aesthetic cultural relevance, they also involve central judgements concerning time and place.

Crossing Genres

Cīrmuk Kamaṭn's Musical Sin

A great *koḷ* player, named Cīrmuk Kamaṭn,[16] was prominent in the lineage of K. Puccan and S. Raman. Each year he used to lead the performance of *arcāyḷ koḷs*, the twelve-god tune suite played underneath the canopy (*arcāyḷ*) at the god ceremony. At the age of eighty, he commenced his annual performance, playing the first tune and the second. But when he tried to play the third, a *tāv koḷ* (funeral tune) "came." "Che che che," he uttered in disgust. "Next year I will die; next year I will not render a *koḷ* here." Cīrmuk died that year.

This story underscores the point that violating rules of place and time for musical performance may precipitate dire consequences. Also, one's memory for the proper context of a piece may fail. In Kota, a melody may "come" or fail to come, just as, in English, memory can "escape" one. A musician may become confused and play a piece in the wrong genre without realizing so right away, even though the genres of "god tunes" and "death tunes" are supposed to be musically distinct. The similarity of melodic phrases across tunes may lead one to take a careless wrong turn.

A Generically Ambiguous Song

The song "They shot the hunting bow" evokes the "Black Cow's Footprint" story via narrative fragments. The listener needs to know the story for the fragments to make sense. Such fragmentary communication is characteristic of *āṭḷ*s, although not exclusive to them. During my stay in 1990–2, Pa. Mathi would occasionally show up at my door and offer to sing; a great boon for me, since, as one of the oldest women in the village, she maintained a relatively broad repertoire of songs. One song took up a traditional theme involving the gods, which would suggest it was a god song. But she rendered it like an *āṭḷ* with flexible meter between verses; sections punctuated by distinct stops and breaths; and tones indefinite and quite close together. The text was also *āṭḷ*-like in focusing on the life of an individual. God songs are usually more generic and collectively oriented, mentioning many people's names (especially women's names), and seldom telling the story of any one person. Ambiguities in text combined with the inscrutable singing style led me, in 2000, to ask Pa. Mathi to identify it.

Both Duryodhana and Pa. Mathi presumed that the "old man" Tuj was a *mundkānōn* and that the events were taking place during the god ceremony because Tuj wore, tied in the front of his head, a *mumuṛy*, a hair knot which is supposed to contain god.[17] God, in the form of a man carrying the bow-and-arrow, a black cow, and the ancestors of the Kotas together made an exodus from one place, Venveṭm, and proceeded to another, Kamaṇvāy. The hunting bow references the Kota father god, *ayṇōr*'s role as protector. The bow-and-arrow is also a reminder of an ancient "tribal" past in which Kotas relied on bows-and-arrows to protect themselves and to hunt.

Next they traveled to Kōkālāṛa (Line 2), where Tuj coaxed the black

Panoramic view of Kolmēl village from the north

Dance day of Kolmēl god ceremony: men dancing
on *ākēr pacāl* (both photos)

The intensity rises; the circle widens.
Kunayṇōr temple visible to left of and just behind large tree on left;
Doḍayṇōr temple barely visible up and to left of Kunayṇōr temple
(both photos)

Naming ceremony. Elders and ritualist lined up from right according to rank

Two (non-Kota) visitors to the god ceremony kneel in deference to K. Puccan

Kota van with Kota bow and arrow insignia and a Tamilized version of their god's name: Śrī Kambaṭṭarāyar

Kota fancy dance dress (*āṭ kupāc*)

Women dancing in the *gagvāl* at the god ceremony in Kolmēl

Villagers in Kolmēl enlarged their *gagvāl*, which could no longer accommodate the number of women dancing during the god ceremony (January 2004)

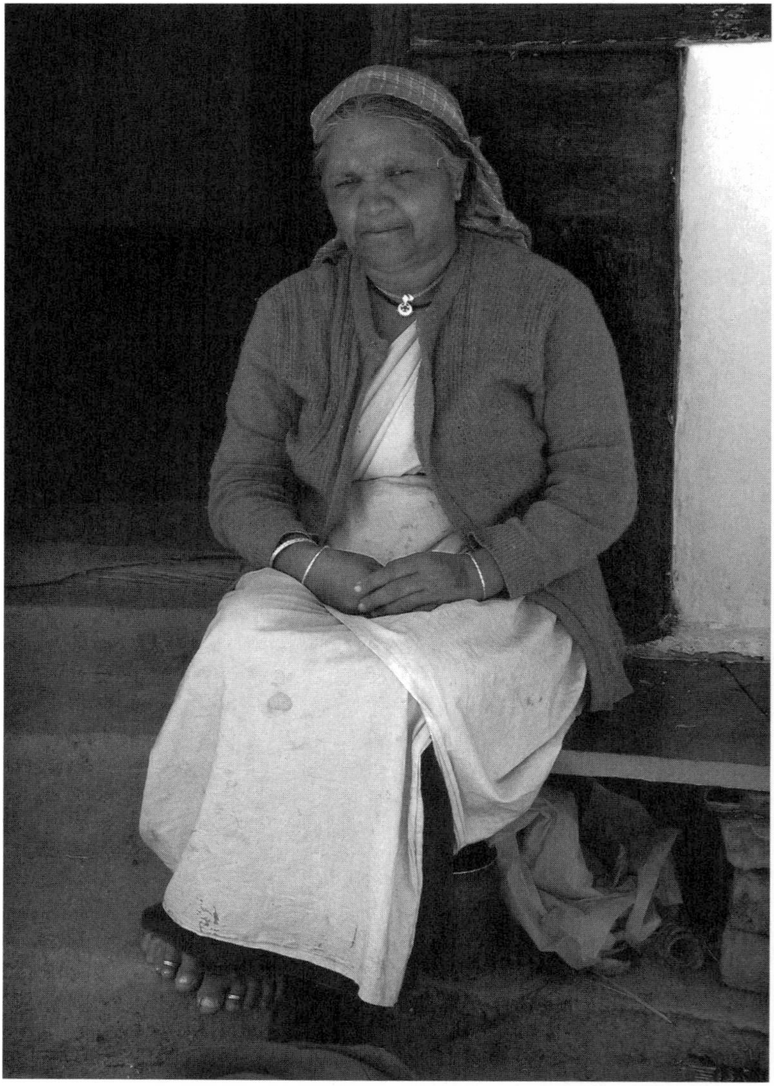

S. Cindamani in 2004

K. Mundan in 2004

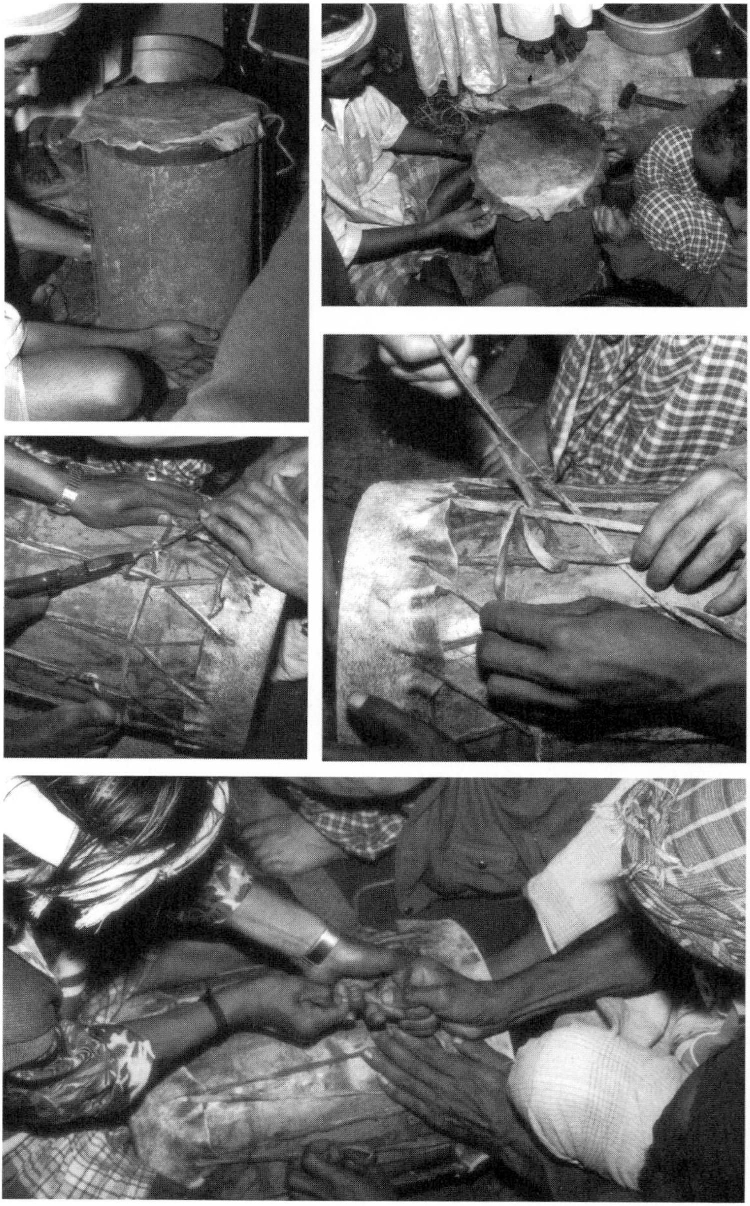

Replacing the skins on a *par*

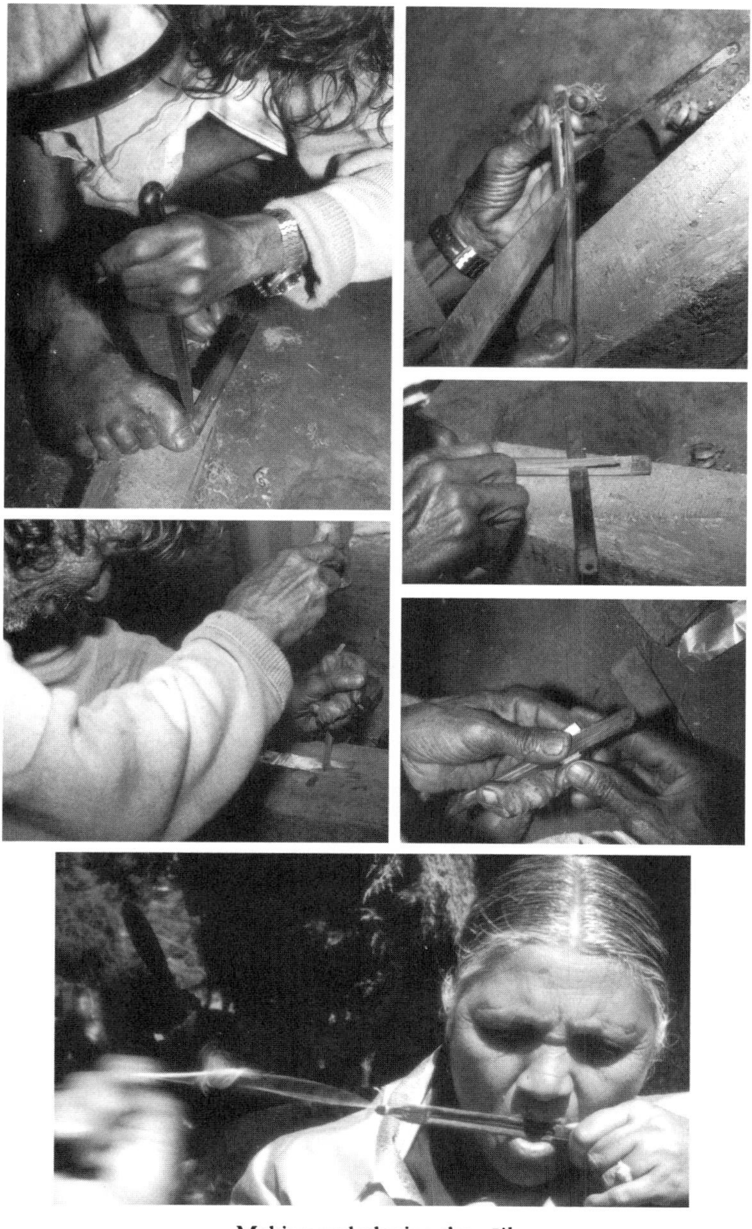

Making and playing the *pījl*

Women washing clothes by *ākēr* water tap, Kolmēl (2004)

Widow crouches in front of her husband's dry-funeral bier, surrounded by family

The millet-pouring tune plays thunderingly and the women begin to cry. Dry funeral, Kurgōj village, November 1997

The *mel pac mog* is instructed to touch the *koṭanm* millet to his forehead

The dry funeral procession commences

Procession to dry funeral ground: umbrella height and pole thickness proportional to age of deceased

Women dancing on the *ākēr pacāl* on the dance day of the god ceremony

Kaṇṇan (2004) wears headphones as he rehearses for the god ceremony. Cassette of the late K. Puccan makes him feel close to his grandfathers

Musicians tighten the skins of their drums by the fire in the *gagvāl*. Kolmēl god ceremony, 2001

Kunayṇōr temple, Kolmēl

Praying toward the temple area (*tak* tree on right)

Duryodhana and his uncle, working in the *kolēl*

"They shot the hunting bow," Sung by Pa. Mathi December 28, 1991 (CD 21)[18]

- = glottal stop in most of the repetitions of the vocalization

a la- a la a la- a la a e le- e le e le- e le e	(vocalizations interspersed between each verse)
1. vil vēṭn iṯr kamaṇvāyk vadvōrē	1. They shot the hunting bow, and came to Kamaṇvāy
2. kōkālāṛk vadvōrē kārāv bacv amn	2. They came to Kōkālāṛā, [with our] black cow goddess
3. tuj vērāḷ kartalk kēvēne kūcānā	3. Old man Tuj coaxed the calf into the calfshed and blocked the entrance
4. kartal pep kuckōṛ mumuyṛōṛ ōnānā	4. He went to the calfshed with the small clay pot for curds and front hairknot
5. kārāv bacv cōym pigālnēnē vadīgā	5. The black cow god comes behind
6. tuj vērāḷe [m]umuyṛōṛ pepkuckōṛ vadānā	6. Old man Tuj, wearing front hairknot, was coming with the curdpot
7. aṇkarāḷ iṉḏ kōkālkāyṛ	7. Older and younger brothers, today, for the sake of the Kota village
8. āygīgē aṇkarāḷ kāl āṛād kan nāṛē aḷāṛād aravangāṛ	8. They come, older and younger brothers A place neither trod upon nor inhabited A forest where men have not been
9. doḍayṇōr guṛyvālkē vadṯ pāl	9. To the Great Father God's temple area [they] came, and milk
10. cordigē kārāv bacv cōymē, la . . .	10. Spontaneously issued forth, black cow god . . .
11. kaṛ vay pay kab iṭd payē	11. The last house in the line is the "house of the erected post"

cow's calf into a shed to prevent it from suckling (Line 3). By preparing the cow for milking, Tuj marked his decision to settle in Kōkālāṛa. Milking a cow cements the relationship between a community and a place, making it not only an *eṛm*, but, more strongly, a *stānm*.[19] Kotas use the latter, Sanskrit-derived term (S. *sthāna*) to refer to a robust kind of anchoring in place. The former, Dravidian term, "*eṛm*," related to terms meaning "place, room, spot, opportunity" (DEDR 434), is temporally more contingent. Kotas might also use the term *doḍeṛm* ("big place") instead of *stānm*.

The status of the black cow as a divinity (Line 5) is somewhat ambiguous, both with respect to its permanence and its gender—sometimes it is called a god (*devr*) and sometimes a goddess (*amn*). The cow is also generally called "god" (*cōym*) as a gesture of respect, but not as a recognition of its divinity.[20]

The older and younger brothers in Line 6 are Tuj and his younger brother, who together went through great hardship traveling in the wild, uninhabited forest (Line 7) searching for a place to resettle. When Tuj approached, the black cow refused to be milked in that place. God entered the cow and directed it toward the future precinct of the *ayṇōr* temple (i.e. the main temple area) in Kolmēl village. The cow started to issue milk spontaneously,[21] indicating the spot was a "god's place," *devrd eṛm* (the term *stānm* would have been appropriate here as well).

When Pa. Mathi heard me recite her words "āṛād kan nāṛē āḷāṛād aravangāṛ" ("a place neither trodden upon nor inhabited; a forest where men have not been") from my transcript of her 1991 performance, she hesitated momentarily, saying "no, no, those words shouldn't be there, they are only used in *āṭḷs*." Such songs often describe the lonely, desolate, forest setting in which a person dies, is bewitched, or comes in contact with the spirits of the dead. They are marked by formulaic place descriptors of emptiness, such as "place where no one ever goes, where the crow doesn't fly." God songs are generally concerned with places of divinity, inhabited places, usually in and around the village. Yet Pa. Mathi had clearly labeled this a god song—not only because of its text, but also because of its performance context. She claimed that the song was still commonly sung by groups of women in the temple area, but neither Duryodhana nor I had ever heard it. There would be no reason to question this genre identification, except for the textual anomaly, and for the fact that the rendition style—flexible meter and intonation—was mournful and *āṭḷ*-like. However, this may have reflected an archaic compositional style and the fact that it was sung by an old woman.

Duryodhana rationalized the textual anomaly: in this ancient period, before the so-called aboriginal tribes arrived, the Nilgiri region was such an uninhabited place. This period of *catym* pre-dated the first onset of human frailty. "Death" was not a fully differentiated category of experience. Pa. Mathi seemed to accept Duryodhana's explanation. The place the song evoked and the song style fitted neither the genre nor the remaining text; it forced us as critical listeners to think. Musical evidence also suggests that this line was not originally part of the song: the section of melody repeated for this line was inconsistent with the song's overall structure of repetition. Pa. Mathi's unconscious associations of the journey and wilderness with an *āṭḷ* may have led her to insert inadvertently this formulaic phrase from the wrong genre and create an awkward fit.

After issuing milk, the cow pointed to another spot and said, in Kota, to found a village there. The first house of the village, the "house of the erected post" (*kabiṭ pay*), marks that spot.

Conclusions: Time and Place, Genre and Gender

The god/death bifurcation of musical genres is morally significant and spatiotemporally constructed. God genres focus on the center and togetherness. Death genres concern extra-village places, journeys away from the village and individuals. Despite ambiguous examples, violations of genre rules may have serious consequences. Mindful performance and close listening are more than merely aesthetic or formal exercises. One of music's critical functions in Kota society is to be reflexively *diagnostic* of time and place. Time and place of performance (or evoked by performance) can serve as the bases for musical evaluation. Musical styles or melodies, conversely, can indicate aspects of time and location: Kotas can learn when and who has died by hearing funeral music in front of the dead person's house; they can find other Kotas at a festival by hearing a Kota group playing or singing.

Within the community, the spatiotemporal patterns by which Kotas perform and transmit music are distinguishable in terms of gender: (1) order: men and women dance to instrumental tunes in alternation—men first, women second; (2) pattern of placement within ceremonies: ensembles of five to eight men perform instrumental pieces which punctuate ceremonies at a variety of moments and in places scattered across the village. Women (in larger groups) perform ritual god songs/circle dances at less varied places and times: mainly at the ends of structural sections of ceremonies; (3) locality of repertoire: men living in the village, generally descendants of its *kēr* founders, tend to transmit songs, *koḷs*, and stories about them that are specific to a village. Women who marry men in villages different from their own teach song repertoires from their natal villages to their offspring and to new female companions.

Kota music shares degrees of affinity with music in the Nilgiris, the South Indian plains, the world of "tribal" music, and South Asia generally. Like some other ritual and folk musical traditions in South Asia, the texture of Kota instrumental music is multilayered. Kotas identify aspects of their musical and dance traditions as explicitly "Kota" and "tribal"; but these valued features are not common denominators of the music produced by all Indian tribal communities. Like some other Indian "tribal" music, Kota music exhibits relative independence among elements of a performance; in the music of Nilgiri tribes, this characteristic is most pronounced in the relationship between a free-floating *koḷ* melody and its accompanying percussion ostinato. The role of the drum ostinato in examples from the Nilgiris and some Indian classical music appears to be one of subtly reining in the melody. Viewed from the melody-maker's perspective, the anchor points at which drum and melody coincide serve as temporary goals, end- and beginning-points for the calculation of phrases. By emphasizing beginnings and endings, embarking on physical and spiritual journeys, citing placenames and strategically using stories of the past, Kota musicians both constitute spacetime and operate within its constraints.

CHAPTER 3

The Morality of Places

Kota spirits of the dead remain so attached to where they once lived that they have trouble departing for the land of the dead. Duryodhana likened such attachments (*gāv*) to the burning desire for water a person experiences after walking in the sun for a long time. *Gāv*, stories tell us, causes some deceased persons to return to their home village as apparitions. The newly deceased are reluctant to leave home. Other spirits of the dead need to lure them away with words of enticement and soulful funeral music. Sitting at the dying one's side, the living refrain from making noises which may distract the departing spirit. If houses and villages make up the physical world, the land of the dead and the world of the gods exist in spiritual topographies. Both kinds of places have moral implications. They have something to do with the way Kotas conceptualize right and wrong, and they affect the ways in which Kotas behave.

Kota notions of moral behavior entail being in the right place at the right time, doing the right things. Presence in one's home village during the god ceremony (*devr*) is so important that an elder formally calls roll near the temples under the canopy (*arcāyḷ* +).[1] (A "+" in the text indicates a site on Map 4.) Those who must be absent feel it acutely. *Tērkārn* Kurval was, in the 1920s, employed by a tea estate to mediate monetary transactions with local villagers. His job often required him to travel. One year, after being deputed to Ceylon (Sri Lanka), Kurval found himself stranded, unable to return in time for *devr*. The *tērkārn* wept bitterly, feeling the pain of separation from his home, his family, his friends, and most importantly from the gods for whom he was a medium. God, it is said, appeared to Kurval in a dream and consoled him with assurances that he would soon find an opportunity to return home. He awoke

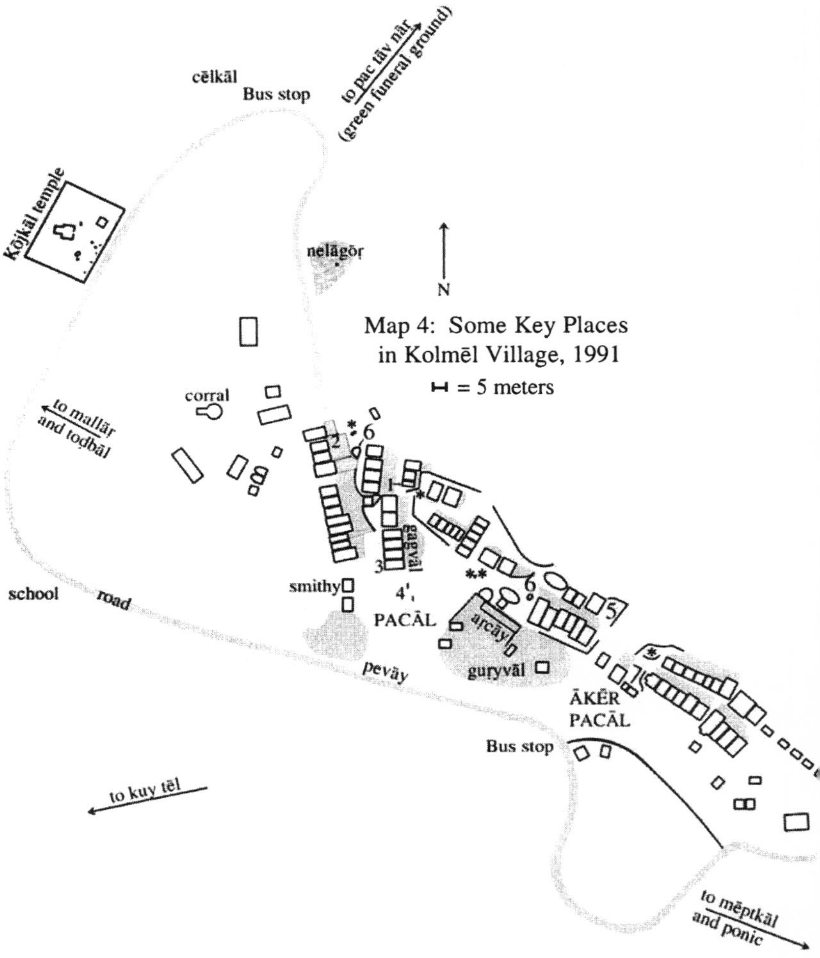

Map 4: Some Key Places in Kolmēl Village, 1991
⊢⊣ = 5 meters

* 4 water taps. Special one for god ceremony marked **
1. tēlvāl (menstrual seclusion house)
2. devr kal (god stone)
3. kab iṭ pay ("house of the erected post")
4. naṭkal (upright flag stones, meeting place)
5. place where women observe nominal seclusion during the god ceremony
6. tondiṭs (two) (where mundkānōns first carry fire during the god ceremony)

and started out for the beach, where he discovered three men about to travel by boat to Ramesvaram in Tamilnadu. Delighted by his luck, Kurval joined them and continued his journey home by train. Even though Kurval managed to return to Kolmēl in time for the temple-opening day, his fellow villagers refused to let him join the ceremony because he had been absent too long. Another *tērkārn* was appointed, and Kurval died as soon as *devr* was over.

Kurval's attachment to the village surely extended beyond the people of the village, for Kotas tend to invest specific topographical features with affective, sometimes nostalgic, significance as well. From childhood, Kotas build up sets of associations with particular stones, trees, and nearby forests where they have played games, tripped and fallen, or kept a tryst. Such associations are enriched by stories and beliefs invoking the landscape. For instance, in Kolmēl they understand the branches of the *toḍbāl* tree (+) to represent ancestral figures.

Each village has a favored location linked to self-definition. Residents of Kolmēl (called Kolmēlōr) give pride of place to their *pacāl* (+), a grassy area in the center of the village. Its physical beauty and its association with divine rituals, playing, leisurely chatting, and soaking in the sun imbue the site with significance. Some of the highly esteemed "god tunes" (*devr koḷ*) are called *pacāl koḷ*s because they are played in this area. *Koḷ*s which may be only played as accompaniment for dance on the *pacāl*, similarly named *pacāl āṭ koḷ*s, are generally more elaborate and longer (CD 11) than their "simple" or "plain" counterparts (CD 22) played in front of houses. Residents of Kurgōj village, in contrast, favor their *mallāṛ*, their many acres of elevated grazing lands bordering upon and interpenetrating the forests of the northern Nilgiris, just south of the Karnataka border.

"The village" can be defined as a "place" in multiple senses. Whereas most Indian villages are composed of multiple castes, often of multiple religions, Nilgiri tribal settlements are generally made up of one community alone. Tamil, Kanadiga, and other non-Kotas who live within the administrative village (Tamil: *kirāmam*) of Kollimalai (the Tamil term for Kolmēl) do not, from the Kota perspective, live "inside" (*uḷguḷ*) Kolmēl *kōkāl*. Yet many of these Hindus, Muslims, and Christians have grown up in houses within a stone's throw from those of Kotas. Most reside near the bus stop in ramshackle dwellings amidst a patch of tea stalls and shops just north-west of the *kōkāl* (*cēlkāl* +). Some run shops;

others work on Kota lands. They are called *kāṛōn*, literally, people of the *kāṛ*, the fields and bush separating Kota villages from forests.

Such outsiders participate in Kolmēl life informally through commerce, but only on the temple-opening day are they permitted to enter the temple area (but not the temples) for worship. For some of them, *ayṉōr*'s divine power is connected with the status of the Kotas as tribal people. Through participating in temple donations, and, rarely, playing music and dancing, these neighboring *kāṛōn*s register their participation as members of the village as a wider geographical and slightly more diverse entity in the real world, even though they can never belong to the village as Kotas define it internally.[2]

The word *kōkāl* does not mean "village" generically, it means Kota village, implying that the seven Kota villages inherently differ from other settlements. The idea that a Kota village is coterminus with the Kota people also emerges from the term *ūr*, which, in Kota, refers to the village as geographical projection of a living community. The complementary term is *nāṛ*, the land of the dead as a geographical projection of the ancestral community and their attendant powers.[3] These moral place-terms appear saliently in prayers and expressions, such as "*nāṛ tiṯ ūr tit*," "look after the village (and god) after taking care of the death ceremonies," or in the distinction between the small-scale *man tāv* (house funeral) and the *ūr tāv* (village funeral), a large-scale dry funeral celebration to which all seven villages are invited.

A Kota village, a place with roots, history and institutional significance, is more securely founded than is a mere topographical locale (*eṛm*). It is a *stānm*. The role of the cow in establishing the village as such is reiterated when Kotas creatively offer "cow leg" as the etymology of Kōkāl. Within the village, the place where the cow issued milk, the *guṛyvāl* (+) or temple precinct, serves as an anchor point for activity.[4] Upon awakening, R. Mathi used to go outside, put her hands together and head down, close her eyes slightly, and pray: first in the direction of the *guṛyvāl*, then spinning to the right in the directions of other significant sites. Afterward she would return home to kindle or stoke the fire in the hearth. Most Kotas pray by the *guṛyvāl* before leaving the village and after returning to it.

If the *guṛyvāl* invites centripetal activity, some of the other places of divinity surrounding the village, the *toḍbāl* (+), *ponic* (+), and the Kōjkāl (Hindu style) temple (+) focus the subject's attention on the village periphery. These locales constitute a kind of village border (cf. Daniel 1984,

77). When Kota men form a procession to play music (the twelve *devr koḷs*), pray, and make monetary offerings to the deities at these gods' places during the rain ceremony, they create a sense of village wholeness in keeping with the aims of the god ceremony (see Wolf 1997b), but slightly different in spatiotemporal form. It is not so much centripetal as circumferential, since the procession circumnavigates the village (along a north-west–south-east axis). The rain ceremony ends at a set of upright flagstones (*naṭ kal* +), where participants share tobacco as a formal enactment of unity. Sulli once said that when Kotas performed the ceremony, they caused rain to fall "only in Kolmēl, not across the boundary" (Wolf 1997b, 268). In this sense the procession ritually constitutes the village's geographical reach.

If processions exemplify ways in which places are given definite form through motion or action, images of motion imbue places with emotive content. Kolmēl was once called *koṛ āṛād kōkāl*, literally, "village-without-umbrellas-moving": the houses were once so tightly packed and abundant that one could not walk through the village with an open umbrella. This "structurally nostalgic" (Herzfeld 1997) place-name richly evokes a lost fecundity. Even terms for smaller-scale locations, such as "meeting stone" (*mandkal*), "man's place" (*gaṇcati*; see Fig. 6), and "dancing yard" (*āṭ kavāl*), suggest ways in which places "solicit bodily motions" (Casey 1996, 24) and are constituted in the experiences and memories of a community by the sum total of many localized actions—here, meeting, being a man or woman, and dancing.

Maps in the Mind

Villages, as internally articulated places, may function like maps in the minds of those who know them intimately. The significance of villages as maps derives from the manner in which agents immediately experience, apprehend, and then deeply conceptualize them over time. As places in the mind, villages are maps somewhat akin to the roadmaps one holds in one's hand. Both chart out, represent, and give emphasis only to particular aspects of the broad swathes of land for which they are named. The village, the dry funeral ground, and the town of Ooty are examples of places that serve as maps when they are envisioned by a Kota and used to navigate to a particular spot. Some places are the spots themselves, articulations, points on those maps, *eṛms*: a big tree in the village, the cremation spot for the deceased of a particular *kēr*, a favorite vegetable vendor in the market. Some of the spots are further articulated, as *toḍbāl*, for instance, is divided into branches which represent village ancestors. Songs too map out a set of locations in relation to one another, usually from the perspective of a particular protagonist. Listening to or singing such songs causes the hearer/singer to chart out the path in relation to his or her own mental models of the territory (cf. Robertson 1979). As these maps are used, they constitute spatiotemporal, and not merely spatial, forms.

Interpersonal (especially kin) relationships are partially mapped in the spatial arrangements of houses in a *kēr*. Household proximity, in turn, has an effect on the ways Kotas understand their social relationships. The Kota term *kavāl condm* refers to the kin-like quality of personal relationships among those who live next to each other, but who are not related to one another through the patrilineal ties that unify a *kēr*. Such unusual living arrangements may come about when a man decides to locate his family in the house, his mother inherited from her father (who lacked male heirs).

Kota ideas of what constitutes a place involve perceptions of topography, interpersonal attitudes, associations with differents kinds of actions, and an emotional component that may apply to all three. Spatiotemporal categories also come to embrace areas of human experience having little to do with literal distance, height, length, duration, or speed. In America, English speakers say, for instance, "I had a good time;" or "I'm in a bad place right now." Through language habits, many of us conflate a variety of attitudes, responses, and meanings created through our actions with the places and times in which these actions are carried out. A Kota equivalent of this can be described in the following model (Fig. 4).

When someone dies, a Kota might use the expression, "kaṭḷ kāl ayko," "it has become bier/cot time." The bier serves as a sign of "what-kind-of-time" it is in a particular place. In that village, the "time" is one of sadness, death, defilement, and so forth, for which funeral music and other rituals are necessary. For the speaker, the bier is also a sign of death, or more specifically, that someone has died. These associations are conflated. "Sadness," for example, is not a quality of "physical space-time" in Fig. 4,[5] but an emotion associated with the experience of losing a loved one that becomes, for the individual, a quality of "bier time." Hence, experiencing a place—or its correlative unit of time—calls to

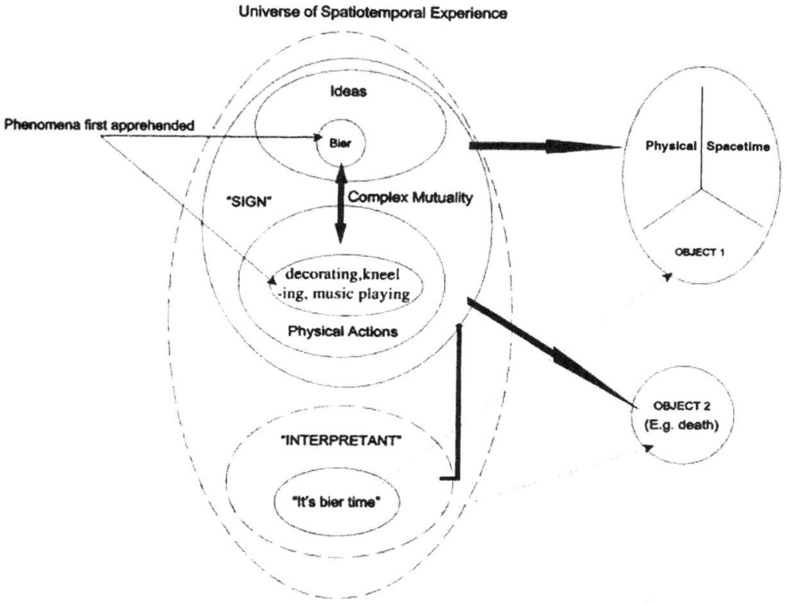

Fig. 4: Bier Time

mind not merely the physical passing of moments or the location of objects in a variegated geography, but other objects of knowledge as well.

Fig. 4 provides one way to think about how phenomena of immediate experience are related through language and action to time, place, and, in this case, death. Three components are central to C.S. Peirce's semiotic model, from which I borrow: the "sign," the "object," and the "interpretant." The "sign" is that which a subject first encounters, be it an image or an idea; the "object" is the immediate referent of the sign, a form of meaning the experiencer attaches to that which he or she has encountered; and the "interpretant," another aspect of meaning, pertains to how the experiencer connects a sign with an object, e.g. through language, gut reaction, emotion, or reflex. The thought, "the music I hear coming from over there means someone has died," is an interpretant of a Kota funeral melody (the "sign" of death) played on the *koḷ*. The thought then serves as a sign for a higher-level interpretant, another thought: "the old man Va. Kamaṭn of *ākēr* must have finally succumbed to his illness." The time it takes to draw such a series of inferences is a measure of the rate at which interpretants are converted into higher-level signs. These interpretants fall within the subject's universe of spatiotemporal experience. However, "objects" are not within this universe because they are not, by definition, experienced directly.

This raises the critical point that different "kinds" of time and space exist only as parts of sign systems. "Physical spacetime," the unknowable sequence and arrangement of all possible events as they have and will exist in the physical universe and to which we shall never have direct access (see Gell 1992, 240), appears as a possible "object" in this model—although an object of a special kind. If the bier signifies "bier time" as a "kind" of time, it does so as a "token" of a "type." This "type," physical spacetime (or whatever we wish to call it), is elusive, not accessible, not within our worlds of experience. One valuable aspect of Peirce's model (simplified here) is that it highlights the multiplicity of possible referents, or "objects," of any given sign, depending on the interpretant.

Let us re-imagine this scenario with further details.

A Kota, call her Mathi, enters a village and sees a bier. Inasmuch as Mathi recognizes the thing in front of her as a bier—and not just a bed—the bier registers in her mind as an "idea." Her recognition of the structure is further reinforced by the sounds she hears and the set of actions she observes—in some of which she could also participate. She hears the special tune played when the corpse is taken from the house and placed on the bier (*tāv kaṛtd koḷ*); she sees persons decorating the bier or kneeling before it. Playing music, decorating, and kneeling are subsumed, here, under the rubric "physical actions." Mathi apprehends these signs through her ears and eyes. Ideas and actions are separated in the model, but the categories are obviously related. A double-headed arrow is meant to indicate the "complex mutuality" of the two: kneeling is a response to the bierness of the bier, and the bierness explains why a person would be kneeling before it.

Mathi "interprets" what she sees via a thought, perhaps verbalized in the expression "it's bier time." The bier and its associated actions thereby become signs of both death and (indirectly) physical spacetime. That is, the signs tells her "what happened" (someone died) and "what kind of time it is" (e.g. the time for doing actions x, y, and z). Perhaps before, perhaps after this linguistically mediated response, Mathi bends over to cry. She reacts to the sight of the bier emotionally. Bowing and crying before the bier are physical reactions that Peirce calls "energetic interpretants." Because Mathi is motivated by sadness (maybe), one can see why Peirce would write that "energetic interpretants" are mediated by "emotional interpretants," i.e. feelings (Peirce 1960, 5.475).

However, Mathi is not an automaton. She also chooses to represent her own public behavior in relation to a set of cultural expectations, which may not be uniform. As a woman she is supposed to shed more tears than a man, but perhaps she does not wish to. If the deceased is a close relation or friend, she may follow the custom of remaining closer to the corpse's head, and for a longer period of time, than someone who is less dear to the deceased.

The expression "it's bier time" refers literally only to time, but it also involves location. The event of a death exerts an effect on Mathi and other people who enter the village over a prescribed period. And it conditions her future acts in other places. If Mathi does not participate in a dry funeral in her own village later that same year, she will be ritually unfit to enter certain "pure" (*cudv*) places, such as the "inner area" (*uḷmaṉḏ*) for feasting in another village's dry funeral.

Space and Spacetime

Kotas travel to and from their cremation grounds (*tāv nāṛs* +), traversing and creating paths, and thereby constituting what I will call "space."[6] Bodies create "spaces" when they move among and between places—as in rituals, processions, sports, paths of commutes, leisurely strolls, or ambulatory jobs.[7] In the rain ceremony, Kotas constitute a "space" by processing from and to certain "gods' places;" this space exists only during the frame of the ritual. The "village" as a place persists; but the borders of the village, the inside and the outside, change depending on how they are defined. Similarly, certain parts of otherwise unarticulated places, including the *pacāl*, are temporarily transformed into spaces for music and dance when women dance in a circle to their god songs. This is a bit different from the *gagvāl* (the dancing ground fronting the "house of the erected post") which perdures as a dancing "place" because of its physical shape (+).

The difference between "space" and "spacetime" is one of emphasis. "Space" draws attention to the temporal contingency of any geographical cutout or three-dimensional movement trace, e.g. the sweep of a hand. "Spacetime" concerns a pattern—physical or imagined—in both space and time. Whereas the "space" of the rain ceremony comprises the area enclosed by cardinal points in the procession, the ceremony's "spacetime" can be described with additional adjectives: short in length (confined to a single day); circumferential, continuous and closed (the procession proceeds from village, to Point A, Point B, Point C, and back to the village); and punctuated by the performance of particular melodies, roughly three at each place. Each melody has its own length and tempo, which will vary slightly from performance to performance.

Women, performing god songs antiphonally, create a form of spacetime by projecting sound from a leader (or small group) to a larger group and back again across the diameter of a circle. The circle starts small and expands, to the extent physically possible, as others join. The size of the circle will ultimately depend on the size of the village and/or the number of visitors. Sometimes the number of participants is so small that women will form a mere arc of a larger circle rather than form such a tight circle that their hands and legs might be constrained. In 2004 Kotas in Kolmēl had to enlarge the size of the *gagvāl* after finding, that year, that the circular wall could no longer accommodate the number of female dancers in the village (see photo section).

Fig. 5 represents, in somewhat exaggerated form, differences between space and place. Space fits only to some extent within the "physical actions" category; we shouldn't preclude such mentally envisioned "spaces" as those through which Kota spirits of the dead traverse en route to the land of the dead. Agents create or outline a particular space by moving (usually physically) through time, but such a space may not exist outside of that movement context. On the "ideas" side of the equation, persons may also envision or conceptualize space in the present (as they traverse it), in the past (in the form of memory or retention), as well as in the future (by way of anticipation).

"Places" concern the ways people conceptualize the world, draw boundaries. Since places persist in time not only as physical entities, but also as mental ones, "places" belong in the "ideas" category. But such ideas of place are not entirely detached from the ways in which persons behave, or physically move, within places. Nor should we forget that some important places are "founded" through physical actions.

"Forms of spacetime" are built on sequences of relative destinations

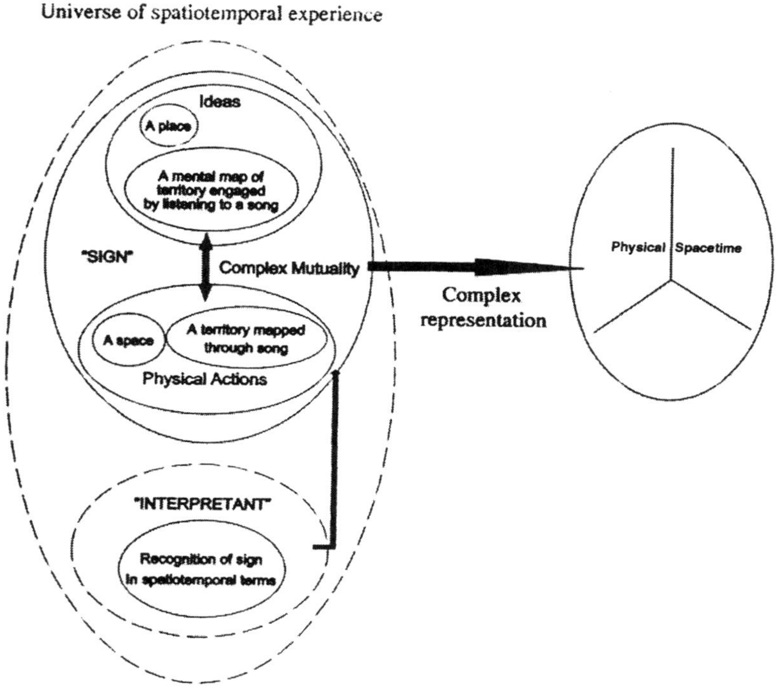

Fig. 5: Place and Space in Experience

(places) and may trace out figures (spaces) on the land. They do not belong exclusively to the action or ideas categories but rather fall within the "universe of spatiotemporal experience." The distinction drawn in Fig. 5 between actions and ideas highlights the difference between tracing bodily motion and emphasizing fixed points. Those "spaces" that are concerned with bodily motion may consist of vector segments (walking in one direction), spins (a person on his or her bodily axis), or sweeps (of bodily limbs, or conceivably of masses of people in formation). "Places" are concerned with valued loci or anchor points. Our notion of spacetime hierarchically subsumes these distinctions between space and place.

We conceptualize spaces and places as part of our larger cognitive maps of how the universe is organized. These maps are representations we form for ourselves of physical locations and relationships among locations that can only be experienced through our sensory impressions, which are "signs." In this sense, "physical spacetime" is an "object" of our spatiotemporal maps. Moving from a specific locus such as the conception of a place or the map of a territory suggested by a song to the more abstract notion of "physical spacetime" requires proceeding through several intervening steps. These are summarized in the model as "complex representation" (to avoid belaboring this discussion with further models).

People and Their Places

Such aspects of morality as assessments of right and wrong and expectations regarding human behavior pertain also to places beyond Kota villages, the most notable of which is the "forest." The distinction between "settlement" and "forest" is an ancient one in the subcontinent, described in Sanskrit literature by dichotomies of *kṣetra* versus *vana* and *grāma* versus *araṇya*.[8]

As Romila Thapar writes, "perceptions" of the forest "were neither static nor uniform" over the centuries. The forest could be "romanticized" as "a fictive paradise, which expunged the inequities of civilized living" or feared as the "habitat of demons." The forest evoked images which were "significant to the self-understanding of the settlement and these change[d] with time and with intention" (2001, 2). Images reflected changing relations between settlement chiefs and kings and the tribal or "forest people" with respect to the hunt. Where the forest people were unpredictable hindrances to the hunt, the forest itself took on the quality of a dangerous unknown: "The king had to conquer [the forest] and refashion the chaos into order" (2001, 6; see also Falk 1973).

A set of common conceptual variables links the historical tradition Thapar describes with contemporary ways in which local inhabitants (and to some extent Indians more broadly) understand Nilgiri geography: (1) The forest and settlement are from some perspectives dichotomous; from other perspectives, they are mediated by a third term or their boundaries are blurred. (2) Places are defined by their topography as well as by the character of real or imaginary beings who inhabit them. (3) The relationship between forest and settlement is framed largely from the perspective of the settlement people.[9] (4) "Forest people" are likened to what Indians now call "tribals" or *ādivāsīs*. (5) The forest is both a source of the unknown, to be feared and controlled, and a source of untapped potential to be exploited.

Two millennia ago, conceptions of Tamil *cankam* poets linked topography, people, and actions under unified categories of thought that were considerably more variegated than those dealing with categories of settlement and forest. Some linkages between persons and places established in this body of literature persist in modern Indian concepts and are relevant to our understanding of how some Nilgiri peoples, and tribal peoples in general, become associated with particular personal and moral qualities. In the region surrounding the Nilgiris, ancient Tamil literature featured the well-known five-fold division of the Tamil landscape called *tiṇai*: (1) *kuṟinci*—mountain region, (2) *mullai*—"pasture-lands . . . meadows . . . half-jungle, half-shrubbery," (3) *marutam*—agricultural zones, (4) *neytal*—the seashore, (5) *pālai*—a place in any of the other regions that has become temporarily parched during the summer or rainless season (Thani Nayagam 1966, 76–7). *Cankam* poets portrayed each of these landscapes in terms of particular clans of people with distinctive occupations; unique flora and fauna; emblematic deities, musical instruments, and scales (Ramanujan 1967, 107).[10]

The scenarios *cankam* poets described were in one sense imaginary, generalized according to literary conventions. But they were accurate inasmuch as the geographic places to which poets alluded really do exist and continue to host some of the same flora and fauna. Some passages on the favored *kuṟinci* region may have referred to what are now the Nilgiri Hills (Thani Nayagam 1966, 93ff.). Literary tropes that *cankam* poets used to connect persons to places resurface in different forms over the centuries. A poet compared "mountain heights" to the loftiness of the chief's "character and his nobility." A millennium later, a similar equation of physical height with social status lent prestige to the title of Nīlagiri Sādāran (Subduer of the Nilgiris) to which the Hoysala King Vishnuvardhana (r. 1104–41) laid claim after capturing the Nilgiri plateau.[11] An association of height with status must also feed into the idea among Kotas that they were once "kings" (*kō*) of the hills. Status accrued to those who ruled the Nilgiris because the hills were something of a challenge to conquer, both for their altitude and for the dangers posed by their animals and forest peoples.[12]

Cankam poets described the chief's subjects as "dwellers of the hills" and hunters. "Near their hamlets are thick dense tropical forests where wild beasts roam" (Thani Nayagam 1966, 95). Poets described peoples of the *kuṟinci* region living in the jungle surrounded by wild animals;

the jungle dwellers were sexually promiscuous, like the lovers in poetry who engage in "union . . . before marriage" (Ramanujan 1967, 106), or the characters in Indian films who dance flirtatiously with colorfully clad "tribal" people on the Nilgiri hillsides of Indu Nagar where love scenes are frequently filmed.

Many of the themes in these Sanskritic and Tamil representations of Indian places continue to find expression in Kota oral literature, everyday practices, and discourse. Like the myriad of Indic themes found in local cultures, including subcontinental inflections of some rather universal understandings of landscape, ideas of place float across time and geography in the subcontinent, taking on definable contours only as they become moored to particular cultures in particular historical moments.

Kota Categories: Village, Forest, and Field

The three main Kota landscape categories are the village (*kōkāl*), the forest (*tēl*), and the fields or bush (*kāṛ*). Kotas also spend significant time in the "bazaar": small markets and towns (the Kota word for Ooty town is this term's cognate, *bajārm*). They recognize by name many other kinds of places as well: natural springs, slopes, valleys and plateaus, and man-made corrals, water channels, and shrines. Kotas draw primary oppositions between village and forest in their songs and folklore as well as in other everyday practices. The forest is: the site of the hunt; the wilderness from which the Kotas emerged to settle their villages; an "object" of the bow-and-arrow as a sign; the site of death stories in *āṭḷs*; a place where spirits of the dead roam; a place of Kurumba sorcery; a place of emptiness, devoid of human activity; a source of food and subsistence materials; and a place of wild animals and hunter-gatherer "tribals." Such associations involve the same conceptual variables Thapar describes in her study of the forest in Sanskrit literature.

In the Nilgiris, the Kotas are in effect both the "settlement people" and the "forest people." Settlement living is a modern condition from the Kota perspective. Forestedness, in relative degrees, serves as a historical backdrop for Kota views on their past ways of life. The relationship of settlement to forest is one of present to understood past. The forest is also a horizon of potential (see Hirsch 1995, 3–4; Carter 1987, 48). It represents not so much what the Kotas "could be" in a largely different future, but rather how they can remain true to themselves through use of the forest and its products. As the Nilgiri Hills become increasingly industrialized and cosmopolitan, urban expansion threatens to eclipse small, local populations. This makes the forest even more important, symbolically.

One way Kotas mediate their relationships with the forest is through their use of thorny species of plants. Thorniness comes to stand for wildness, both symbolically, in songs and stories, and physically, since Kotas collect many thorny species for everyday uses such as tying bundles of wood. In the old days, Kotas used nettle fiber to make clothing. Today they use threads and swatches of such fabric (long since abandoned for making clothing) in death rituals as reminders of their former self-sufficient lifestyle. Ritually, thorny plants are like moral barbed wire: they ward off the contagion of death (*kēṛ*) and potential ill-effects of menstrual blood (*tīṭ*).[13] In Kota eyes, the forest has never been tamed entirely. It remains a source of fear (especially at night), a place where tribes of sorcerers may still be found. Kotas construct Kurumbas and Irulas—who reside on the slightly wild Nilgiri slopes—as tribal "others" of a negative kind, "savage, uncivilized, violent" (Babiracki 2000/2001, 36). Kotas are, from this perspective, "settlement people." Inasmuch as Kota villages protect them from Kurumbas, such villages constitute what Michel de Certeau terms a "proper," "a *place* that can be delimited as its *own* and serve as the base from which relations with an *exteriority* composed of targets or threats . . . can be managed" (Certeau 1984, 36).

Forests (Tēl): Nilgiri forests are of three types. Moist evergreen forests were prevalent until the mid nineteenth century on the Nilgiri slopes to the elevation of the plateau (5,900 ft), but are now rare. Dry deciduous forests and thorny thickets grow on the Mysore plateau. *Shola*s or low forests on the Nilgiri plateau contain small and medium-sized evergreen trees with several strata of varying density (Lengerke and Blasco 1989, 52–9). One needs a machete and hatchet to cut one's way into such thick forests. Surrounded by grasslands, *sholas* are found in coombs—small valleys between hills where natural water springs from the ground. The Kota term *tēl* refers to any forest of thick trees.[14]

In the region of Kolmēl, the nearest *shola* forest is called the *Kuy tēl* (+), which takes approximately forty-five minutes to reach, walking briskly to the south. I accompanied Duryodhana on several occasions to this forest to collect *vag* wood for making *koḷ*s and to search out medicinal herbs. Another area, including dense forest and sparse plateau, is located directly up the slope to the west of the village in the direction of Ooty. Kotas obtain bamboo for making *pulāng*s from this highland region, *mallāṛ* (+).

Kāṛ: Cognates of *kāṛ*, found in most Dravidian languages (DEDR 1438), point to a continuum of possible moral and physical geographies. The primary meaning of *kāṭu* in Tamil, and across the languages, is a forest or jungle, from which derives the Tamil term *kāṭar*, "ones of the forest" or hill tribes. *Kāṭu* can also mean a desert or wasteland, the emptiness of which resonates with that of *āṭḻ* landscapes: uninhabitable places, places devoid of civilized people, places of death. Related terms also mean wild, rustic, untamed, or "other," as in the Kota term for a non-Kota, a *kāṛōn*. In Malayalam and Telugu, cognate terms also refer to places for disposing of the dead—related again to the idea of forest or bush in *āṭḻ*s as a place where people die, where those who kill people live, and where one may encounter spirits of the dead.

In Kota, the words *kāṛ* and *tēl* are not synonymous, but their connotations overlap. Kotas use the word *kāṛ* both for forest and for a region that is neither village nor forest: bushlands, wild, untamed brush and trees where wild animals might be found. They also use it to refer to cultivated fields, especially with the more specific term *kāṛ-kar*, "field-border." The uncultivated *kāṛ* stretches out indefinitely and contains a variety of physical features; a cultivated field has a border.

Musically Implicated Places

Kota men gather materials for constructing musical instruments from particular fields and forests at different elevations and parts of the Nilgiris. They depend on being able to find such animal and vegetable products as deer antler or wild boar tusk (for the *vāypor*, or pirouette, which is now sometimes made of plastic), quill from feathers of crows or other birds (for the *garl* which connects the reed with the neck of the *koḷ*), the reeds for the *koḷ*, and deer, ox, or goatskin for different parts of various drums. Materials for making instruments implicate urban landscapes. Skins may be purchased in slaughterhouses or the bazaar. Drum-makers scavenge cylinders or purchase them in shops or from hawkers of recycled chemical containers. Instrument-makers also appropriate plastic or other metal pieces that have been already manufactured for other purposes. The bell of an air horn, for instance, makes an excellent bell for the *koḷ*.

The form of spacetime associated with instrument-making is ever shifting. The *vag* trees whose trunks Kotas used to hollow for drums are now scarce, so they now only use metal cylinders, which are readily available. As the technology of instrument-making has modulated, so has the geographical path of the maker. Similarly, material availability has changed in that certain items can usually be found in some bazaar, if one is willing to search and pay the asking price. The instrument's "value" now combines cash purchase, skilled craft, and the labor of traversing the landscape in search of specialized or high-quality natural materials. Finding such materials still depends on a Kota's observant habits of living, his paying attention to items deposited on the ground, making note of where a rare plant tends to grow,[15] or saving products of the occasional hunt.

Places are musically implicated not only through the sourcing of instrument-making materials but also via the stories songs evoke. In the following *āṭḷ*, the (anonymous) composer associates social and spiritual otherness with the bush (CD 23):

"Stone field, thorn field, Kanm father"
***Āṭḷ* (mourning song) genre. Pa. Mathi, Singer**
(February 11, 1992)[16]

la la . . .	
kale kāṛe muḷe kāṛe kaṇmayyo	stone field, thorn field, Kanm father
enīṇe enīṇe ponayyo	my father, my father, Pon father
(a) alāde nāṭike vadvīme kaṇmayyo	you came to a bad land, Kanm father
enīṇā enīṇe ponayyo	my father, my father, Pon father
alāde kāṭike vadīme ponayyo	you came to a bad bushland, Pon father
maṇḍdēcile oḍāce kaṇmayyo	by your head, one woman, Kanm father
kāldēcile oḍāce kaṇmayyo	by your feet, one woman, Kanm father
amide kēr amīr kēr kērīle	in our *kēr*, "Amirker"[17]
(a) tāv ācr vadege kaṇmayyo	a funeral is going on, Kanm father
enīṇā enīṇe ponayyo	my father, my father, Pon father
(a) irk indēl anōr eyṛāḷ	tonight, two brothers, two men
orkṉāṇtl orgādi kaṇmayyo	don't sleep deeply! Kanm father
avḷ oḍalk mark made acvēndē ponayyo	I fed her sleeping potion,[18] Pon father

This typical *āṭḷ* is set in a threatening (thorny) environment, a wild place in the bush, far from the village. Two brothers, Kanm and Pon, meet two women of the Irula tribe who feed them *piṭ*, a millet and rice mixture. Satisfied with their meal, the two men gradually nod off to sleep with the two women sitting opposite one another at the men's heads and feet. From this position of spatial control, the two women commence acts of sorcery in order to capture the brothers as their husbands. The spirits of the dead manifest themselves in the men's consciousness and sing, warning of the danger. Spirits communicate musically using funeral tunes or mourning songs, regardless of whether the story ends with the demise of the central character(s). In this story, the spirits instruct the men first to return quickly to the village, for someone had died and the brothers needed to attend the funeral. To assure the men's safe passage, the spirits give the women a tranquilizing herbal drug.

The malevolent forces of the bush are represented by otherness of ethnicity and gender. Although Kotas do not fear Irulas as much as Kurumbas, they do believe Irulas possess supernatural power. The idea of women taking domestic and sexual possession of Kota men reverses the commonplace of Kurumba stories, in which Kurumba men try to molest Kota women sexually. Fear of evil here is connected with the fear of miscegenation and the risks of venturing into uninhabited lands which lie beyond the village.[19]

Song Maps

A song or *koḷ* story may function like a map. It may also, by naming places along a path, stimulate a Kota listener to navigate through his or her own mental map of a territory. *Āṭḷ* composers and singers use place names to move their songs forward, providing vivid details to localize a narrative in a village or region.[20] This is not unlike the process whereby Australian aboriginals sing the names of geographical features created by ancestors in the mythical period known as "the dreaming."[21] Similarly, Kota god songs (*devr pāṭ*) often refer to divinities in terms of their locations[22] and thereby map a geography of divinity.

One of the most widely sung god songs belongs to the village of Kolmēl. The text invokes god at significant locales, which are either at village borders or the sites of trees.[23]

A *mundkānōn* offended god by praying before the *veḷk* (oil lamp) after committing some unspecified "mistake" and caused the flame, a manifestation of god, to disappear. Grief stricken, his wife and female counterpart, the *mundkānōḷ*, went around the village crying "lamp, lamp, where are you? Come god!"[24] She looked for god's flame at the foot of particular trees and known places of divinity, eventually finding the flame at the site called *ponic*. Like other Kota moral stories, which are often associated with music, *veḷke veḷke* links the absence of god with improper behavior, and the presence of god with pious devotion and special features of the landscape.

"Lamp, lamp, where are you?" (CD 2)

Refrain (3 times antiphonally):	
veḷke veḷke ēy ōḷīme vā cōyme	lamp, lamp, where are you? Come god!
[a la la la la kuī . . .]	[expression of excitement inserted at various points, here during the second iteration of the refrain]
Verse (1)	
tīṛ markāl ōḷīmo vā cōyme	you're at the foot of the Tīṛ tree, come god
Refrain (3 times antiphonally)	
Verse (2)	
vācēry markāl ōḷīmo vā cōyme	you're at the foot of the Vācēry tree, come god!
[Verse (2) with Refrain (3 times) reiterated 2 more times, then Verse (2) with refrain once]	
Verse (3)	
padne markāl ōḷīmo vā cōyme	you're at the foot of the *Celtis tetranda* tree, come god!
Refrain (one time)	
(recording fade-out)	

The theme of Kota gods being hidden or formless is a recurrent one in Kota songs, stories, and self-descriptions. Hiddenness is a source of Kota gods' powers. God keeps humans at bay, always searching, always conscious of their behavior, by remaining out of view. The spatiotemporal forms of Kota worship, in some sense, respond to this belief. Kotas draw divinity into places by praying in particular spots, processing through and around them, and emphasizing centripetal forms of action.

K. Puccan, after singing "*veḷke veḷke*" and narrating its story, began to describe the rain ceremony, thereby suggesting that the song and the rain ceremony were conceptually linked. Both draw their meaning from the divine significance of particular places in and around the village. Singing the song constitutes an act of worship not only through singing, *qua* singing, but also through invoking god, referring to a divine story, and naming divine places. The geographical emphasis, in the case of the rain ceremony, draws god's attention to the place as one needy of rain (see Wolf 1997b).

Place through the Senses

Sight is one of the more obvious senses through which Kotas understand place, particularly with respect to the experience of divinity,[25] but places can be sensed in more subtle ways as well. The Kota term *cēv* refers to a spot (of variable size) that cannot be specified descriptively, but only deictically or in relation to a known place. One can meet at the *cēv* of a particular tree or one can point to an inexact spot where one feels pain in one's back. Kotas also have a concept of spatial memory, *nēk*, which is not tied to vision. The ability to locate objects and paths in the dark is of significant use in a society whose members privilege their hunting prowess and facility with moving about in the forest—even if there is very little of it left.

Smell is significant in Kota topographical markings of self–other relationships. Once, when passing another community's village, Duryodhana remarked on its distinctive odor, for non-Kotas smell different. A well-known *āṭl* recalls the story of Dēcmāngy, a girl whose beauty attracted the envy of her peers. Knowing the nasty ways of jealous girls, Dēcmāngy's father admonished her to spend time only with boys. Ignoring her father's advice, she set out to collect clay with some female friends and was berated by one of them for allegedly sleeping with a non-Kota. The companion stung her with the phrase "the stench of a 'new' [i.e. non -Kota] man reeks" (*ocāḷceṯ nāyro*), which was so insulting that Dēcmāngy committed suicide.

In rainforest settings, where it is easier to hear than to see (see Feld 1996), some cultures may be "disposed to order reality in the acoustic mode" (Gell 1995, 249). Kotas are not greatly reliant on sound for survival, but they do interpret aspects of time and place through the sounds they hear. CD 24 presents a sampling of *kuytēl* forest sounds. On CD 25 Duryodhana playfully imitates animal sounds heard in the *kuytēl* and the village. (1) The *karvaky*, "black bird," issues a wake-up call just before dawn, a time called *kōjām* ("cock-time"). To see the *karvaky* bird in the village is of no consequence, but to encounter it as one leaves the village is believed to augur ill. (2) The sound of the crow is the second wake-up call. A Kota is not considered lazy if he or she waits for the sound of the crow to arise. When the crow "cries out" (*kirco*), the meaning is neutral, but when it "caws" (*kardo*) the sound is taken as a bad omen. (3) The owl, which is said to "make sound" (*pāṛdo*, cognate with verb "to sing"), signals an even more inauspicious time. (4) The sound of the *pemaṇḍvaky* is believed to be good at any time. Duryodhana narrates (CD 25:4a) how a Kota man completed a successful hunt but could not find his knife to cut up the meat. He heard the song of the *pemaṇḍvaky*, typically in triple meter, which sounded to the hunter like a message in the Kota language telling him the knife's location. The bark of a dog is considered positive, but its howl is a sign of dread. If a fox is seen as people leave the village, their mission will be successful, so if someone has good luck another might say, "Hey, you've seen a fox, go on!" (*eh, ni nayr kaṛvī, ōg!*). Many of these aural and visual animal signs are effective at spatial and temporal borders.

In a Kota village, residents read sounds subtly—or not so subtly. Some shout from one end of the village to the other, communicating without words. In the early 1990s Duryodhana's mother used to call him by shouting "yayō . . ." and he would recognize the tone of her voice. The sound of a bus in the distance is all the advance notice Kotas in Kolmēl require to catch it on time. South Indian villages generally announce festivals, weddings, or funerals through loud sounds. Local codes will dictate how members of one village should respond, by avoiding or attending the village, or sometimes by competing with still louder music.

Place and "Pollution"

No moral forces with respect to "place" are as powerful as those covered by the subtle Kota terms *kēṛ* and *tīṭ*, which are associated with death and childbirth "pollution" respectively.[26] Differences between *kēṛ* and *tīṭ* depend on the entities involved, the places in which they can exert effects, and the ways in which they can be removed.

Kēṛ helps articulate the realms of god and death. One Kota model for this articulation focuses on the unfortunate anomaly of someone dying during the god ceremony. If the effects of death (*kēṛ*) cannot be separated from divinity in the village through creating a temporal gap—performing a sequence of rituals and waiting until the passing of the moon—it can be separated by creating topographical, tactile, and sonic boundaries. Four men, appointed to do all the funerary rituals, set up a fence in the village and ensure that all the funeral proceedings take place silently within it. Mourning participants and the four men assiduously avoid stepping into the village or touching other villagers until the end of the god ceremony.

Kēṛ is related to Dravidian words meaning "to perish or rot" (see Ta. *kēṭu*) and comes to mean both "ruin, loss, damage, adversity, death" and the "evil" which causes such a state. The Kota word *kēṛ* refers to a contagious condition, associated with a corpse, that is said to create possibilities for future adversity and be repugnant to the gods. This contagion spreads through time and across the landscape according to rules that are extremely complex, have varied over time, and apply differently to different categories of persons.

At least three spans of time and two dimensions of space (indicated parenthetically) come into play when observing *kēṛ* rules: up to one or more years (intra-village), up to one month (intervillage), or a matter of days (intra-village), respectively. (1) The entire village in which a person dies is rendered ritually unfit to celebrate god-related rituals until its members, after some years, perform the dry funeral (*varldāv*). (2) Kotas from other villages who have entered a Kota village within the month of a death are prevented from participating in certain rituals. (3) Some *kēṛ* is removed during the days of the *pac tāv*, or "green funeral," at which time participants cremate the corpse, ceremonially feast, and ritually bathe (Wolf 1997a, 272).

Non-Kotas are not conduits for *kēṛ* so I did not need to exercise caution when traveling outside the village during *devr* for fear of unintentionally coming across a funeral: *kēṛ* would not stick to me. Kota adults are personally impervious to certain ill effects of *kēṛ* after a funeral is over—rather as a person may carry a disease non-symptomatically. But *kēṛ* does adhere to adult Kotas, who can pass it on to other people directly and through common meeting places. An adult returning from a cremation ground may "infect" young children, causing them to attract harmful spirits (*pēy-picāc*). Paradoxically, young "lucky" (*rāci*) children, who are still "innocent" of the ills men perpetrate upon one another, are also said to resist the harmful potential of death. For this reason, such children or youths act as the principal ritual officiants for both green funerals and dry funerals, where they are called *tic pac mog*, "fire-grasping child," and *mel pac mog*, "breast-clutching child," respectively.

Music, Emotion, and *Kēṛ*

The word *kēṛ* also means the Toda dry funeral and came to be associated with Kota music-making during ostentatious Toda buffalo sacrifices. Kotas also staged such ritual buffalo fights for their own *varldāv*s until recent decades. Through this semantic slippage, musical pieces performed for the buffalo rituals came to be called *kēṛ koḷ*s. Many were instrumental renditions of *āṭḷ*s; among those songs, some were addressed to favorite buffaloes and were not about deceased persons at all (see Wolf 2001). *Kēṛ koḷ*s, then, have come to be regarded in Kolmēl as less lachrymose kinds of funeral melodies than other *tāv koḷ*s (funeral tunes). Sadder tunes are called *dukt koḷ*s ("sad tunes") to emphasize this difference. *Kēṛ* in this sense is not a form of evil, defilement or contagion, but rather a selected set of ritual imperatives that are of a mixed emotional nature.

The dry funeral ground is a place of *kēṛ* in the sense that it is a place in which *kēṛ koḷ*s and their associated rituals are performed. It is not a place of *kēṛ* defilement, but a zone through which Kotas create a transition between the period infected by death and the period in which they become in a position to worship in the god ceremony.

Tīṭ, the defiling potential of women who are menstruating or who have just given birth, like *kēṛ*, can be transmitted through touch, but its onset cannot affect an entire village, or even the members of a household—naturally so, or the village would be in a continuous state of pollution. Yet *tīṭ* is in some ways more dangerous than *kēṛ*, at least to adult men. The touch of a menstruating woman, in a number of stories, is responsible for the death of a man while hunting (see Mandelbaum, April 14, 1938, pp. 6–7).[27] Strongly valued as a sign of the Kota past, hunting comes to be closely associated with the gods, who taught Kotas how to live in the Nilgiris. Since menstrual restrictions are observed before the gods, it is not surprising that they should also be observed in such a dangerous activity as hunting, where one would hope to have god on one's side.

Tīṭ is symbolically connected with the forest through the term for the house in which women separate themselves from the village during menstruation: the *tēlvāl*, literally the "forest-entrance." Even after hospital births (which most today are), mother and child undergo a purificatory ritual there before they enter the village. One of the interesting aspects of this ritual is that it implies *tīṭ* can affect people through objects backward in time and through spatial proximity. The water for the ritual is collected from a lowland area and not from a more "pure" area above the village, where water flows from a spring and supplies the village—almost as if the act of drawing such village water for *tīṭ*-related purposes would defile the village. The ritual also exhibits the common theme of forest products as both dangerous (as thorns) and protective or purificatory. Fire transforms substances; exposure to fire (without actual burning) serves to remove *kēṛ* and *tīṭ* from objects and people.[28]

The moral effects of *tīṭ* vary according to location. Women who live on physically and conceptually "high" (*mē-*) *kēr*s (subdivisions of the three main *kēr*s) must observe menstrual purification rituals more assiduously than others because they live in proximity to sites of importance. *Korykēr* (the upper line of *īkēr*), for instance, is the location of the house of the "big" (*doḍ*) *mundkānōn*, the one who serves the gods *doḍayṇōr* and *amnōr*.[29] Similarly the *gagvāl* (in the lower line of *īkēr*) is ritually high because it fronts the "house of the erected post" (Map 5). The lower line of *ākēr* and the clusters of houses that lie off the main rows of ancestral house sites are considered ritually lower than the others. To an extent, they are also physically lower: from the north-west "entrance" to the village (the *kēr vāy*, or "*kēr* mouth") through the village to the south-east, the village gradually descends. Only beyond *ākēr* does the village landscape ascend once again.

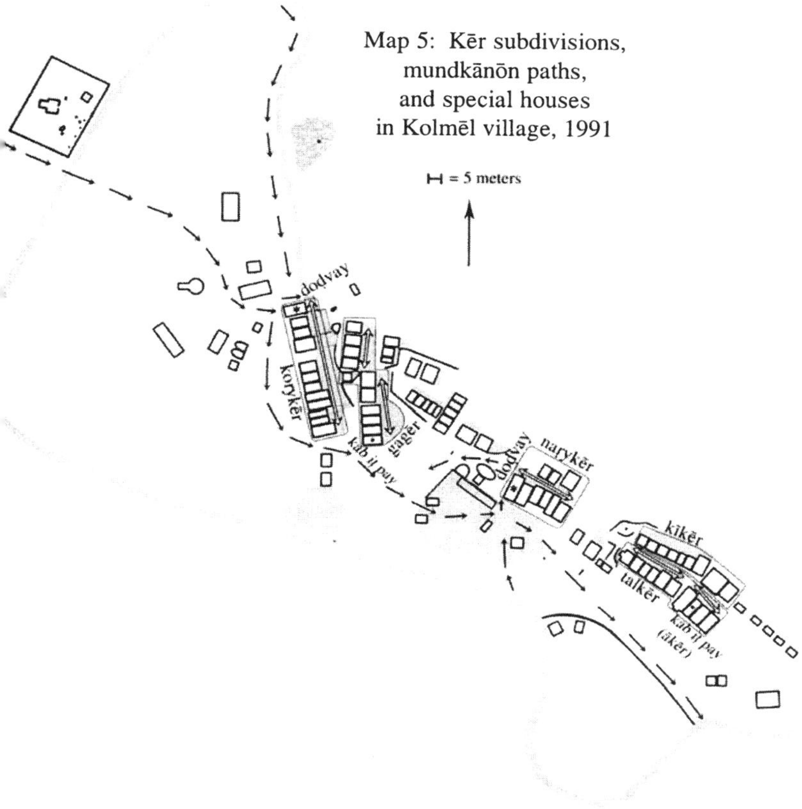

Map 5: Kēr subdivisions,
mundkānōn paths,
and special houses
in Kolmēl village, 1991

This map, showing subdivisions of the three *kērs*, builds on the layout in Map 2. *Ākēr* is divided into *talkēr* ("head" *kēr*) and *kīkēr* ("low" *kēr*). *Īkēr* is divided into *korykēr* and *gagēr*. The unidirectional, solid arrows delineate paths upon which the *mundkānōns* may walk during the god ceremony. (They may not walk on *kērs* during the god ceremony.) The double-headed, hollow arrows show *kērs* upon which *mundkānōns* ordinarily can walk. These *kērs* are ritually and physically "higher" than the others, owing to the presence of special houses: the *mundkānōns*' houses, called *doḍvay* ("big house"), are marked with asterisks, and the *kab iṭ pays* ("house of the erected post") are marked with bullets. The site of the first house in the village, the *kab iṭ pay* proper, is at the south end of *gagēr*. The *kab iṭ pay* in *ākēr* is on the site of the first house in that exogamous division.

At ordinary times, the *mundkānōns* walk only on the ritually higher *kērs*—*korykēr, gagvāl, naṛykēr, talkēr*—where *tīṭ* rituals are observed assiduously (Map 5). Other forms of action which contribute to and result from the status of these four *kērs* include communal dancing, storing of musical instruments, and pouring of memorial millet during the *varldāv*. The spirit of the dead as manifested in this millet, more than the original corpse, is an object of veneration, not a source of pollution.

Tīṭ affects a person differently than *kēṛ* and can be transmitted differently as well. Suitably controlled, *tīṭ* would seem less repugnant to god, judging from a special *devr* ritual. All women nominally observe seclusion by occupying a lower area of the village on Friday and Saturday preceding the temple-opening day (+). Those who are still menstruating will silently absent themselves from dancing on the *pacāl* but will, in name's sake, still fulfill the duty of participating in the ceremony.

The capacity of intra-village places to "solicit bodily motions" (see Casey 1996, 24) changes over time. So, while the "high" *kērs* are, at ordinary times, ritually pure, they are at some special times, just ordinary. The village as a site of everyday goings-on—sex, menstruation, death, and all manner of behavioral misconduct, ritual or otherwise—is at odds with the ideology of how one should comport oneself in god's presence. Hence the *mundkānōn* should not walk on any of the *kērs* during the god ceremony and must instead ambulate around the village, avoiding the houses. He may walk through the *kāṛ*, along the road, or through the *pacāl* and temple area (Map 5).

The temples serve as anchor points for village geography in that each temple is associated with ritualists from particular kin groups, and those kin groups are distributed according to the *kēr* system around the village. (1) The *doḍmundkānōn* tends the *doḍayṇōr* and *amnōr* temples. He hails from *gagēr* (the *kēr* of which the *gagvāl* is a part) but his official house, the *doḍvay*, is in *korykēr*. (2) The *tērkārn* who tends these temples comes from a *korykēr* family. (3) The *mundkānōn* in *naṛykēr* tends the god *kunayṇōr*'s temple. (4) The *tērkārn* in *ākēr* is the mouthpiece of *kunayṇōr*. This distribution of responsibility among kin groups is an example of "interlocking," which gets activated when the village performs the god ceremonies.

Naṛykēr is literally and geographically the "middle *kēr*." The deity *kunayṇōr*, who originated in Porgāṛ village, once spoke through the mouth of a *tērkārn*, saying he would rather live in Kolmēl, where "the *ōmayṇ* is extremely loud and beautiful," as Raman put it.[30] *Kunayṇōr* was assigned to the *naṛykēr* subdivision of Kolmēl since that relatively newer group had no deity of its own. *Kunayṇōr* demanded a special "style" of dance, according to Raman (who used the English word "style"), meaning a special time and place carved out during the daytime exclusively for dancing. On this penultimate "dance day" (*āṭ nāḷ*) of the god ceremony, neighboring communities join in dancing, and village musicians will formally welcome respected guests from the municipality or neighboring villages. The part of the *pacāl* reserved for this activity, called the *ākēr pacāl*, is east of the *kunayṇōr* temple and just above (south of) *ākēr*.

This *ākēr pacāl* is a medial zone, a part of the *pacāl* which borders the temple area (*guṛyvāl*), the *kēr*s, and extra village areas. Like the *kēr*s, the *ākēr pacāl* and the *guṛyvāl* are defined by Kota actions while also exerting a moral impact on how Kotas comport themselves. Under ordinary circumstances, one does not enter the *guṛyvāl*, except during the god ceremony.[31] Only those who are ritually clean (and not drunk, for example) may enter, and only while wearing their traditional forms of dress: white *varāṛ* (cloak), *muṇḍ* (waist cloth), and no footwear. The *ākēr pacāl* shares qualities with public areas beyond the village in that it may be traversed at any time; one may park vehicles there or tread on it with shoes—unless one of the important festivals or a funeral is taking place in the village. It also serves as a shortcut for pedestrians traveling to and from the neighboring Oranayi village of Badaga Lingayats.

The *pacāl* is differentiated in two other noteworthy ways. Men will typically seek privacy for conducting village council business at the *mēptkāl* ("upper *pacāl*"), located south-east of and above the village. Its literal elevation makes it appropriate for men and for such lofty matters as legal deliberations. *Mēptkāl* (+) is opposed to *kīptāl*, the lower part of the *pacāl* that borders the road. Employing spatial iconisms in the 1990s, young men fashionably termed good, desired, or exciting things as "*mēptāl*," and those lacking such qualities as "*kīptāl*"—a linguistic equivalent of the gesture-indexical "thumbs up" or "thumbs down" in America.

The Kota House

The spatial organization of Kota houses is significant. They ideally face east, as facing the rising sun is auspicious and the path of light into the house is important in diurnal time reckoning. R. Mathi could reckon time within about ten minutes by observing the glimmer of light falling into the kitchen from the small skylight in the ceiling above the stove. Kotas also use the sun for calculating directions. East, called the "rising side" (*utn mūl*), is the direction Kotas face for some prayers, e.g. when harvesting *āminj* (a kind of millet). Men also face east when sounding the *ērdabaṭk* drum. This is considered a form of respect for the drum and for the object of the drumming (the gods, or the deceased). The

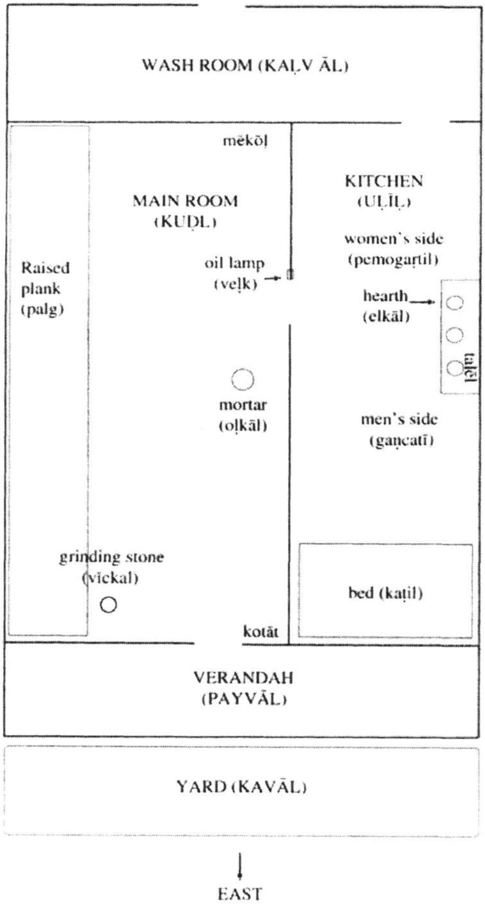

Fig. 6: A "Traditional" Kota House

special "respectful" term for playing the *ērdabaṭk*, "ēric-," means in other contexts, "to place on top of," thus reinforcing the iconism of height with respect.

In addition to high and low, the terms *mē-* and *kī-* are also used for West and East. Other terms for directions derive from the orientation of the body when one faces the sun: (1) South-east: "right belly side" (*valaḷmūl*), (2) South: "right shoulder side" (*valmūṛmūl*), (3) South-west: "back of right shoulder side" (*valmūṛnmūl*), (4) West: "setting side" (*mārnmūl*), (5) North-west: "back of left shoulder side" (*eṛnmūl*), (6) North: "Left shoulder side" (*eṛmūl*), (7) North-east: "left belly side" (*eṛaḷmūl*).[32] In this way, individuals orient themselves bodily in relation to the sun when they leave the house in the morning.

Kota houses are traditionally fronted by verandahs (*payvāl*), many of which are now gradually being converted into rooms and extended outward onto the *kavāl*. The entrances of such newly styled houses become small halls and storage-rooms for footwear and sundry materials. Just to the right is often an *āfic* ("office") or *doḍ kuṛjil* (big small room). The *āfic* holds a cot, a table (sometimes folding) or desk, and/or a metal bureau. The "house of the erected post" and other houses in the *gagvāl* are enjoined from converting their verandahs into rooms because they lie in the oldest part of the village, where Kotas have to some extent compartmentalized their architectural traditionalism. More practically, the verandahs provide important vantage points for observing the dance during the god ceremony. To extend the front of the house would also encroach on the dancing area. In general, Kota verandahs are important sites for all-night music-making during funerals, when men will crowd together on the ground with drums and *koḷs*. The wattle and daub walls provide musical resonance and warmth. Ideally the music will be played in the verandah of the bereaved's home; if a modern *āfic* is in the way, though, musicians might move over a house or two or play outside.

Beyond the verandah or entrance hall is the *kuḍl*, the main, public room of the house, where a family entertains guests and performs child-naming and other household rituals. A *palg* (plank, 3–4 feet off the floor and about the same in width) was, until recently, common along the length of the left wall. Those who sleep on the *palg* are of superior status in gender, age, or ritual position to those who sleep below it. The female medium for the spirits of the dead, the *pēnpacōḷ*, was said to have typically planted herself below the *palg*, perhaps in deference, before shaking with possession and tunefully expressing the ancestor's words. Few houses still have the traditional *palg*; some have placed a wooden cot in this part of the room.

The *kīkōḷ*, "lower part of room" closest to the front door (not labeled), is only incidentally in the easterly (*kī-*) direction and may be physically lower for drainage purposes; "*kī-*" refers to the ritually lower status of this part of the room, where refuse is swept. The right side next to the door when one enters, called *kotāt*, is considered less clean than the left side; small piles of dust are sometimes left temporarily against there before being removed from the house. Toward the center of the room on the right, just before the entrance to the kitchen, is a stone mortar (*oḷkāl*) set in the mud floor. To the left, when entering, is a grinding stone (*vīckal*).

The right side of the far end of the front room opposite the door is called the "upper" side or corner (*mēkōḷ*) because it is ritually superior. When a large group of people sit along the walls, as in the child-naming ritual, they line up according to seniority with the most important men in the *mēkōḷ* (see photo section). In descending rank, they circle around counterclockwise to the left, past the door, skipping the site of the dust pile, and then along the right inner wall ending at the entrance to the kitchen. Men are supposed to occupy the part of the room closest to the *mēkōḷ* when women are present, and Raman hangs his *koḷ* on this part of the back wall as well.

Traditionally, the kitchen is to the right, north of the *kuḍl*. Its name, *uḷīḷ* (lit. "in inside") reflects the idea that this is the heart of the house. The threshold to this inner place is an open doorway with a crevice on the left-hand side, about shoulder height, called *madl*, where the small oil lamp, *veḷk* (mentioned earlier in connection with a common god song), is kept. Women light this lamp daily at about six p.m.

The hearth, called the *elkāl*, is on the north wall of the kitchen. To the right of the hearth is the traditional place in which men must sit, the *gaṇcatī*; some families keep a cot on this side of the kitchen. Raman spends his evenings lying here reading, practicing the *pulāng*, listening to the radio, or writing in his diary. The opposite side, *pemogaṛtil*, is the "woman's side." Women rarely merely sit in this spot, as do the men on the other side; they squat and briskly move around, feeding wood to the fire, stirring food, cutting vegetables, grinding spices, and cleaning. They may store vessels on this side of the kitchen. R. Mathi kept a grinding stone and several steel storage containers of drinking water there. Directly behind the kitchen on the woman's side is a low doorway to the *kaḷv āl* (“wash room”), used for bathing, changing clothes, storage, and occasionally sex. A back door leads to a stone rain-gutter on the ground and often a small garden.

The *talēl*, the “head” of the hearth on the top right next to the men’s side, is the most ritually important spot in the house. A site of divinity, Kotas worship this spot during the god festival and for harvest festivals. During the festival of *pabm*, each household places a sweet pancake (*piṭāṛ*) made of *āminj* millet on the *talēl* as an offering and bows down before it (see Emeneau 1944–6, IV: 299).

Divinity is also said to be present in the *aṭṭ*, rafters of the house directly above or near the kitchen where pots and dried straw are stored for use in the god festival. These objects are kept above human beings, who occupy themselves with mundane activities in the household below, as if divine qualities adhere to these objects before and after they are actually used to “make god” in the god ceremony. When sounds issue from that region which are not attributable to wind or movement within the house, Kotas say “*devr erygo*” (lit. “god descends”).

In modern expanded houses, the room hitherto used for culinary and ritual purposes is made into a bedroom and the bathroom is expanded and made into a kitchen. The hearth might in this case be fashioned out of cement and attached to a substantial chimney and supplemented by gas or kerosene stoves. In the house of a retired employee of Hindustan Photo Films, a modern fireplace fueled with wood is used for cooking food and a separate gas stove is used for coffee and tea. In the new-style houses, the upper right-hand part of the mantel still serves as the *talēl*, but the rest of the mantel may support a variety of items such as a clock and knick-knacks.[33]

Sometimes a separate bathroom (but, as of this writing, almost never a toilet) is attached in the back on the opposite side. More commonly, a square of raised clay surrounds a drain and this is used for bathing, sometimes blocked off with strips of cloth. Orientations of remodeled houses vary. Whatever its location, the hearth is the anchor point for men’s and women’s spatial orientation and thus provides the basis for hierarchical seating when it is necessary to demonstrate respect for an honored guest.

A Structuring Structure?

These household spatial patterns invite consideration in light of Pierre Bourdieu’s well-known analysis of Algerian Berber (Kabyle) houses.

Bourdieu regarded the house as a "structuring structure," akin to a "'book' from which the children learn their vision of the world." Children "read" this book through their bodies, their "movements and displacements" both outlining or creating "space" and acting in terms of the structures previously created (Bourdieu 1989, 90). Practically speaking, in the Kota universe, the idea that men, gods, and respected elders should be to the right and up within a particular frame of reference, and women to the left and down, is reinforced in the most basic household activities and arrangements. But this orientation is hardly surprising given the status accorded to the right side of the body in Indian, especially Hindu, society at large (Mandelbaum 1970–2, I: 195); this is also in keeping with Dravidian language (including Kota) terms for the right hand which derive from terms meaning "strong, strength" and Indian areal linguistic terms for the right hand as the "eating hand" (Emeneau 1987).

Bourdieu had in mind more localized analyses of action, however, when he observed that the "internal organization of the house is exactly the reverse of that of external space, as if it had been obtained by a half-rotation on the axis of the front wall or the threshold" (Bourdieu 1990, 281). The significance of this transformation lay not in the mere homology, but in the forms of action that the Berber adopts in entering and leaving the house, "movements of the body, such as a half-turn, which play a well-known role in rites, where objects, animals or clothing are constantly turned upside down or back to front, to the left or the right, etc." (1990, 10).

In view of Bourdieu's insights, it may be significant that (1) Kota directional terms are consistent with the orientation of one's body when leaving the house in the morning; (2) When Kotas enter their houses, they should first pay respect to elders/men who would be located ahead and to the right, or after turning (usually right) into the kitchen, to the right of the hearth; (3) Kota dances begin with a spin to the right; and those arriving generally join with the other dancers when they are spinning in the right direction; (4) Kota men expose their right shoulder in tying their *varāṛs* for certain types of god-related rituals and perform ritually significant actions using the right hand, right foot, or right shoulder. This logic, which Bourdieu himself calls "fuzzy" (1990, 87), can be extended only so far, however, because a spin to the right (in the dance for instance) often calls for a balancing spin to the left. Kotas sometimes spin to the right in prayers, too, but the directions to which they turn for prayer are sometimes dictated by where deities reside (e.g. in mountain peaks) and the direction of the sun. Considered in broader terms, the spatial outlay of the Kota house may indeed be a "structuring structure" in Bourdieu's terms, but as agents have multiple orientation systems from which to choose, it is by no means certain which, if any, particular system, or in this case bodily habit, will predominate at any given moment. Furthermore, as Kotas enlarge their homes, they will also be modifying the "book," if not rewriting it altogether.

Other Sites of Importance

Village geography is spotted with a variety of other small but significant sites. The smithies (+ see photo section), for instance, are associated with the gods; men working inside must not wear shoes and must refrain from eating meat; women may not enter at all. Near the houses of the *mundkānōns* are *tondiṭs* (+), raised, stone-encircled areas for fire during the god ceremony. These too command sartorial and other behavioral demonstrations of respect; but they are also sites of informal social gathering for men and boys. A form of *pachīsī*, the ancient Indian game marketed in America as Parcheesi (Ko. *cukāṭ*), which Kotas traditionally play with cowry shells, is scratched on one of the stones. Such games, found in significant spots such as this, reinforce the association between divinity and human play (Wolf 2001, 398–9). Men lie across such areas lazily on warm sunny days.

Certain kinds of sites command respect for their intrinsic qualities, such as association with cows, and are hierarchized according to location and use. Places for penning up cows and buffaloes (+) owe their status to the connection between the gods, the ancestors, and bovine species generally. *Mundkānōns*' cow pens, where cows are milked for a special "milk-placing ceremony," are treated with more reverence than ordinary ones. Sites where water enters the village from the seven mountain springs hold similar ritual importance. Of the four village taps (+), the one just north-east of the *pacāl* commands special reverence. Kota men wash divine coin offerings there before publicly presenting them before the *mundkānōns* at the god ceremony.

Finally, each village contains places with unique historical significance, which usually illustrate divine or ancestral power. The landscape comes to encode moral issues associated with important incidents. A "god stone" (*devr kal* +), inscribed with the Tamil words "*maram pēci*" ("tree speaking"), commemorates a story of two brothers who were n on speaking terms. To separate grains from their husks, Kotas trad tionally spread grain on the ground and drove oxen over it. The tw brothers found themselves unable to divide the threshed grain witho speaking. Finally, the wooden post used to tether the oxen, animated b the voice of god, spoke up and resolved the dispute. After the post di integrated with age, it was replaced with a cement post inscribed i Tamil. Such static sites as the speaking post are not re-presented i ritual: they stand as moral reminders every time Kotas pass by. Th land grounds moral stories.

Summary and Conclusions

Kota places are invested with "morality" in many ways. (1) Stories whic name places may illustrate a moral principle; the place recalls the stor and encodes the value. (2) Being in a place engenders a set of sent ments (security, lonesomeness, fear, etc.) fostered by a belief concern ing the behavior of its constituent humans or animals. (3) Places ar hierarchized (with temporal contingency) according to activities of pe sons involved with different kinds of "pollution" and those dealing wit divine matters, and (3a) according to orientation (up–down, east–west and (3b) the preferred location of respected individuals and their home or things.

Music feeds into the construction of Kota places as moral, in tur by (1) serving as a conduit in the oral transmission of moral storie (2) providing a formal performance mechanism for reiterating the name of significant places, evoking their meanings aesthetically, artisticall and verbally; and (3) serving as a ritual and everyday means of diffe entiating places qualitatively as well as hierarchically, not only throug kinds of performances but also through the making, placement, and sto age of musical instruments.

Finally, the value, moral or otherwise, of places for Kotas lies in set of affective attachments (or repulsions) that are connected sensori ally with people's bodies, whether through sight, smell, sound, or gen eral orientation in three-dimensional space.

CHAPTER 4

Knowing When and Where

In this chapter I focus on the origins of Kota music, how Kotas learn, compose, interpret, and analyze music, and what, for Kotas, constitutes musicianship more generally. With these in view, I also address the following questions: how do spatiotemporal constraints on Kota musical performance affect the performer's ability to remember and pass on repertoire? How is musical learning more generally modulated by spatiotemporal considerations? How does a performer shape a piece during performance? What kinds of information travel with musical pieces when they are taught?

Gaining Knowledge, Controlling Time

Kota views on how one obtains musical knowledge reinforce widely held ambivalent beliefs about music in the Indian subcontinent. While musical knowledge and one's capability to acquire it are linked to divine grace, music is also a learned skill that requires hard work. S. Cindamani once said that ability to compose or "build" (*kaṭ-*) music requires a "cleverness" (Ta. *tiṟamai*) obtained by virtue of god's power (*śakti*) and compassion (*karuṇai*). Kotas emphasize this view with respect to god tunes, which were first learned through dreams or trances rather than directly composed. Raman, however, intimated his confidence in composing in any genre, for *koḷ* composition is the province of the skilled musician. These views reflect differences in musical performers' control over time. If musicians must simply wait for divine inspiration, they will not know when musical knowledge will "come." If music is a skill or craft, one may choose when to work on a new piece, just as one might set out to fashion an iron implement in the smithy. The same ambiguity surrounds one Kota's understanding of where Kota music originated:

> How did the Kotas learn? . . . [the gods] gave us learning, but is there any "record"? No. What "record" is there? My son Gundan is here, I tell him. Gundan tells his son. My grandfather tells my father; my father tells me; I tell my son. This is the power (*cakti*) of Brahman [the power underlying the universe]. How do people learn to play the *koḷ*? My grandfather says "will you learn?" and teaches me. One man who knows *tabaṭk* will say, "hey man, you go play." This is our "record." For the rest of it, as for the [details of the] "record," there is no need to tell! There is no writing, there is no reading, only the power of Brahman . . . how did God teach us *koḷ* playing? Was it through mourning songs (*āṭḷs*), through dreams, or was it directly? We picked up his teaching just like we learned blacksmithing. Do we learn from *gurus*? No, our learning comes from *ayṉōr-amnōr*, our grandfathers and grandmothers, of that era . . . following the "rules." [Our ancestors] knew nothing of cheating, stealing, or killing. We live with *catym* and *nīdy* (justice). That's all.[1]

The speaker, S. Cindamani's late brother, Caḷn, initially uses the English word "record" to refer to a historical document. Then he reconfigures "record" as a kind of "proof," which exists in the very *form* of oral tradition—the intersubjective passing on of knowledge. Caḷn uses forms of learning to link the moral conduct of present generations with the innocence of previous generations, thereby articulating another aspect of Kota "structural nostalgia." Kota music does not have a separate origin story because it is closely linked with blacksmithing, other forms of artisanship, god, and Kota identity. It is inconceivable that "*kōv*" existed who were not a community of musicians, blacksmiths, and other artisans.

The idea that a deity transmits new melodies through the medium of a *tērkārn* provides a perspective on how musical transmission may be constrained in spatiotemporal terms: a new repertorial item could emerge in times and places reserved for possession during the god ceremony. When Raman teaches his son Duryodhana a piece on the *pulāng* his act will engage a different place—probably Raman's home or some convenient place nearby. A musical act in one place, the *guṛyvāl* or the home, at a particular time sets up the possibility for future such acts (more possession, more practice at home) whose frequency and character become clearer as these possibilities are or are not realized. In these respects, musical transmission both takes place in the physical dimensions of time and space and constitutes a spatiotemporal form that constrains future musical actions.

Composition and transmission are related processes. While songs are frequently composed and disseminated around the seven villages, mostly by women, *koḷ* repertoires are more conservative, not as subject to observable change, even over a decade. We should not assume that this repertoire has always been so slow to change. A rare passage from the fieldnotes of David G. Mandelbaum records an interview with Naṛykēr Kamaṭn, one of Puccan's teachers, who claims to have been one of the main *koḷ* composers of his period:

> In Kolmēl only I have made seven or eight new tunes and Koḷkaṭ Tūj [S. Raman's father] has made one . . . I have dreamed three *devr koḷs*. I dream that I am playing the tune on a [*koḷ*] and when I wake it is still going thru my head and I whistle it and play it on the [*koḷ*] and then I know it. Other tunes I have made while I was aimlessly whistling (he whistles thru puckered lips). (Mandelbaum, May 11, 1938, p. 5)

This musician "made" new melodies either in his head or through the approximating medium of whistling. He did not do so by experimenting on the instrument—just as learning and rehearsal are not generally accomplished on the *koḷ* but on something softer. This passage also raises the issue of auto-transmission: Naṛykēr Kamaṭn inscribed a new melody on his memory while going about everyday activities and then finally cemented this knowledge by performing the piece on an instrument.

Spatiotemporal Factors Affecting Musical Learning

Kotas view singing and dancing as passively acquired talents. Learning some musical instruments involves more commitment; the more specialized the skill or the piece of repertoire, the greater the spatiotemporal constraints for learning and the greater the reliance on specific teachers. S. Cindamani presents a special case of cultural learning because she could afford the leisure time to absorb traditional forms of knowledge gradually, without the responsibilities that normally hampered girls of her age. The single daughter among the ten sons of her father, Kabāln in Kurgōj village, Cindamani never went to school. This was atypical among Kota women of her generation, born *circa* 1944. As she put it in 1997, "When I was young I used to hang around with the old ladies . . . I was the only girl of eight siblings. My mother wouldn't ask me to do even one lick of work. 'Where are the old men, where are the old women' [I would ask], for having fun (*tamāc*) I would roam around. I was free, full of amusement. Now would people let *her* [Cindamani's niece, who was sitting next to her] be like this?" This childhood leisure provided Cindamani the opportunity to interact creatively with adults and learn from them in a way that other children of her generation seldom could. By breaking free from "traditional" shackles of everyday household responsibilities on the one hand, and school on the other, she was able to gain an informal education in aspects of culture it normally takes years to imbibe: music, dance, and storytelling.

Families, as one might expect, tend to share aspects of their musicality. Members of a village, like an extended family, also share common ways of rendering repertoire and more broadly share interest in activities that come to distinguish one village from another. Kolmē musicians, for instance, are known for the excellence of their god tunes. Ticgāṛ village women are renowned for their neatly synchronized dancing; Kurgōj villagers relish association with the rougher and more raucous aspects of being a Kota tribal: interest in hunting and drinking, skillful craftsmanship, tending of semi-wild buffalo herds, and elaboration of rituals and customs connected with death—especially their *tāv koḷ*s and *āṭḷ*s. Cindamani and her brother Mundan continue to maintain performance knowledge of two rare instruments, *pījl* and *bugīr*. The survival of *bugīr* and *pījl* performance in Kurgōj village is part of a broader congeries of practices connecting Kotas with their past.

Sustaining Skills: Kotas generally learn drum "beating" (*oy-*) or *koḷ* "blowing" (*irp-*) on their own, receiving guidance on occasion from those with more experience. *Koḷ* playing ("blowing") is more difficult, so novices may seek guidance from more skilled players. They start with the bamboo *pulāng*, which can be played in the home at almost any time without causing alarm, as it is not very loud. It is also easier to play than the *koḷ* because its reed, slit from the instrument's bamboo tube, requires little adjustment. The *bugīr* can also be used as a practice instrument, but it requires a great deal of skill to produce a tone.

K. Puccan started playing the *pulāng* at age twelve, consulting his mother's maternal aunt's son, "Knife Nose Kamaṭn," and Naṛykēr Kamaṭn, who would provide feedback by either humming the melody or demonstrating it on the *pulāng*. Puccan said he and his playing partner, Veḷn, who lived in the line of houses below, became *geṭygārns*, "clever fellows," "hot-shots." After that, Puccan took only about "eight days" to learn the *koḷ*. It was easy for him to switch from one instrument to the other since he had mastered techniques of fingering (*verl iṭd*) and circular breathing, or "holding air" (*cīl pacd*). "Eight days" is a Kota expression that stands for a "short period of time." It generally takes quite a while for a novice to attain a good tone on the *koḷ* even after learning the *pulāng* well.

Graduating from the *pulāng* to the *koḷ* presents a practical problem because the *koḷ* should not be played in the village unless it is called for ceremonially. A funeral tune, played loudly on the *koḷ*, would be taken as a sign of an actual funeral and would alarm villagers, make them sad and worried. Puccan and Veḷn used to practice in a forest below the village and then, after returning home, use the *pulāng* or their voices to check the accuracy of their playing with their teachers. Such ambulations in and out of the village required leisure time on their part and the teachers too would have needed to be around the village and available for consultation. Puccan's life was pastoral; he had ample time to pass playing the *pulāng* while out in the fields tending animals. Those Kota men whose agrarian lifestyle allows them to maintain a regular rhythm of alternating between field and village are well disposed to perpetuate the *koḷ* tradition. So too does living in immediate proximity to one's teachers and playing partners—though Kota villages are small and one's comrades are never far away anyway.

Puccan learned *devr koḷ*s from Naṛykēr Kamaṭn and *tāv koḷ*s from S. Raman's father, Tūj (the same Koḷkaṭ Tūj mentioned by Naṛykēr Kamaṭn above). The "best" *koḷ* players in 1938 knew the *tāv* and *devr koḷ*s; these are generally the longer, more involved pieces connected with special rituals. One indicator of aptitude has had to do with where and when one is encouraged to demonstrate one's knowledge. The *pacāl* is associated primarily with important moments of communal music-making, at which time only the more experienced musicians are encouraged to play. Hence, when a musician is first permitted to perform god tunes and special dance tunes on the *pacāl*, this is a kind of musical coming-of-age. Puccan first played on the *pacāl* when he knew all the important *devr koḷ*s, at age twenty-five (around 1937).

Snatching a Moment: Puccan encouraged his sons to study hard and seek gainful employment outside the village. Without their father's flexible village–field routine neither brother could commit himself to *koḷ* practice. Puccan's first son, Varadharajan, became a successful doctor and, eventually, Chief Medical Officer at Hindustan Photo Films, some ten kilometers beyond Ooty. Throughout the 1990s and until the present writing he has been returning to his village home every Sunday and never misses important village events. Like many others, Varadharajan learned to play the drums when he could snatch a moment. He usually spoke with me in English.[2] "I think you might have seen that small kids are playing *dobar-kiṇvar* every day in that *pacāl* during [the god] festival season [casually, in between other events]. Likewise I was also playing *dobar-kiṇvar*, playing there. The knowledge I don't know from which age, probably after five-six years."

After such casual sessions of what often amounts to pounding on instruments, those who wish to hone their skills may seek the guidance of more experienced players. As the beginner progresses he gradually joins in communal music-making. Novices, though, must fit their interludes of practice between major rituals of the god ceremony. Performances of moment-specific repertoire combined with non-musical activities co-create a ritual frame within which these kinds of rehearsal become appropriate. This temporary and contingent rehearsal space, in turn, contributes to the ways in which the *pacāl* comes to be conceptualized and defined more permanently as a place in the memories and experiences of Kota villagers.

Places outside the village also become associated with kinds of musicianship. In earlier times, less experienced musicians were usually deputed to perform for Toda or Badaga funerals. There they could develop their performance chops outdoors in lively performance settings without the same expectations of excellence that might be demanded within a Kota village. Nowadays, less experienced musicians might still be sent out for minor functions—for the benefit of patrons, for example, that Kotas do not know or respect. For a more high-profile function, as when the Kotas were invited to perform for the president of India at the Ooty Botanical Gardens, the seven villages hold a *kūṭm* to select representative musicians. In 1990–2 these were usually Raman and Duryodhana.

Those who wished to learn the *koḷ*, but who, like Dr Varadharajan, did not have the flexibility to spend time with a teacher or gain further experience *in-situ*, have had to resort to other means. K. Jayachandran, of Porgāṛ village, used a cassette recorder.

Learning from Recordings

K. Jayachandran had been studying in a Tamil-medium school when, at the age of eighteen, he decided to discontinue his pre-university course and seek employment. Working diligently and benefitting from his status as a member of a Scheduled Tribe, Jayachandran rose in the ranks of government service and eventually entered the State Bank of India system. The State Bank's policy of transferring those who are promoted led Jayachandran to live away from his village for several years. During this time, Jayachandran witnessed the erosion of his village's musical culture. As he explained it to me in English: "Actually in my village, the elderly people they never allowed anyone else to touch that *koḷ* and all when I was in my childhood. One Mr. Kanaḷ Kamaṭn and Kavundan Māgāḷi, they were the *koḷ* players. But they never gave at all. They continued to play until they attained sixty or seventy years of age. So I was forced to learn it after they became elderly people. At that point they were no longer able to play." In Hindustani musical *gharānā*s and elsewhere in India, protection of musical knowledge is common even if it is not happily accepted by all. Many Kotas consider this kind of secrecy to be culturally inappropriate and indeed socially counterproductive. Kota villages need competent *koḷ* players for special ritual purposes as well as to provide lively dance music. "I was forced to take a tape recorder and borrow the *koḷ* [repertoire] from Kollimalai. Puccan is my father-in-law, so I used to record *koḷ*s on cassettes and take them to my village and hear him. I became successful in *āṭ koḷ* because it is a must for us [to dance]. *Devr koḷ* I can manage, but *tāv koḷ* alone [is difficult for me] because I have been transferred to Jolarpet which is too far away from my village."

Regularly recurring ceremonies and celebrations allow those living away from the village to schedule their return. Deaths, while sometimes predictable, are never events for which one can easily plan. Jayachandran could not attend many Kota funerals and for this reason could not imbibe the funeral repertoire. The spatiotemporal form of an annual occasion sequence, its regularity or irregularity, could have a significant impact on the perpetuation of certain musical genres, particularly if more and more Kotas are constrained by the locations of their jobs. Residential patterns affect the lead time Kotas need to schedule leaves of absence for major ceremonies and the time required for travel.

Jayachandran's strategy of learning from tape recordings presents the potential pitfalls we find in other modernizing traditions, in that a single recorded performance might be privileged when a number of acceptable variations exist. It has obvious advantages, however, and could even, in this case, serve as an impetus for cross-village musical fertilization. But was the Kolmēl repertoire going to usurp entirely that of Porgāṛ? Did any remnant of Porgāṛ's earlier *koḷ* repertoire survive? I asked Jayachandran if he recorded performers from his own village. He said no, "Only Puccan . . . My guru is Puccan. . . . The only *devr koḷ* I picked up—gradually by listening in my own village—is the *ōlāguc koḷ* [temple-opening tune]. The [others], especially *devr koḷ* and . . . *āṭ koḷ* I learned from Puccan . . . through the tape recorder."[3]

Just as Naṛykēr Kamaṭn needed to develop a method of remembering the tunes he himself composed, so too did Jayachandran need a means for transferring the "knowledge" recorded on tape to his own mind, and a means of bringing that knowledge to bear at the right moment in a performance. I asked him: "OK so suppose now it's *devr* [god ceremony] time in Porgāṛ, and it comes time to play the *aṛcāyḷ koḷ*s. Now this *ōlāguc* you have in your mind, but these other *koḷ*s you learned from Puccan. Those are a little bit more difficult, perhaps?"

> The *devr koḷ* is somewhat tough. Suppose if I have a doubt . . . I'll set up with the tape recorder (laughs) on the day itself. For example, in our village, we have another *koḷ* also, that *kū murc koḷ* ["tune for breaking up clumps of cooked grain," used for offering grain to the gods] in fact. I am not knowing that *koḷ* in my village, so that I collected from Kollimalai village. That particular *koḷ* I am not able to pick up because there is no time for me to practice. The dance and all very often we used to do it, so automatically . . . [it was easy to learn the dance *koḷ*s]. But this is special: [for] this particular ceremony [only] we used to play it, no? So that once in a year (says somewhat laughingly), at that particular moment I used to [practice by listening to a tape recording].

> When I was first learning, I also used to practice before *devr* time with the help of the *pulāng*. To make it cent per cent I used to play. But nowadays I have become experienced no? Forever I can remember.

I asked him whether he used the syllables "gag gil lil lil" as some other musicians do. The syllable "*gag*" generally corresponds with a "*gag*" tone—used for melodic punctuation and generally played by covering all six holes of the *koḷ*. The other syllables, "gil, lil, le," etc. correspond to relatively higher pitches, but not in one-to-one correspondences. *Koḷ* players and even perceptive non-players remind one another of melodies using such vocalization techniques. Jayachandran laughed, and responded: "That 'gag gil' business, I [do it by] whistling." (Many *koḷ* players whistle to remind themselves of a tune just before playing it.)

I asked him to whistle the *ōlāguc koḷ*. He said "in our village, we have got some sort of *ōlāguc koḷ*," by which he meant an inferior or simpler kind (Ta. *oru mātiri*) in comparison with that of Kolmēl. The Kolmēl tune is "very good and quite toughest also to learn," has more parts (*dāk*s) and requires "the help of some guru." Jayachandran then whistled the short melody, which is, I suspect, quite old, for a version of it is included on recordings made by Thurston and Rangachari (*circa* 1905), probably at the old site of Porgāṛ village, in modern-day Kotagiri.[4] A version of the same is also played in Kināṛ village, which village tends to share rituals, *koḷ*s, songs, and kin with Porgāṛ, its closest Kota neighbor.

Jayachandran set out to use this new mixture of local and imported god tunes "to develop the younger generations" in his village. He's established a new ritual of "playing at least three to four *koḷ*s before the dancing during the festival days . . . to collect people for dancing." In Kolmēl, he noted, they play the "*padneṭ devr koḷ* [eighteen-god-calling tune]" (CD 26), because they believe that "eighteen *murti*s [gods] are with us while we dance for the great almighty, *ayṉōr amnōr*." In his village "they have discontinued it, no? So automatically I don't know what is the purpose, exactly, no?" but he feels that those in Kolmēl "may know the purpose because still they are continuing the practice."

So, although Jayachandran wished to reinvigorate interest in "traditional" cultural knowledge, he recognized that meanings and understandings can vary locally and over time, and that "original" meanings and practices may become irretrievably lost. But he believed it possible to create new meanings. This dual goal of attaining new education in the broader Indian context and returning to the fundamentals of Kota culture guides many Kotas who are economically and socially successful outside the village.

How Kotas Analyze Their Music

Jayachandran's comment on the small number of *dāk*s in the Porgāṛ tune raised questions about what he meant by the word *dāk*, which generally applies to both melodic and percussion patterns, and to sub-units that comprise melodic patterns. I asked Jayachandran to clarify:

> In Tamil we call these sections *pallavi*, *anupallavi*, and *caraṇam*. . . . There are six holes on the *koḷ*. The middle [three] fingers [on each hand] no? . . . So the right hand finger, the border finger and the second finger . . . may [be used to play the] *pallavi*. If we go up and up . . . *anupallavi*, then *caraṇam* comes. That is what Tamil songs [are] also like: *pallavi* gradually starts, then [the] *anupallavi* will [have] more effect than [the] *pallavi*. The *caraṇam* has got most effect than this *pallavi*. The *caraṇam* is the ideal . . . It concludes that real song.

Jayachandran's strained attempts to make this terminology fit are not without merit. *Pallavi*, *anupallavi*, and *caraṇam*, are generally differentiated by range in Karnatak music. Jayachandran projected the idea of a three-part registral structure onto the *koḷ* by dividing the six holes into three two-hole units. Just as Kotas conceptualize pitch, like register, in spatial terms (a *meṭ* is a series of steps), musicians conceive melodic units on the *koḷ* in terms of where the holes (Ko. *kaṇ* "eye") are located. These may not correspond with discrete notes because players may obtain multiple pitches, and produce waves (*alykd*) and tremolos in the vicinity of a scalar position, by altering their embouchure and air pressure (*cīl*). In songs, whose melodies do exhibit more-or-less discrete notes, the term *kaṇ* is used to refer to lyrics. *Kaṇ*s in both cases, then, are units of melodic articulation.

When I asked Dr Varadharajan about pitch, he employed the common metaphor of physical height,

> My father . . . used to go [vocalize] "lillil le lil lil lil lil lil, lil lil lil le lil lil lilll, il likl lil le lil lil lil lil likilile lil lil" . . . he used to go topmost and

> he comes down (CD 10). That tune actually sometimes it goes and comes down . . . My father used to say, that *eṛkay dāk* you should go up. Left will go up sometimes, so its pitches are high . . .

Varadharajan's reference pertains to hand positions: the three middle fingers of the left hand cover the three holes on the *koḷ* closest to the player's mouth; the three corresponding right-hand fingers cover the remaining holes. "*Eṛkay dāk*" is the *dāk* or section played by the left hand. This is also termed *mēl dāk*, "upper section/type." An entire *koḷ* could be called a *mēl dāk koḷ* if its pitches lie in the upper register. "*Valkay dāk*" is the section played by the right hand. Since the climactic sections of *koḷ*s are in the upper, or *eṛkay* register, and since it is very difficult to control the reeds when one is forcefully blowing in this register, only the best *koḷ* players can successfully negotiate it. Varadharajan criticized another player's abilities, "See, you can watch [his] *koḷ* [and compare it with] my father's *koḷ*." The inferior player "goes up [only] to some extent and comes down . . . I think [he] is not getting it high enough."

When our conversation turned to musicianship on the drums, Varadharajan was not one for false modesty. "Actually," he said, "I am [the] best drummer in *dobar*. I will say I am the number one in *dobar* in all seven villages." So I asked him, "What makes somebody number one?" "Rhythm," he responded, by which he probably meant an accurate sense of timing. The other criterion had to do with the blending of the ensemble into an internally differentiated, unified whole. The *dobar* provides the bass, but "all instruments are needed to get a good music. [A] single *koḷ* will not make a good music, [a] single *kiṇvar* will not make a good music, [a] single *dobar* will not make a good music . . . each single component has to be given . . . Here everybody says 'Varadharajan is good in *dobar*, so for whatever function let him come.'"

Despite striving for symbolic equality in some forms of ritual, and notwithstanding the social unity they articulate through "interlocking" in a well-balanced ensemble, Kotas do not overlook the talent differentials among musicians. The community "gives a certificate" by permitting someone to play during central group functions and by asking for particular musicians over and above others. They ask for Varadharajan because, "If I go there, the dance also changes . . . the others feel the drum." "My hands are biggest!" he said. "For *dobar* to make a sound you need good [fingers and big hands]." His love for music and his devotion to god, he feels, is translated into the force with which he drums. His hands bleed, but he does not feel it. The forcefulness affects others.

Loudness, Extension, and Structural Nostalgia

For many Kotas, loudness of sound is an effective means to call god, just as the *ōmayṉ* is effective in reaching the heavens. But for Varadharajan loudness is more than this. While driving from Ooty to his house, Varadharajan played music loudly on the radio and told me of his love of volume. Sound is "music," he said, sound is "good" and should be loud, "like a breaking sound." The drum should "beat most violently," particularly the "bass sound. See, whatever bass: cinema songs, or Tamil songs, Hindi songs, whichever songs, all rock songs, whichever it is it should be . . . loud! It should be banging! It should be breaking! Violent! And I like it. I am accustomed to that also."

Why would Varadharajan hold such strong feelings about volume? He related a well-known story that may help explain some of the cultural underpinnings of this preference (which other Kotas share):

> Oṭāṭe Kamaṭn, my grandfather's grandfather, was a Kolmēlōn. He was visiting his widowed mother, who was living in Mēnāṛ village. It was temple-opening day *(guṛyterd nāḷ)*, Sunday. In the olden days they used to play four, six, sometimes eight *kob*s at once for this temple opening. At present no one is able to make this much sound. From Mēnāṛ, Oṭāṭe Kamaṭn heard the sound of the *kob* coming all the way from Kolmēl. He started chanting "*ōḷy ōḷy*." These fellows in Kolmēl were cleaning the temple saying the holy syllables "*ōḷy ōḷy*," so this same thing he was doing in Mēnāṛ. This shows how much sound there was at that particular period, say about thirty miles from here! In that particular period, how much efforts have been given for sound. So that man was able to hear. Nowadays I think that sound is not coming.

Varadharajan explained that Kotas of the old days could project their sounds over long distances because they used to eat a great deal of meat. "That is what, as a doctor I say." Today's weakness, in his view, stems from smoking and drinking. His community's inability to play as ɔudly as their forefathers is a symptom of bodily infirmity. Volume is positive attribute of sound because it embodies strength. Volume is a ıeasure of *catym*. It is one of the terms by which Kotas articulate their tructural nostalgia (Herzfeld 1997), their sense of remembrance, repliated in each generation, of the power possessed by Kotas of the previus generations.

Multiple sonic gestures come to reference and implicate one another ı Kota ritual. The *kob*'s significance depends upon additional cues. It ıay communicate that someone has died in one context, or that the ɛmple is being opened in another—in which case the *kob* blast is a call ɔ god. Varadharajan's ancestor in Mēnāṛ responded "*ōḷy ōḷy*" because e knew the god ceremony was under way in Kolmēl.[5] Another such ffering of abstract, non-musical sound, is the calling out of "*a hau au.*" This is called *edykd*, or literally, "jumping high," probably beause it sometimes includes raised, dance-like steps as well. "Jumping igh" is performed enthusiastically in a variety of ritual contexts and ppears to celebrate (and respond to) the process and/or completion of ertain actions. Kotas attend not only to volume and to the intrinsic signicance of certain sounds but to sound qualities such as timbre as well—ften with acuity. Once, when R. Mathi heard the blast of the *kob* anouncing the temple-opening, she was supposed to respond by tossing ıe *vatm* millet (reserved for the upcoming feast) into boiling water. But er response to sound was not merely functional here: listening to the ıusic accompanying the dance that followed the temple-opening, she ɛmarked on the poor sound of the *tabaṭk* and asked if the head had been amaged (it was).

Musical Evaluation

Kotas describe well played music as "tasteful to hear" (*ōriṛḷk cayvāyṛ ṛo*). Such music is played in synch, with a steady and strong tone, for long period of time, and with artful ornaments. Less finely wrought ıusic may satisfy a ritual requirement, but the sadness of funeral muic will not be savored, will not "taste good to the ears" (*kevk tucūḏo*), vill not be "fragrant" (*gaml gaml*). These terms for taste and fragrance lso index music's potential to excite the dancers or focus the mind on od, as per the genre and ritual context.

In both funerary and god contexts, the non-human entities involved (spirits, gods) are said to appreciate the appropriate music aesthetically, to yearn for it, to have "desire" (*anglāpm*) to hear it. Kotas perform music for the ancestors or gods and in return receive the benefit of welcome for the deceased into their midst (ancestors and gods) and their blessing. Additional, almost symmetrical, aesthetic exchange obtains when spirits of the dead beckon the dying with funeral music, sing to the ill in dreams, chant through a female spirit medium (formerly); or when the gods (through the possessed *tērkārn*) teach the Kotas a new melody to be used in worship.

Dayṇ: *Voice Quality*: Musicians pay careful attention to the features of their own sound production. When Cindamani and Mundan concluded their performances of the same piece, vocally and on *bugīr* respectively (CD 27 and 9), they expressed exasperation. After singing with increasing intensity and gradually rising pitch throughout, Cindamani truncated her rendition when her voice became strained and scratchy: "My voice quality (*dayṇ*) is not good, enough please [stop recording]." *Āṭḷ*s are often open-ended, their performed length depending on the knowledge, creativity, and energy of the singer. Mundan, who was repeating the same melody without much variation, complained, "this is difficult," the piece "should be played on the *koḷ*." He was grousing about the limited range of the *bugīr*, with five (in this case) instead of six finger holes. Sustaining melodic activity in the upper range of the instrument is difficult in any case. With the *koḷ*, the player can maintain air pressure by buttressing his lips against the *vāypor* (pirouette); the *bugīr*, which is played by vibrating the lips, as one would in blowing into a conch shell, is more difficult to play in the upper register.

What Kotas mean by the term for sound quality, *dayṇ*, can be further explained through reference to Cindamani's procedures of composing songs. First, Cindamani said, she must "build" (*kaṭ-*) a *rāgam*. Only if the *rāgam* (melody) is "good" will the song be, as she put it, well "set-up." When asked to clarify what she meant using Kota language terms, Cindamani replied "*dayṇ oyḷām ikvōṛo*" (the *dayṇ* should be good). She insisted that in the dialect of her village, Kurgōj, *dayṇ* is used to describe vocal *rāgams*. Cindamani sees melody and vocal quality as a single seamless entity when it comes to musical evaluation.

The Kota word *dayṇ* derives from the Sanskrit *dhvani*, meaning "sound, echo, voice, tone, tune, thunder,"[6] and retains a similar potential for semantic slippage between "tone" and "tune." Although Cindamani told me the term *dayṇ* applies only to the singing voice, *koḷ* players use it to describe the "voice" of their instruments as well, especially the quality of the "*gag*" sound. If the reeds are faulty, or if air is leaking from the instrument, the *gag* sound will not attain its desired fullness and clarity. Men and women are also said to have different *dayṇ*s, different "voices."

Cindamani said both *āṭl*s and *devr pāṭ*s would be "beautiful" (*pacand*) if the *dayṇ* were rendered well (*dayṇ oyḷām ītāme*). Different *dayṇ*s produce different affects. The proper *dayṇ* for an *āṭl* is "sorrowful or grieving" (spoken Ta. *tuyaramā*) and communicates anxiety or worry (Ko. *arkl*). God song *dayṇ*s are celebratory (spoken Ta. *koṇḍāṛvā*) and convey pride (*angārm*). *Dayṇ*, then, is a "grain" of voice (Barthes 1977) as well as a melody.

Fig. 7: "En Aṇ Caḷo," as Sung by S. Cindamani

How a Performer Shapes a Piece in Time: Composing, Singing, and Rendering

If *dayṇ* is the most important component in Cindamani's composition how does she go about setting words? Cindamani "by-hearts" (i.e. memorizes) the words and then, having internalized the melody, thinks of beautiful way to "place" them.[7] The boundaries of "singing" (*pāṛ-*) c "song rendering" (*pāṭ et-*) and "composing" (*kaṭ-* "to build, tie") blu somewhat. Kotas frequently render a song they haven't themselve "composed" by stringing together a few main ideas or textual phrase to fit the melody; but they do not always do so in the same way, as i Mangiammal's rendition of Raman's song (Chapter 2). Some singer insisted that song components are fixed in order and not merely pu together according to the whim of the singer. Some verses must com before others, especially narrative songs or songs naming a sequenc of places on a path. But not all songs that are supposed to be fixe actually are so.

This notation combines tablature with staff notation. The icon to the right of the treble clef represents a *bugīr*. It is lined up with the staff to show how a hole on the *bugīr*, covered by the player's finger, corresponds roughly to a note. Reading from the top of the instrument down, the fingers correspond to the holes (dots) as follows. Left hand: index, middle, then ring finger; Right hand: index, then ring finger. The absence of a position for the note C in this tablature represents a physical gap on the *bugī* between the fourth and fifth holes. In the analogous positions on *pulāng* or *koḷ* this gap would be fillec by an additional hole and played with the middle finger of the right hand.

Fig. 8: "En Aṇ Caḷo" Played on Bugīr by K. Mundan

Listening Guide and Musical Discussion of Mundan's *Bugīr* Rendition (Fig. 8)

Extreme rhythmic and tonal flexibility and weak forms of internal articulation make this *bugīr* example extremely difficult to notate. The impression of the melody gained from reading this notation may also be difficult to match to the recording. To get a sense of how I hear this example, I suggest first listening to the recording without the notation. Let the "pickup" note pass and begin snapping your fingers in groups of four when you hear the note G according to the following pattern of pulse groupings: 3 + 2 + 2 + 3, where 3 + 2 = mm. 56. Focus first only on the first phrase, which repeats. You should be able to get your snaps to line up with some of the internal articulations of the phrase, and be able to maintain the snapping pattern in the repetition. Now look at the notation. The accent marks show where the first two of your snaps, in each group of four, should have more-or-less lined up with the melody. These are anchor points.

The second repeating section (Measures Five through Seven and Eight through Ten) becomes more ambiguous because the melody does not provide anchor points. The accent on pulse eight, F, in Measure Five militates against feeling the slightly flat E that follows as beat one in the next rhythmic cycle (Measure Six). The trill and its release on E similarly destabilizes the metrical feeling in Measures Six through Nine. A fermata appears at the end of Measure Seven and its analogue, Measure Ten, because the following note is often delayed. Despite these ambiguities, I predicted that this piece would be accompanied on the *koḷ* by a 10-pulse *cādā dāk* pattern and that the performer would realign his melody with the pattern on the opening phrase, which is from my perspective more regular. In January 2004 I tested this hypothesis by playing the recording for Mundan and asking him to accompany it on the *tabaṭk*. His choice of *cādā dāk* confirmed my analysis. The *tabaṭk* pattern cut across the melody, sometimes lining up as in my notation, sometimes not. This characteristic drifting of the melody seemed exaggerated in this case, as Mundan was not trying to "anchor" his melody on an actual percussion ostinato when he performed it for the original recording. Mundan did have to adjust his drumming a bit to make it fit the melody, but for the most part he maintained a continuous groove and let the recorded melody go in and out of synch.

The ways in which Cindamani and Mundan express their musicality go a long way toward explaining singing, composing, and instrumental performance among the Kotas more generally, for which the same verb *et-* is used.[8] A musician internalizes a melody and then performs it by accommodating the melody to the constraints of text, instrumental technique or range, and/or the sound of accompanying instruments (especially drums). This process of accommodation is often one of anchoring, where a string of words is fit (perhaps awkwardly) to land up on a particular point within a metrical structure, or a melody stretched to correspond with a drum stroke or hand clap.

Examining parts of Cindamani's and Mundan's performances allows us to probe deeper into the idea of Kota musical "rendition" as a particular kind of negotiation of musical elements in time. Cindamani's performance also enriches our picture of the *āṭḷ* in terms of its spatio-temporal form, the ways in which the genre invokes certain kinds of

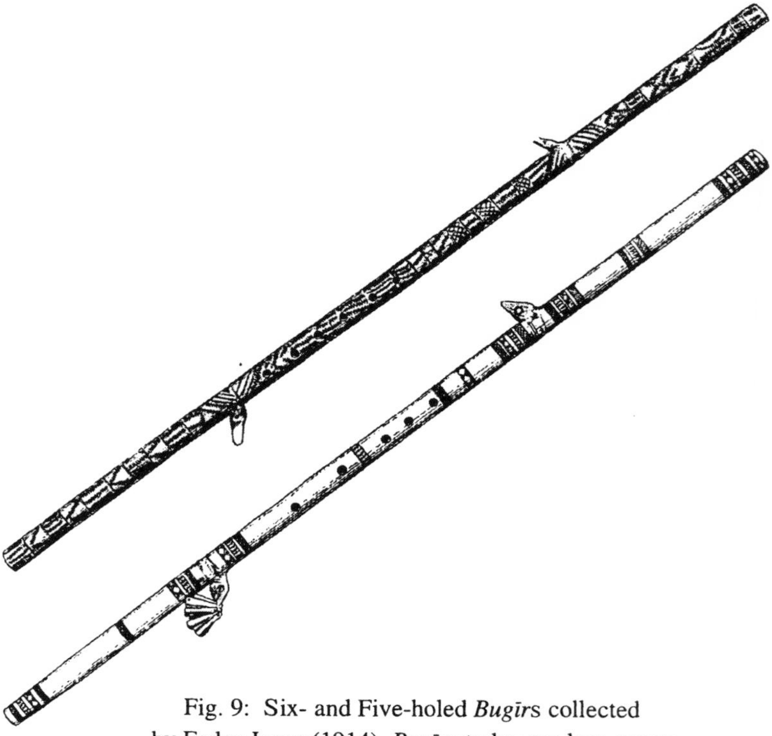

Fig. 9: Six- and Five-holed *Bugīr*s collected by Fedor Jagor (1914). *Bugīr*s today are less ornate

places, and how it plays upon the memories of listeners to create affective complexity.

"En aṇ caḷo"
Song associated with Kurgōj village. Text as sung by S. Cindamani (June 7, 1992; CD 27)

(a) la la la . . .	
1. (a) enaṇ caḷō (refrain, sung 4 times)	1. My older brother Caln!
2. (a a) uruḷēnē piṭāṛē (a) eytiṭē (a) tinēne (a) iḏēnā enaṇ caḷō, enaṇ caḷō	2. "Eat the fried sweet in the pot hanging in the rope sling," I said, my brother Caln
3. (ā) pālēnē uṉire iḏirē (a) paṛydēnā (a a) enaṇa (a) enaṇ caḷō (o) enaṇ caḷō	3. "Drink milk," I said My brother Caln
4. (a) edīyē oygūḏār iḏāmē (a) cēlkāllē	4. If you ask where he's gone, "to the Celkal"
5. oygūḏār ināra enaṇ caḷō enaṇ caḷō (a a) la la la . . .	5. "He's gone," they say My brother Caln la la la . . .
6. (a) edīyē oygūḏāmē naṛdiṭḷ oygūḏārō enaṇ caḷō (a) enaṇ caḷō (a) la la la . . .	6. If you ask where he's gone, "He's gone to the Nardit,"[10] they say My brother, Caln la la la . . .
7. (a) edīyē oygūḏām tēlviyḷē (a) oygūḏārō (a) enaṇ caḷō (a) la la la . . .	7. If you ask where he's gone, "He's gone to the Telviyl," they say My brother, Caln la la la . . .
8. (a) edīyē oygūḏāra enaṇ caḷō (a) enaṇ caḷo	8. If you ask where he's gone My brother, Caln
9. (a) imbayṯl oygūḏārō	9. "He's gone to the Buffalo grazing land,"
enaṇ caḷō enaṇcaḷo (a) la la la	they say, my brother, Caln la la la . . .

Discussion and Textual Analysis of Cindamani's Rendition

A sister mourned over her older brother as her village mates were carrying his corpse home from Kalāc village, where he had just died. Understood to be based on an actual funerary lament (CD 27), this *āṭḷ*'s words, phrases, and fragments of melody would have been cobbled together by the singer later, while recalling her spontaneous tuneful wa ing over the corpse. Its limited range and long, sustained pitches le themselves well to instrumental rendition.

For the composer, the song may carry bodily memories of weepin For the listener, instrumental and vocal renditions of an *āṭḷ* may conv only the more generalized emotionality associated with the genre. T song may also trigger specific memories of the individual, dependi on the time elapsed since the death of the song's subject, and the a quaintance of the listener with that subject's home village. But it is qui common for individuals to play and sing pieces associated with tho long dead, with whom neither listener nor performer has any person connection.

This song is structured around a series of hypothetical questions (" you ask where he's gone, he's gone to . . .") using the narrative strate of focusing the listener's attention and contextualizing forthcoming i formation: a sequence of place names. These are either the places t sister actually came across when looking for her brother, or ones ass ciated with her elder brother's peripatetic ways, about which she wa reminiscing nostalgically. Lines numbered 2 and 3 are also ambiguou the sister was either fondly recalling, in a general sense, times in whi she cooked for and doted on her brother (by preparing sweets); or s may have been recounting specifically what happened when Caln, nev to return, left the house, eating a sweet *piṭāṛ* and drinking milk in prep ration for his journey.

Musically, the *āṭḷ* "En aṇ caḷo" exhibits trademark features: a str phic setting, a single narrow range, long sustained pitches, metric flexibility, and glottal articulations at the ends of some phrases and pr ceding meaningless initial vowels (the parenthetical "a" sounds). T effective range of this song (C-sharp to a very flat G) is relatively na row. In the instrumental version of "En aṇ caḷo," the melody is artic lated differently and does not follow word divisions. Their sharing melodic resources allows us to compare how melodic ideas are resolve differently depending on whether they are rendered vocally or instr mentally.

Comparison of Two Renditions

The opening measure of both renditions is a prolongation of a sing tone. In the instrumental case, the "recitation tone" G is approached b a leap of approximately a minor third, both at the beginning, and at eac repetition of the opening phrase.[11] This same equivalent of roughly a major or minor third always appears in the beginning phrase of the song as sung as well. The second measure of the song (vocal) moves the melody up by roughly a neutral second and then descends by two more from the original F. The same generally holds for the instrumental version, with two slight differences: the melody doesn't clearly rise by a neutral second, and the penultimate note is a *gag* tone (slightly sharp B). The former can be explained partially by the fact that there are only five holes on this *bugīr*. With all the fingers removed it is difficult to get a clear, consistent tone (the indefinitely pitched A grace note was produced with all fingers raised). Also, all Kota wind instruments are played with a great deal of ornamentation, so that a sung pitch could easily be represented by an ornament starting from a lower neighbor. The *gag* tone is a cadential marker, a typical form of phrase articulation in instrumental music. Here it signals either the repeat of the first two measures, or a change to the next section.

The next instrumental section (Measure 5) starts for all practical purposes on G.[12] The melody moves from an emphasis on a lowered F-sharp at the end of Measures 5 and 8, down to a sustained "tonal envelope" with D-sharp as its lower limit in Measures 6 and 9. I mean by the term "tonal envelope" a characteristic pulsating with the breath. Experienced *koḷ* players called this "shaking" or "making waves" (*alykd*). In a funeral melody, the technique adds a touch of poignance (*dukm*). In a god tune, "shaking" evokes a devotional feeling (*bhakti*), according to Duryodhana.

Skilled players accomplish prolongation of positions on the *koḷ*, *pulāng*, or *bugīr* by touching on melodically neighboring positions using their fingers, or approaching neighbor tones asymptotically with breath pulsations. When a senior musician corrects a junior musician whose pitch is a bit sharp or flat he may tell him to "let the breath out well" (*kāṯn oyḷām viṛkoṛo*); when the up-and-coming *koḷ* player Kaṇṇan (see photo section) instructed the beginner, Vāsu, in 2001, he used the English word "free," *kāṯn "free" ā viṛkoṛo*, "you should play without restraint." To use less air pressure, a musician would say *kaymāyṛ viṛkoṛo*, "let it out less." "Tonal envelope" is neither of these, but rather an alternating between "letting out well" and "letting out less." The choice of whether to use tonal envelope or neighboring finger positions depends on the position on the instrument, the choice of the player, or the particular piece being performed.

Returning to the analysis of the instrumental version, Measure 7 provides a cadence leading to a repetition of the three-measure segment (Measures 5 to 7) in Measures 8 to 10; the analogous cadence in Measure 10 leads back to Measure 1 or serves as a conclusion for the piece. The two *gag*-tone motives frame each section: the second motive in each section (Measures 7 and 10) is more developed and lends a firmer sense of conclusion and return than the first (Measures 2 and 4). The tune's beginning, middle, and end are well defined through these motivic articulations.

Measures 3 and 4 of the vocal rendition resemble Measures 5 and 6 in the instrumental in that both feature a descent of roughly a third, a slightly flat E-sharp to a C-sharp and a slightly flat F-sharp to a D-sharp respectively. The strongest similarity between the renditions rests on the emphasis on the lowest melody-note of each, the C-sharp and D-sharp (emphasized by the trill/envelope) respectively. Absent from the vocal rendition are the two cadential *gag*-tone figures at the ends of sections. Such cadential figures (usually with *gag* tones) are typically added when a vocal melody is adapted on the *koḷ*, *pulāng*, or *bugīr*. They give an instrumental melody its idiomatic clarity. Disregarding the cadential figures leaves two melodies with essentially the same contour, but varying in articulation and rhythmic structure.

In the case of the vocal example, since the text is variable, the precise articulation of the melody undergoes some mutation over the course of a performance. Articulation on the *bugīr* is accomplished by individual puffs of air combined with the timing of finger placement (*verl iṭd*). It doesn't sound as if Mundan is thinking "textually" while playing, but even if he were, the larger constraints of the 10-pulse *cādā dāk* (3 + 2 + 2 + 3) need to be taken into account. All Kota instrumental music is conceptualized in terms of such patterns, whether or not they are actually realized on the drums in a given performance. In transcribing this piece, I first tested each of the two likely patterns—a slow *tiruganāṭ* of eight pulses or a slow *cādā dāk* of ten pulses. Knowing that one of the two patterns underlies the rendition informed my decisions about notating rhythmic values. The melody is rhythmically flexible, especially since there is no actual accompaniment to provide rhythmic anchoring. Players orient their performances to framing patterns of drum beats only when those beats are actually present. In appropriating the *āṭḷ* onto an instrument, the player has to stretch and compress motives or add or subtract articulations to make musically sensible phrases begin and end within the instrumental rhythmic framework. For vocal music, especially the *āṭḷ*, which is rendered solo, the text provides the meaningful rhythmic framework. In each case, the vocal or instrumental idiom has given a single melodic idea its characteristic rhythmic form.

Responding and the Metaphor of a "Gap"

Performers of music and dance often realize a set of musical ideas, patterns, or resources in response to others (see Blum 1996). When this is done effectively, Kotas aesthetically appreciate the result. One of the critical variables in this regard, from Varadharajan's perspective, is the insertion of "gaps," sometimes unexpected holes in the rhythmic texture that serve to give a performance momentum, drive, and interest. Varadharajan also used the English word "gap" in a larger-scale temporal sense as well, providing us a metaphor that links spatiotemporal forms in different time scales.

Varadharajan justified his self-estimation in terms of how the dancers appear to respond to him. Kota music is a process of stimulation and response,Varadharajan explained, "so we have to give the tune which actually creates a nerve tone. Each and every person feels this thing." Kota music resists fixity because, as Varadharajan put it, "we don't know any books on this music." When Varadharajan said "tune" he meant "drum rhythm," just as in casual South Indian English, speakers may use "tune" and "rhythm" interchangeably. In Kota, both rhythms and melodies constitute *dāks*, i.e. "types" or "patterns." Drum sounds are differentiated not only with reference to a sort of temporal map or grid, into which particular articulations might be mentally fitted—the conception of rhythm that Brăiloiu was justified in criticizing—but also in terms of timbral and pitch differences. Percussion patterns are like melodies. Hence, when Kotas imitate the sounds of the ensemble, they make drum sounds that are pitched. Almost any Kota child can imitate the sounds of Kota drums. Dr Varadharajan provided examples of such vocalizations (CD 28).[13] One "type of music," he said, is "**d**ob.ba**d**oba.**d**ob.ba**d**oba.". Another type is "**d**ubeke**d**uba.**d**ubeke**d**uba.".

"Is that for *dobar* only or is it for the whole thing?," I asked, wondering whether people imitated individual drums. "For whole thing," he replied. "'**d**ubeke**d**uba.**d**ubeke**d**uba.**d**ubeke**d**uba.' This is one sort of sound.

'**d**ub.k**d**ub..**d**ub.k**d**ub..' This is another idea for sound." He said that they can arrange the same sets of syllables in different patterns; "with slow gapping, gapping and gapping" they make "adjustments" to the sound. Each syllable represents a pulse in this notation, as does letter "k" and a dot (indicating a rest). Bold face indicates primary syllables of emphasis. The tonal contour generally proceeds from a high position on the first stressed syllable to a lower pitch on the second stressed syllable. The last $\frac{6}{16}$ rhythmic unit sometimes ends with a slight rise in pitch on the elongated "ba.".

In "**d**ob.ba**d**oba.**d**ob.ba**d**oba." a characteristic hemiola effect is created by the $\frac{3}{8}$ feel of the syllables in italics and $\frac{6}{16}$ metrical framework outlined by the syllables in bold: "***d***ob.*b*a**d**o*b*a.***d***ob.*b*a**d**o*b*a.".

The hemiola is less pronounced in the second and third vocalizations because what Varadharajan calls "gaps" are filled in by syllables. The appearance of two dots at the end of "dub.." in the fourth vocalization is an indication of "slow gapping" as Varadharajan put it. The two examples were of *cādā dāk* used for dancing, but Varadharajan was less sure when classifying rhythms as either *tiruganāṭ dāk* (simple duple) or *cādā dāk* (compound duple) as his father was wont to do. "We have not learned 'this one is *cādā*, that one is *tiruganāṭ*' because guidance was not there," he said.

Based on the *koḷ* and *tabaṭk*, Varadharajan said, the *dobar* player inserts appropriate variations, such as "**de**.dedede**d**ubba.**de**.deke**d**eba.**d**edeke**d**ubba.". Here, the underlined syllables and dots are uttered at twice the rate of the non-underlined ones. This variation provides the additional cross-rhythmic twist of dividing some of the $\frac{3}{16}$ segments in half (i.e. $\frac{3}{32} + \frac{3}{32}$).

I then asked Varadharajan to vocalize the *cādā dāk dobar* part alone: " '**d**un.ge**d**uba.**d**un**d**ege**d**uba.**d**un**t**aṛi**d**uba.**d**un**d**ege**d**uba.**t**un**d**aṛi**d**uba.' I think this is that," said Varadharajan, adding that other variations are not significantly different. He pointed out that younger players try to be innovative by keeping "one or two sounds" and then leaving a "gap;" they'll strike the drum and "then say [for the] next two beatings, they leave it, or four they leave it, then [on the] sixth [beat] they'll give it [a stroke]." This will be "stimulating," he said, but the "tunes" will be the same. There will be "Some filling and gapping, like "**t**entaka**d**ibbo.**t**inkata**d**ibbo.". He explained this because some young musicians had told me they were playing new drumming styles, including one that originated in Ticgāṛ, traveled to Mēnāṛ and made its way to Kolmēl.

aradharajan did not accept the idea that Kota music might be changg, or rather, that existing variations constitute significant forms of difrence which are tied to local village practices.

Varadharajan thought that there were other kinds of "gaps" in the ounger generation as well, namely in terms of *koḷ* knowledge (he used e English term gap in both ways). In 1991–2 a *koḷ* player showed up te for some ritual and was not playing particularly well that day. The ders were grumbling that they shouldn't have to rely on only a few rresponsible) players and that if the younger generation did not start arning to play soon, there wouldn't be anybody to fulfill the ritual nctions in the future. Varadharajan recalled this:

> Yes, there was that period, actually when my father became old, actually there was a gap. I think everybody, seven villages, everybody felt, so there's a gap. I'll say for 100 per cent *koḷ*, so they will say my father is 100 per cent. So these fellows are only 10 per cent. [Some are] 40 per cent or 50 per cent, not 100 per cent. [Other new players] are only 60 per cent, not 100 per cent . . . they are fulfilling the gap . . . but they are not knowing. [Different kinds of] *koḷs* are there, separate songs are there, *tāv koḷ* is there, *devr koḷ* is there. For serving food, separate *koḷ* is there. See everything he [Puccan] was knowing. But these fellows they mingle this *koḷ* and that *koḷ* everything they are mingling. But correct is, my father's. And everybody knows about it.

In the performance of a percussion ostinato, the careful placement of hythmic gap creates musical interest. The creation of gaps characters the "new" styles of drumming—which Varadharajan does not think as "new" at all, because in his view the underlying rhythmic structure nains unaffected. Temporal "gaps" in the transmission of oral knowge have an effect on the ability of performers to play well on the *koḷ*. ese gaps do not provide interest, inasmuch as they are not musical; they produce community-wide anxiety—just as musical gaps proe small-scale moments of tension. The broad anxiety is apparently viated, now that younger men are taking the time to learn, and are ceeding.

Cultural Implications of Admixture

ingling" is a not a neutral process in India. In the South, Brahmans pecially, but not exclusively) talk about foods in terms of their unique special tastes: foods should not be mixed up; side dishes with rice should maintain their individuality. Traditional caste interaction operates in terms of similar parameters: who can marry whom; who can accept food from whom; and in what form can food be accepted all depend on carefully constructed notions of difference. And *rāgas* in South Indian music too must be kept separate. South Indians feel that North Indian *rāgas* lack purity, that they are mixed. We see similarity in Varadharajan's view of *koḷs*, a conservative one that is not entirely shared. It is a hegemonic view, though, that gains strength from its source in the playing style of Puccan.

What Varadharajan calls "mingling" is the result of a musician beginning to play a *koḷ* in a recognizable fashion, and then wandering somewhere else toward the end. In some cases, this wandering is the result of imperfect knowledge. Others feel that they may show individual creativity by departing from the main tune in this way. Returning to Puccan's comparison of playing *koḷ* to taking a path across the village: one can either take a direct route—play the *koḷ* correctly, straightforwardly—or take detours along the way. Puccan played with a great deal of melodic ornamentation; but the underlying melody remained more or less fixed. He objected to performances that departed from the melody.

From Mandelbaum's frustratingly truncated interview with Naṛykēr Kamaṭn, we get the impression that departure from the main melody was a conscious form of variation in an earlier era: "(Here I tried to find if they improvise.) The *melpackoḷ* that I showed you was only that first bit. The rest was just fancy and the men who can do it are the best players. The fancy seemed to consist . . ." (Mandelbaum, May 11, 1938, p. 5) [Entry ends here].

Another form of criticism lodged against *koḷ* players has to do with their inability to hold down a repeated melody in proper relationship to the drums. (The criticism can also be lodged against the drummers, who sometimes start in the wrong place.) In 2001, for instance, Kaṇṇan had trouble keeping the temple-opening tune consistently in phase with the percussion ostinato (CD 1 and 29 discussed in Chapter Five).

Varadharajan asserted that so long as melody and drum pattern start together correctly their continuous alignment will be automatic. The key is starting in the right order and waiting for the *koḷ* player's cue, a "small tone—some place [where the melody] goes up." The *tabaṭk* player then makes the sound, "dak da dak," and then the other musicians know when to come in. The temple-opening tune is preceded by a melodic gesture that cues the *tabaṭk* player (listen to the very beginning of CD 30). If the *dobar* starts, Varadharajan said, "the entire rhythm will go." So he would watch his father, who would say "you stop it you stop it" if the *tabaṭk* player entered at the wrong time. Then Puccan would tell someone else to start, indicating with a nod of his head at the right moment. Important here is the close interrelationship of drummers and melody-makers. Alignment is important, but it is not as if either the melody or the drum pattern can be simply superimposed one on the other. They mutually affect one another.

What Gets Transmitted with Music: The Shape of a God Tune Narrative

When a Kota learns a *koḷ*, he does not simply learn the melody, how to distinguish it from other similar melodies, and how to coordinate with the drummers, he also learns when to play it, and why that piece is important. Transmitting information about music has its own performative form. The cultural themes associated with musical pieces reinforce those expressed in ritual. The following story of the "instrumental melody of going to the herd of Kirpuṭn's son" (*kīrpuṭn meyṇ gubḷk oygd koḷ*), for instance, emphasizes the connection between proper behavior and divine efficacy. Like many songs and stories, the narrative unfolds geographically. K. Puccan told the story in Kota to me and to several young Kota men (for the first time) as follows. Puccan's rhetorical style, common in South Asia, engaged listeners with questions, making them listen and follow each episode:

> The villagers here owned many cows in those days. Once, a disease came to the cows—by disease I mean a throat disease . . . to the cows . . . a throat disease and diarrhea, cow diarrhea. All the cattle died here.
>
> What'd they do? They looked to god, asking the diviner, "Why are our cows dying"? Then the diviner for "big father god" shook. God possessed him, saying,
>
> (*Puccan assumes the diviner's voice*)
>
> "Disease came to the cattle because you are not in a state of oneness . . . From now on, after this diarrhea goddess leaves the village not even one of those cows will die. Not even one. Not even one."[14]

The diviner sang this melody as he spoke. He continued:

> "In a Badaga village near the Kota village of Mēnāṛ there is a man known as the son of Kīrpuṭn, owner of many thousand cattle . . . He is exceedingly cruel to them. Furthermore, if even one neighboring cow strays near his herd, he'll heat his seal and brand it as his own."
>
> (*Puccan grins broadly and laughs*)
>
> He went on deceiving like this, Kīrpuṭn meyṇ. Where? In the Mēnāṛ area. Like that he acted unjustly.
>
> (*Puccan speaks again in the voice of the diviner*)
>
> "Today I'll go enter his herd, I'll send this goddess there. The goddess is coming. She is now crossing the river, now she's going to Kurmūṛ, now she's going to Caṇḍāny stone."
>
> (*The account mentions other villages and geographical features along the way to the south-west, towards Kīrpuṭn meyṇ's village*)
>
> "I am carrying this goddess and traversing the entire route. She has now entered his herd."
>
> That very day the disease entered Kīrpuṭn meyṇ's herd. As soon as it entered, within eight, fifteen days a thousand cattle died.

For Kotas, divine grace depends on communal unity and justice. The story reinforces the idea of the Kotas as a moral community, distinct from some of its neighbors. Given the importance of the cow not only as a reminder of village origins but also for its economic role in providing milk, curds, and dung, the notion that someone might be cruel to a cow evokes a strong sense of pity and adds weight to the image of Kīrpuṭn meyṇ's cruelty.

In total, the gods were said to have taught about sixteen god tunes to the Kotas, a few melodies via the mouths of possessed *tērkārns*, others through dreams. The stories associated with some tunes and songs concern one or more characters who traverse a set of locations. The locations are means of creating narrative tension, translating the sense of movement along a physical path into a temporal sequence in the time-frame of the story's telling. In other stories, as in that for "*veḷke veḷke*," the locations themselves are important.

Conclusion: The Where and When of Knowing

The temporality of Kota everyday routines have an impact on how Kotas learn music and what genres they learn. Puccan's pastoral experience as a child and Cindamani's responsibility-free childhood allowed both to learn their respective arts deeply and thoroughly—although in different ways. Cindamani's knowledge exemplified a "music comes naturally" model: she was able to absorb the traditional knowledge around her. Puccan, who exemplified a "musical knowledge is gained by hard work" model, attributed his knowledge to the teaching of a guru. Modern, semi-urban routines led such musicians as Varadharajan to learn drumming in the off-hours of the god ceremony, and Jayachandran to record pieces and practice at home. In both cases, spatiotemporal constraints for musical performance in the village have made it a challenge for those who were living away from the village to learn and remember instrumental music. Varadharajan and others who practiced in between "important" events during the god ceremony constituted these periods—and the *pacāl* as a place—as ones for practice. In these ways, Kota processes of musical transmission have both taken place in the physical dimensions of time and space and constituted spatiotemporal forms that have constrained their future musical actions.

As musicians grow more experienced, they earn the right to play music in a wider range of places and time slots—indeed they undertake the responsibility to play the most important kinds of music whenever it is required. Novices might practice drums or *koḷ* on the *pacāl* during off hours, or they might practice using the *pulāng* during their spare time. They may seek guidance at home from a relative after dinner when the family is gathered around the hearth. Gradually, they participate more fully as musicians in village functions, perhaps accompanying dancers in the domestic dancing ground (*gagvāl*); in earlier times they would also have traveled outside the village to perform their traditional duties as musicians at Badaga or Toda funerals, or to perform ad hoc for a variety of functions as they do today. Finally, musicians would be permitted and indeed encouraged to play on the *pacāl* during important rituals of the god ceremony.

Part of learning how to be a musician or a dancer is learning to negotiate the delicate balance of fixed and malleable elements in time; this negotiation is key to "rendering" (*et-*) instrumental melodies and songs. For Puccan, rendering a *koḷ* excellently meant taking a "direct path," playing a piece exactly the same each time. His teacher, in contrast, located skillful musicianship in the ability of the player to depart artfully from a fixed core. A singer like Cindamani renders a song by particularizing a melodic idea, using syllables and words. With the constraints of syllables removed, a musician rendering a song on the *koḷ*, *pulāng*, or *bugīr* uses the articulations of the percussion *dāk* (either played by drums or implied) as anchors, and structures sections of melodies with cadential, *gag*-tone patterns.

However Kotas gain their musical knowledge, whether from sitting attentively with one or two teachers, or picking up fragments from many singers or instrumentalists, they tend to absorb a range of extramusical associations. The stories concerning the origin of musical styles and pieces have cultural value in and of themselves; one need not be a musician to possess such knowledge, for origin stories encode central values; the melodies, and their names, act as reminders of these stories. As they are retold, these stories connect the potentially unruly present to the more righteous past. Loudness of sound relates to both musical and historical sensibilities. Practically speaking, Kotas reckon loudness in terms of the distance a sound can potentially travel. Kotas constitute loudness nostalgically, in their collective memory, as something desirable, which can be produced only by large and powerful men. Loudness has come to join with other manifestations of *catym* that connect Kotas with their past and their gods.

At least three kinds of stories and/or ideas travel with musical pieces when they are taught: stories of specific origin (who composed a piece, and under what circumstances); stories of more general origin (the idea that gods are ultimately teachers); and moral stories that happen to be tied to a piece, but which could easily stand on their own and which carry themes of central concern to Kotas culturally. Each kind of story has a different spatiotemporal form and represents a different way of remembering and thinking about music.

CHAPTER 5

Points of Anchor

Kotas embody the process of "anchoring" when they make music rather than describe it by a particular term in their language. Duryodhana synchronizes a relatively free-rhythmic *koḷ* with its percussion ostinato by firmly placing his finger over a hole of the *koḷ* at just the right drum stroke. In between such "anchor points," he exercises freedom to stretch and pull (*iḷv-*) the melodic rhythm. Sometimes a *koḷ* player will begin and the *tabaṭk* player will insert his first stroke in the wrong place. If that happens, Duryodhana explained, a second *koḷ* player might start the piece again to coordinate with the *tabaṭk* player; the first *koḷ* player would then synchronize himself with the second. *Koḷ* players mark anchor points linguistically when they ask the *tabaṭk* player to clarify the main beats, or the *kiṇvar* player to make their appropriate strokes "shout out;" these are verbalizations of what psychologist Jamshed Bharucha (1996) calls a musical "yearning" for anchor points. But such speech acts index mere moments in an otherwise continuous and dynamic process. If the instruments are not properly linked, Kotas say, the music will break down.

An "anchor" often means a "reference point;" "to anchor" means "to fix in place." Bharucha develops the concept of a melodic anchor as reference point to explore cognitive processes associated with tonal music perception, focusing primarily on how listeners enculturated to Western tonal music "yearn" for "unstable" tones to be resolved in proximally pitched stable ones, or "anchors." Bharucha usefully frames his discussion in spatiotemporal terms that have more general applicability. Humans orient themselves toward the "most salient object" in the "general direction" to which someone or something points. "In the case of melodic anchoring," he writes, "the nonchord tone is the pointer or attention-getting cue and the salient object is a mental object—a strongly activated mental representation" (1996, 387).

The Kota *koḷ* player performs his melody and anticipates an appropriate structural drum beat as a "mental object." Kota melodic phrases create patterns of expectation that are resolved with other notes or phrases in an analogous manner.[1] Bharucha emphasizes the systematic features of anchoring: where one tone is located with respect to another in a composition. Anchors in Kota music, by contrast, are actively created in performance rather than inherent in compositions. Kota performers use them to navigate through a melody in relation to the drums, or through a dance in relation to both melodic phrases and drum cycles. Male dancers will synchronize from time to time, but in between may, within limits, explore their own patterns of relationship between steps, spins, and melody cycles.

By regarding an anchor as a kind of cognitive reference point, Bharucha explores a theme common to an extensive literature on time-reckoning and spatiotemporal orientation in anthropology and sociolinguistics.[2] But the term "reference point" seems insufficiently dynamic for the processes of ebb and flow, gravity, give and take, or fluidity and fixity, which the term "anchoring" can evoke. When a ship drops anchor, it shifts with wind and tide within a limited perimeter. Just as a ship's anchor may drag slightly as the ship pulls, the "anchor point" may be subject to subtle movement as well. An anchor's position may change more dramatically, as per the orders of the ship's captain. Analogously, Kota musicians exercise choice in lining up their melodies one way rather than another in relation to the percussion ostinato, choosing different points of anchor.

We need not think about anchor points in relation to brief spans of time or narrow regions of movement. The more any event serves as a point of departure for planning other events, the more it "anchors." The short-term timing or long-term scheduling of such an anchoring event affects an entire temporal cycle, just as choosing a beat on which to moor a *koḷ* pitch has implications for how the rest of the melody will line up in synchronized repetitions. Such an "event" may be as fleeting as a drum stroke or as substantial as a national or religious holiday.

Metaphorically, a field of force seizes upon articulations that "anchor." Affect contributes to such fields of force, as Leonard B. Meyer has so effectively shown in his insightful writings on the play of expectations in music. Many local forms of meaning are invested in the manner in which individuals (or complex agents) regard the "most salient object in th[e] general direction" in which they look, whether these are musical directions in a Western tonal context, sites marked on the paths of pilgrims or tourists, or the center of activity in a group gathering.[3] All salient articulations in the world as we experience it, in this sense, constitute spatiotemporal anchors. Broadly conceived, anchoring is a widely shared human process, not limited to one area of human activity or one cultural group. What do actors reveal about themselves in creating and interacting with anchors? In what ways do individuals or groups produce "themselves or aspects of themselves" (Munn 1986, 11) when they engage in anchoring?

Houses provide excellent case studies. Janet Hoskins uses an anchoring metaphor to describe the coordination of relatively fixed and fluid structures in an Eastern Indonesian society. She finds the house "is the temporal center of gravity in Kodi social life." Hoskins writes, "its continuity provides an anchor for more free-floating notions of individual life projects and obligations . . . it is a mark of prestige and achievement for a house to be filled with 'heavy' valuables which cannot be easily moved along alliance paths" (Hoskins 1993, 24).

Kota houses anchor in different ways. A Kota "house of the erected post" (*kab iṭ pay*) exerts an especially powerful effect on Kota behavior. Kotas invest notions of time continuity into this house through storytelling, initiating and concluding rituals, dancing to particular melodies, and storing instruments. They create "aspects of themselves" involving the various sign relationships between themselves and bovine species, the place of the "self" within the Kota kinship system, and the location of the individual within the generational hierarchy. The virtual "field of force" surrounding the *kab iṭ pay* varies when compared to that associated with such anchoring places as the *mundkānōn*s' houses, the *toḍbāl* tree, and the grassy *pacāl* in the village center.

Anchors have different qualities and magnitudes and may change their character over time. Different places in the village vary in significance over the course of the god ceremony. Rituals during the first few days occur in and around individual Kota houses. Then, at night, men and women concentrate dance on the *gagvāl*, in front of the *kab iṭ pay*. Kotas associate pureness and respectworthiness with the area, so these become "qualities" of the place. Such qualities are intensified during the god ceremony, and augmented by the sense of joy or bliss (*ānandm*) Kotas associate with dances for god. This is significant when contrasted with the more restrained sensuality of a green funeral. And yet funerary dancing may take place in front of that same *gagvāl*, for the spirit of the dead person is, at that time, being entrusted to god.

As a domestic place, the *kab iṭ pay* is more mundane than the temple area, the *guṛyvāl*. This is why the temple area was once cordoned off at non-god ceremonial times of the year and why the *mundkānōn* cannot walk in the domestic yards during the god ceremony. Shifting anchor points centripetally from the domestic areas to the temple during the god ceremony involves a qualitative shift in experience. The *gagvāl* continues to exert a pull on ceremonial participants throughout the ceremony, though. As the ceremony nears completion, dancers move to the *gagvāl* to dance in street clothes, a sign of return to normalcy. The *guṛyvāl* and the *gagvāl*, then, each possesses its own form of virtual gravity.

Two senses of the term quality are relevant here. One is "an attribute, property, special feature or characteristic."[4] A thing embodies such qualities palpably: sandpaper has the "quality" of roughness; the *pacāl*, "green area," is green. Another meaning of "quality" involves sense and resonance, feelings, and associations. "Sadness" comes to be felt as a "quality" of bier time (*kaṭl kāl*); agents conflate the feelings associated with someone dying with the period of time during which various types of social-cultural practice are enacted. As the anthropologist Henri Hubert wrote, the period conventionally associated with an act becomes "contaminated" (*contaminer*) by it, or, pervaded by its qualities (1905, 14; 1999, 56). Similarly, the actions conventionally or habitually performed in a particular place, or sung about a place, come to imbue that place with the qualities agents associate with their actions or songs.

Anchoring Places of a Kota Culture Hero

A series of places is associated with a legendary culture hero, named Koṭērvaykīṇ, who set off into the hills with his bow and arrow, leaving his nine-month-pregnant sister alone in the village. She followed him, crying, eventually becoming overwhelmed with thirst in the dry and parched land. Koṭērvaykīṇ shot his arrow into a boulder and unleashed fresh spring water. He then caused seven steps to appear in the rocky face of the hill and climbed up to fetch water for his sister. The steps, which are still visible, are said to be used by the souls of dead Kota men as they ascend the slope on their journeys to "that land" (*ānāṛ*, land of the dead).

Koṭērvaykīṇ disappeared and his head became a mountain peak near the village of Mēnāṛ, the name of which, significantly, means "upper land," and which is considered the first and, administratively, "head" (*tal*) Kota village. Within the duration of his sister's consuming the water Koṭērvaykīṇ traveled to Kināṛ village ("low land"), at the opposite end of the Nilgiris, where his feet became another mountain peak. Head and feet hence anchor Koṭērvaykīṇ's body within the Kota domain. Put another way, the story makes Koṭērvaykīṇ's body "flexible" so that it fits fixed anchor points (villages) on the landscape and makes the land the Kotas inhabit a "body" politic.[5] If the black cow's footprint story grounds the identity of each Kota villager in a particular village, then, this story binds all the villages together into a collectively held region.

Kotas talk about Koṭērvaykīṇ's act of collecting water for his sister as one of kindness and love for his sister, which was enabled by his great *catym*. The framing of the story phenomenologically equates the duration of the drinking, and its associations, with the spatiotemporal expansion and transformation of Koṭērvaykīṇ's body. His "body," in turn, serves as a mnemonic for collective memories of the Kota past, evoking senses of power, size, *catym*, tribal prowess (through the symbolism of the bow and arrow), and closeness to both the gods and ancestors. Kotas sing an *āṭḷ* that indexes this legend in a typically fragmentary fashion (CD 31):[6]

"āḷ āṛāde arvangāṛe"

(excerpt, with slight syllable alterations to clarify the Kota words)

āḷ āṛāde arvangāṛe yama	A forest where men have not been, mother
kan vīṭāc kanōṛ keṭō	A girl pregnant for the first time, along with her child, is deteriorating
o̱de minge nīr etugo yama	take one gulp of water, mother

Kotas casually picnic at the site described in this story. The spring and the steps stimulate Kotas to think about the grandeur of their history and the potency of their gods and ancestors. As if mimetically capturing something of this miraculous event, Kotas carry water back from this spring for young children in the village to drink. The song evokes pity for the suffering sister; the place poignantly reminds Kotas of generations of ancestors who crossed that spot; and the story evokes a "structural nostalgia" for the *catym* these ancestors possessed. Inasmuch as a Kota casually ambulating in the vicinity will be drawn to the spot, it serves as an anchor.

Holidays

Variations of the anchoring concept apply well to some large-scale structures of time, which involve deliberate planning, calculating, even debating. Holidays such as Christmas possess anchoring characteristics. In the United States, its field of force takes subjective forms, such as participants' anticipation and excitement, and practical forms, such as the rush to buy gifts. Christmas operates on surrounding periods of time dynamically, is heavily marked, and has qualitative associations: it creates an occasion for school vacations, compels employers to cough up fiscal bonuses, and calls to mind special foods, smells, clothing, decorations, and music.

Holidays vary in their "qualities" and in the degrees to which they anchor. Christmas is officially celebrated on a fixed date in the US, regardless of the day of the week.[7] Christmas and certain other holidays are "strong" enough to make fresh articulations for themselves each year within the frame of the work week: one year Christmas may fall on a Tuesday, in another year on a Saturday, and so forth. President's Day—lesser in degree and different in quality from Christmas—is conceptualized on a particular day but *observed* on a different one. Because such lesser holidays anchor less—i.e. have less capacity to change the character of events surrounding them in time—the work week (a stronger force) determines the day on which they are observed.

The process works somewhat in reverse for Easter in that the day of the week is important and has the capacity to affect the date from year to year.[8] Thanksgiving in the US is another example of a holiday calculated according to the day of the week. This scheduling has implications for the way in which Americans organize their work and school breaks. Like Kota ritual frames (e.g. free time in ceremonies used for rehearsal), the Thursday of Thanksgiving creates a tantalizing potential for a vacation on Friday, whether or not this is realized and regardless of whether a given institution officially sanctions an additional day's leave. Easter and Thanksgiving, as observed in the US, share with Kota ceremonies an emphasis on the day of the week's relationship to the beginning of a month (in an appropriate calendar) rather than on a particular date in a month.

The Kota year is "anchored" by *devr* (god ceremony) and the *varldāv* (dry funeral), which must be celebrated during particular annual lunations or not at all. By contrast, an ear-piercing ritual is not an anchoring event for Kotas. Sometimes appended to *varldāv* or other observances, the ear-piercing ritual demands no fixed position in the calendar and has little bearing on other events. What is important, however, is that the status of an event as an anchor might change. The seed-sowing ceremony, *ēr iṭ pabm*, apparently served as a strong ritual anchor for the year; it once depended on its own natural anchor, the "blossoming of a certain tree" according to Emeneau (1937–8, 114). Now the ritual is observed more flexibly in time: it signifies a ritual beginning but not an instrumental beginning because the environment has changed, new agricultural technologies have been developed, and crops are more diverse. The seed-sowing ritual is occasionally appended to the more elaborate ceremony, *doḍpabm*, which follows a month after *devr*. Yet this seed-sowing still exhibits anchoring characteristics in that it sets up expectations for a later ceremony, the harvest ceremony (*veḷ īt pabm*), to complete the agro-ritual unit associated with certain kinds of traditional crops. Not only can anchors change, they may also be somewhat unpredictable, as when a musician makes an unexpected move to which his ensemble mates must suddenly respond, or when an eclipse or a death interrupts, and changes the flow of, everyday life.

Tempo, Convergence, and Closure

Agents frequently create instability when they try to join relatively fixed and flexible structures, sequences, or time processes. They may engage in "anchoring" when they try to resolve this instability. Temporal flexibility in many musical traditions is reined in through shared points of reference which may operate as "anchors." Lewis Rowell represents contemporary "composition . . . as a field within which the placement of individual events is unpredictable;" when improvisation is featured, composition "can well be seen as a kind of situation—a happening or encounter that is based on a minimal script." In a stream of such sound events, articulations of beginning, ending, and attack often become points of anchor, which are important to "the establishment of a metrical framework or some other hierarchy of controlling periodicity" (1981, 201).

Hebrew cantillation shares aspects of "free-rhythm" with Hindustani and Kota musical styles; the two former differ in the ways in which linguistic constraints govern their relative degrees of "freedom," but these differences should not obscure the general point. Judah Cohen describes a cantorial instructor at Hebrew University in Jerusalem, who drew a line on a blackboard to illustrate the temporal flexibility of his melismas: "What you do in that time is not important; what's important is that you start here and you finish here. . . . So I could elongate some vowels but if I elongate some vowels I have to speed up on some other vowels" (2002, 166n. 25).

The lability of the calendar over the course of human history as it is adjusted to fit astronomic reference points provides a large-scale analogy with music. Only in 1582 did Pope Gregory XIII finally respond to Roger Bacon's 1267 appeal (regarded as heretical at the time) to "fix" the solar calendar so that Christians could celebrate their holidays on the "correct" dates (Duncan 1998, 1). In some calendars of the world, natural phenomena related to the agricultural seasons and the movement of the sun serve as anchor points. In others, such as the Islamic lunar calendar of 354 days or the Kota lunar calendar, anchor points are determined by the waxing crescent moon. The flexibility of these points stems from the fact that an authority must actually *observe* the crescent moon to confirm the onset of the month; this may vary by one day. (Clouds make issues of precise determination even more difficult.) A lunar month in the Islamic calendar will not always fall in the same season of the solar year. A particular conjunction of one date in the Gregorian lunar calendar and another in an Islamic lunar calendar will return every 32 solar years (Duncan 1998, 134). In the Kota case, months should correspond fairly well with seasons, so Kotas have needed to regularly realign or "anchor" their monthly calendar with reference to other calendars or regularly occurring natural phenomena.

The aforementioned calendrical and musical systems exhibit different kinds of flexibility—the former systems often involve long-term mathematical approximations and the latter may be more perceptually oriented (but could involve numerical calculation as well). But both share the goal of representing closure.[9] Both also involve manipulation of what Bourdieu calls *tempo*. In using tempo to refer to the rate of virtually any kind of event in relation to another, Bourdieu draws attention to the effect produced by strategies of delay or anticipation, "holding back or putting off, maintaining suspense or expectation, or on the other hand, hurrying, hustling, surprising, and stealing a march, not to mention the art of ostentiatiously giving time ('devoting one's time to someone') or withholding it ('no time to spare')" (1989, 7). Time is made meaningful through agreed-upon anchors, points of reference, attack, or boundary; if Kotas mismanage the tempo of their practices, if they stray too far from these agreed-upon points, they make un-musical music, dance sloppy dances, misalign rituals with naturally occurring events, and quite possibly, create ritual mistakes that are spiritually threatening.

One way to explore the relationship between musical and other temporalities is to analyze the micro "structure of conjuncture" (see Sahlins 1985), when an activity "anchors," locks into a position in a given framework or set of competing frameworks. How are convergences constituted, represented, valued, and perceived in local terms? In Javanese culture, for instance, Judith and Alton Becker argued for the significance of musical coincidence whereby "simultaneous occurrence [generally] is a central source of both meaning and power." Relatively independent "melodic sequences" simultaneously conclude on the pitch of the *kenong* (a kind of gong). The "iconicity of sounding gongs with calendars (and other systems within the culture)," they write, "is one of the devices whereby [gongs] resonate with import beyond themselves" (1981, 208; 210). In this case, calendars and music share a cognitive cultural entity.

In the Kota case "coming together" or "joining" (*kūcd*)—as in making "one mind" or "one heart" (*o̱d manc*)—is a central socio-religious value. Men and women dress in white and pray at the same time after the *mundkānōn* utters "*elm ceydvīrā*?" (are we all joined?). Dances begin ritually with the "leg joining dance" (*kāl gūc āṭ*), synchronizing the group with alternate steps, right and left, moving in the direction of the circle. Kotas formally share food or tobacco to perform their closeness "persuasively" (see Fernandez 1986b). These types of joining vary in specific form, but are related for Kotas as simulacra of conviviality and commensality.[10] All symbolically ensure a harmonious future, in part because social "unity" is pleasing to god. Coming together musically, two *koḷ* players should play in perfect unison; drummers should play with rhythmic accuracy and interlock; and melodies should remain in phase with their percussion ostinatos by returning to "anchor points." For the sake of unified action, it really does not matter where the melody is anchored to the percussion pattern, just that it is.

"Out-of-phaseness" in the Kota instrumental tradition constitutes a form of musical instability. When individuals are playing out of phase, they may generate change—possibly by choosing new anchor points—as they seek stability. This is especially likely to happen as the tradition passes from one generation to the next. Just as instability between melody and percussion provides the basis for musical reorientation, so too do choices among multiple models for time-reckoning provide actors the basis for altering their calendars.

Anchoring in Ceremonies

The Temple-opening Tune: The central composition in the Kolmēl repertoire is the "temple-opening tune" (*guṛy terdd koḷ*).[11] It is relatively slow, complicated, and long—about one minute for a full cycle of the melody. Relative length and slowness tend to correlate with ritual and/or emotional importance. This is no exception. Slower, more intricate melodies, such as the temple-opening tune, often demand more attention on the part of the *koḷ* player to keep the melody anchored on key drum strokes. More rapid melodies, such as some for the dance, cycle back quickly. They lock in place with the percussion pattern homogeneously throughout. Anchoring in such brisk tunes is less of a problem.

The opening of the temple, which occurs only once a year, is part of a bundle of activities which constitute the "making" or "doing" of god and which establish god's presence in the *guṛyvāl*. The temple-opening tune is "central" in that musicians play it during all activities that accompany temple-opening—activities which are performed in the middle of the ten- to twelve-day ceremony. The temple-opening tune is also the first in the suite of "god tunes," performed on key evenings during the god ceremony and on a couple of other occasions.

For rituals subsidiary to the temple opening, men play the *aṇviṛcd koḷ* ("channel-clearing tune" CD 32), which is musically marked as shorter than the temple-opening tune, but is built from the same musical resources. Musicians add or omit parts of one or the other melody in the confusion of performance during the ceremony. The process of maintaining either melody in phase with the percussion ostinato remains a challenge because neither tune is played exactly the same in each iteration, except by expert players. When a part gets left out, or an extra part added or repeated, the musician may need to sustain a tone here and there, waiting for the return of the proper position in the percussion cycle.

The CD provides seven instrumental renditions of these related melodies (CD 1, 8, 15, 16, 29, 30, 32) plus one that is sung (CD 10).[12] Mandelbaum's wax cylinder recording of the *aṇvịrcd koḷ* (CD 32), the oldest example available, dates melodic ideas in the temple-opening tune to at least 1938. The recording is too distorted to transcribe. Dr Varadharajan recorded a rendition in the 1970s that he considers ideal (CD 8). Now that Puccan has died, young players are using this and other recordings (including my own) to learn and refresh their knowledge of all the god tunes. The transcription from Varadharajan's recording shows the basic contour of the melody, some of the microtonal variations in one of the cycles and the important "anchor" tones, indicated by a vertical shaded bar (see Fig. 10). Each cycle varies slightly from the transcription.[13] The notated quarter tones and microtones approximate the melody's tonal variation and character, but their tonal values do not remain constant each time the melody is repeated. This transcription uses measures to represent cycles of percussion ostinato and emphasizes only key positions within it: four strong strokes outlining the framing pulse pattern of 3 + 2 + 2 + 3. Within the percussion frame of reference, these four strong strokes are the "anchors;" the intervening strokes on all the drums can be swung a bit.

The remaining recordings provide examples of different ways of anchoring the melody to the percussion pattern. Notice the ways in which the other performances differ from the transcription of CD 8. CD 30 of Puccan and Raman performing during the god ceremony of 1992 exhibits slight heterophony. Perhaps swayed by Raman's different take on the melody, Puccan maintains a looser hold on the melodic anchors around which he and his late playing partner had organized their 1970s performance. Raman demonstrates the *koḷ* with drummers outside the village on CD 15. In Puccan's absence, Raman aligns the melody in an entirely different manner. On CD 1, recorded at *devr* in 2001, the then novice *koḷ* player Kaṇṇan and a partner perform during the cane-and-bamboo-bringing ritual. On CD 29, from that same god ceremony, the musicians were sitting and should have been able to concentrate. Yet in both cases the melody remains loosely moored to the percussion; the versions are not yet stabilized. Raman's *pulāng* version (CD 16) and Puccan's vocal rendition (CD 10) show how the melody becomes even more rhythmically "free" without explicit drum beats on which to anchor certain tones. A *koḷ* player *relies* on the drummed framework; he establishes the initial pattern—first beat and tempo—and then fits the melody into the framework.

The notation of the temple-opening tune in Fig. 10 combines the graphic virtues of tablature with the tonal specificity of staff notation. Each position on the staff represents a stop (*kaṇ*, "eye"). A stop corresponds with a finger position (which is what makes the notation a kind of tablature) but not necessarily with a single note. The next Kota analytical level is *dāk* or *meṭ*, which Kotas translate as "step" when referring to "melodic section." Both terms refer to units of variable size, ranging from a few notes to a complete melody. My labeling of sections by letter is compatible with this set of Kota terms for melodic structure.[14]

Guide to Notation of *Guṛy terdd koḷ*

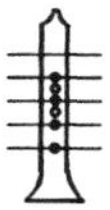

Correspondence between staff and covered holes of the *koḷ* (note produced with all holes open indicated on upper E)

Anchor point

Approximate pitch variations:

𝄰 = three quarter tones sharp

𝄲 = one quarter tone sharp

𝄳 = one quarter tone flat

♭↑ ♭↓ ♮↑ ♮↓ ♯↓ = slight difference in pitch, sharp or flat, as per the arrows.

In this excerpt, the musicians first play to Measure 23 and then return to the beginning. In the second iteration of the melody, they skip to Measure 28 after Measure 23. The melody then returns to Measure 11 and continues to the end of Measure 27.

Fig. 10: *Guṛy Terdd Koḷ* (The Temple Opening Tune)

11
D'
E'
F
2
13
(D")+1
F
F-1
C"
8vb
15
C2
C1
C2
3
8vb
17
C2
C21
C21'
C1'
8vb
19
C2'
8vb

Fig. 10

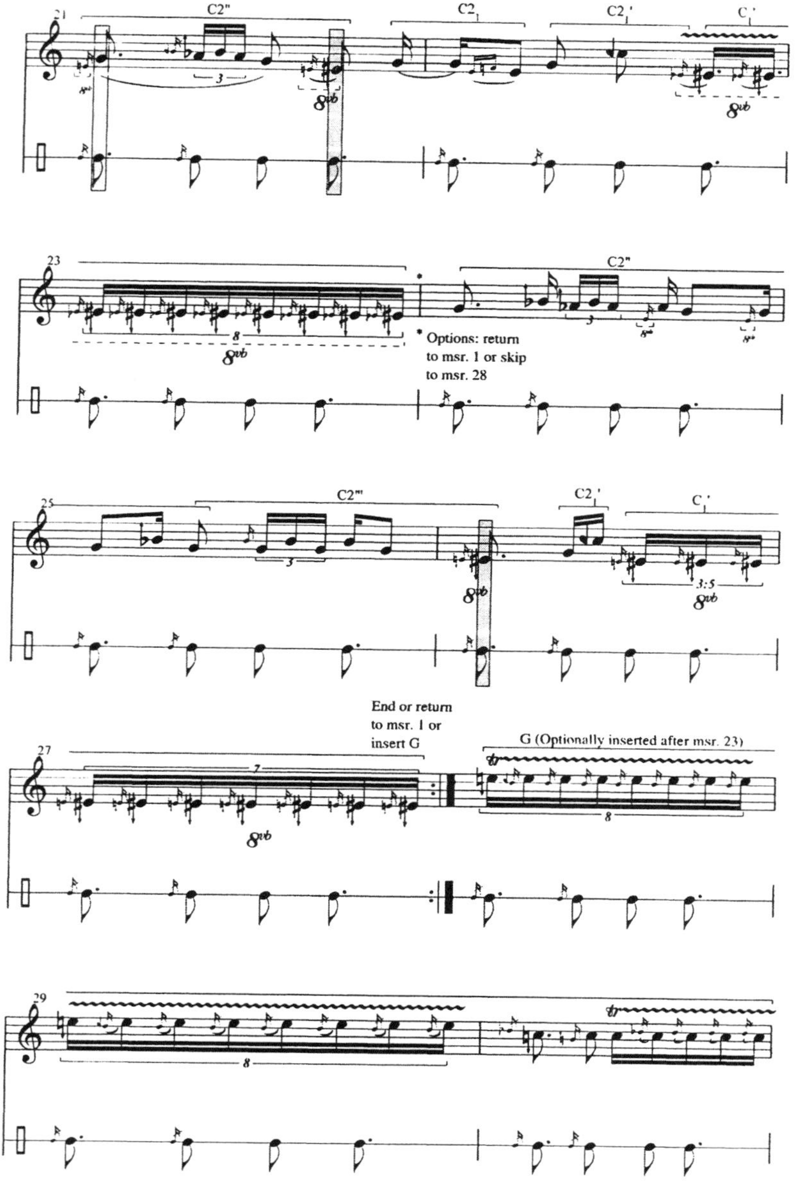

C2"
C2₁
C2₁'
C₁'
8vb
Options: return to msr. 1 or skip to msr. 28
C2'''
End or return to msr. 1 or insert G
G (Optionally inserted after msr. 23)

Fig. 10

Fig. 10

In using these terms, a player might launch the criticism, "you've left out a section" ("*kaṇ viṭvī*" or "*meṭ viṭvī*"), or "look, you are singing/playing having left out one step" (*meṭ viṭṭ pācī / eytī nōṭ*). If the musician changes the melody or percussion pattern someone will say, "he changed the *dāk*" (*dāk mārīko*) or if he is unable to render it properly, someone might say "look, the *dāk* is not coming" (*dāk vārā nōṭ*). After making such a mistake a musician will either fudge a transition (tread water, if you will), or, as Naṛykēr Kamaṭn explained, insert an improvisatory flourish. An anchor point becomes especially important, then, when a musician takes liberties with a melody and needs to restabilize himself.

Musicians commonly use the lowest position on the *koḷ* to punctuate phrases with *gag* tones, alternating honking and squeaking in ways that resemble what bagpipers call "cranning."[15] *Gag* tones, repeated insistently and often cross-cutting the drum pattern, figure prominently in cadential passages; the action of playing such tones is called *gagarcd*. The rhythmic tension may be relieved when a *gag* tone or a tone that follows one serves as a melodic anchor, hooking the melody firmly with the drums.[16] Musicians may realign their melodies in these cadential sections.

Kotas use the onomatopoeic *gag* sound almost like a solfege syllable for low, punctuating pitches in a string of sung phrases (CD 10). Before beginning to play, Kotas make the sounds "gā, gā," that is, do *gagarcd*, to make sure the reeds emit the proper sound, that there are no leaks and that the *gag* pitch issues forth clearly and forcefully.[17] A related gesture is the warm-up pattern called *koḷ ākcd* (*koḷ* preparation), which varies slightly by player. In Kolmēl it is important that the *koḷ ākcd* for a god tune is distinct from that for a funeral tune (CD 32, 30, 29).

I have labeled the tune in sections and motives to show how it exploits transformations of a few core ideas. The beginning is clearly marked with a three-measure-long section that repeats. The end consists of extended closing gestures (C sections) with motives of increasing *gag*-tone density, which cross-cut the metrical framework. The final *gag*-tone cadence is marked with a dramatic leap. Features of balance, motivic conservatism, and *gag*-tone cadential building are characteristic of many substantial Kota instrumental melodies and are less pronounced in shorter pieces. Another characteristic is the return of a musical unit with part of the melody replaced with a "tonal envelope," or heavily pulsated (*alykd*), sustained tone.[18]

The optative insertion of the relatively long, contrasting Section G is significant as one of the few contextually-specific musical variations in all of Kota musical culture. The *mundkānōn*s throw a handful of thatch onto the temple roof in memory of temple-rethatching in the past. At that moment, the *koḷ* players insert Section G, thereby indexing the action of throwing, and iconically drawing attention to both the upward trajectory of the thatch and the hierarchical importance of this moment in the ceremony. This exemplifies anchoring at both micro and macro levels. At a micro level the temple-opening melody is anchored by correspondences between note and drum stroke; at a macro level it is anchored by the correspondence between Section G and the extramusical activity of thatch-throwing. The temple-opening tune and its variants are performed on several different occasions in the ceremony, but the additional section (ideally) is added only in conjunction with the thatch-throwing ritual.

Before and after the moment of anchoring can also be viewed from multiple analytic levels. In almost any melody, the moments adjacent to the anchor may involve, at minimum, the preparation for attack and the process of release. Anchoring in slow Kota instrumental pieces involves three stages: (1) Before articulating the anchoring note, a performer may need to calculate where the beat will fall; this may take musical form in the acceleration or deceleration of attacks leading up to the anchoring moment; (2) At the moment in which the melody is anchored, the performer must be acutely attuned to meter (correspondence with the beat) in a way that he would not have been a moment before; (3) After articulating the anchor, the performer can once again relax his attention on meter and focus on the free-flowing melody. His memory of the anchor does not appear audibly important in the moments that follow.

Taking note of Rowell's view that beginnings and endings are important in compositions where the placement of events is otherwise somewhat unpredictable, we should view the beginning of any Kota instrumental performance as an anchoring moment. First, musicians prepare their instruments—tauten the drum heads before the fire (see photo section), get their *koḷs* to sound properly. These sounds contribute to performers' and bystanders' senses of anticipation. The relationship between preparation and attack lends character to the anchor, the moment of beginning. In this way, the process of *ōmayṇ* is a far stronger gesture in time and place during the god ceremony than is any beginning of any sequence of melodies on its own in other contexts. As Varadharajan explained, by rule there should be complete silence before the *ōmayṇ*; then, all at once, all instrumentalists should play as loudly as they can. Once that beginning sound is made, and the *first three* dance melodies performed, the players are free to tune their instruments, make intervening sounds, and choose what comes next.

The *koḷ* player begins the melody, and if necessary, nods his head, using his *koḷ* like a baton to indicate where to strike the first beat. The *koḷ* player is then guided through the melody by the percussion pattern he has set in motion. He subtly readjusts his playing to line up with the pattern. *Koḷ* players and drummers are dependent upon one another when they perform together: the double-reed player must first create the temporal form within which he organizes his musical timing; and his actions, in three-dimensional space, must be coordinated according to the same pattern.

The freedom Kotas may exercise in choosing anchor points is also illustrated in melodies other than the temple opening tune. In a previous publication, I provided an example of another god melody that lined up with its percussion ostinato differently in two villages (see Wolf 2000/2001a; CD 33, 34). In some Indian "tribal" musical traditions, as in this Kota example, elements of a performance, such as beats in a cycle, melody, and dance steps, operate somewhat independently of one another. I suggested that such independence may not be a diagnostic feature of tribal traditions at all, for it is common to many Indian traditions. A difference is that in the classical traditions the relationship among many of these elements is more formally regulated. More broadly, though, the relationship among elements in a performance is always a potential musical issue. It has become more so in recent years in Western art music (as Rowell implies), where performers have to interact with one another (and/or with electronic media) without the benefit of a common, articulated, metric grid for reference. To the extent that the relationship among elements is only loosely controlled, there exists the possibility for a continued tension among them and the possibility for change—owing either to new choices for alignment, to error, or to poor senses of temporal memory among musicians. The variable stability between melody and percussion ostinato in the temple-opening tune examples illustrates a range of options. The other god-tune example, drawn from two villages, shows that two types of alignment may both be correct: they are two musical choices for stability. Both show that certain Kota melodies have an inherent instability, which can be resolved by "anchoring" in different ways by different players.

Anchoring of Larger Performance Units

Anchoring concerns not only timing, but also time of day. Kotas reserve certain dance tunes for dance performances at the conclusion of particular rituals. On Sunday night, after the day-long temple-opening rituals, women mark another anchor point by dressing up in their finest gold and silver jewelry. Accompanied by the *aṇviṛcd koḷ*, the shorter variant of the temple-opening tune, women carry heavy head-loads of "god firewood" which they have collected for the next days' feasting. After depositing the wood, women dance a special dance as a form of honor and spectacle for the gods. The actual dance steps are no different than the steps of dances they usually dance. The difference, what makes this an anchor, is the scheduling of the dance, one of the melodies used (exclusively for this dance), and the way women tie their white cotton clothes—waist tight, with a knot on the shoulder. This activity is a center of attention, a high point in the god ceremony. Onlookers and invited guests collect to watch while it is still light outside. The evening activities, which Kotas prefer to keep to themselves, have not yet begun.

Anchoring in a sequence of instrumental pieces involves the choice of aesthetically appropriate chains of pieces, contrasting perhaps in melody but accompanying the same dance, or containing a similar melody but differing in tempo or rhythmic pattern. Musicians remain sensitive to contextual cues that require a particular piece—or a specific sonic gesture—at a particular moment. The temple-opening tune anchors by virtue of its magnitude and also by its position as first in the sequence of twelve *devr koḷs*. Puccan used to play the twelve in a sequence whose logic was guided by the sharing of melodic ideas between some adjacent pieces; the first piece in each such a pair would presage the second. Dances ritually begin with three types, called *kālgūc āṭ, tiruganāṭ*, and *koynāṭ*, which are danced in order. After playing a tune appropriate to each type, performers may choose what *koḷ* to play rather freely, though a set of common transitions linking one *koḷ* to another tend to generate a few predictable sequences, more or less in the way one *devr koḷ* tends to lead to another. In a typical sequence, a *koḷ* player signals he is about to change from one dance tune to another by playing a sustained tone (CD 35).

A string of Kota instrumental melodies may be likened to a series of colored points on a line; for melodies, like colors, have "qualities" that differentiate one from another. These qualities are both musical and indexical. Ritually important tunes are named accordingly. As a listener follows this colored string, the order of pieces creates a subjective sense of changing time that is rather different from the sense of recurrence one experiences when listening to, for example, the return of key drum strokes in a repeating ostinato. It matters not whether musicians play Tune A for three minutes or fifteen minutes before moving on to Tune B; the order of change from A to B, and then B to C, is important for this notion of temporal subjectivity.

However, this linear representation of *koḷ* performance only takes us so far, for performers move their bodies in three-dimensional space and stand in significant spots. Not only may Tune B be different from Tunes A and C in certain respects, Tune B may also need to be performed in a different physical location from Tunes A or C. During a funeral, musicians sit on the *kavāl* and, at first, play funeral *koḷ*s according to their choice or by request. As villagers prepare to carry the corpse to the cremation ground, though, musicians' choice of what to play will briefly narrow. Let us imagine that *koḷ* players have been performing a sequence of funeral pieces of their own choosing up until the last such piece, Tune A. The moment the bier is lifted, *kob*s are sounded (indicated by the letter K) and musicians must play the *tāv īt koḷ* ("corpse-lifting tune"), Tune B. A few moments later, the procession starts moving from the *kavāl* in front of the home of the bereaved toward the cremation ground; musicians then play the *tāv ītr oybd koḷ* ("corpse-lifting-and-going tune"), Tune C. Following this, *koḷ* players perform another series of optative tunes while the procession is moving. This goes on until another important ritual moment anchors the sequence, calling for another contextually-specific melody, Tune D.

One spatiotemporal form associated with such Kota instrumental performances is the rhythm of change between repertorial freedom and prescription. This can be represented as follows, where "O" stands for musicians' options of pieces and other letters stand for specific pieces that must be played at specific times (and often at specific places). E is the bier lighting tune, after which no other funeral music is played. The sound of the *kob* blast creates another level of spatiotemporal articulation. When the blast corresponds with a critical moment, as it does here, it constitutes an anchor:

O O O O · · · A (K) B C O O O · · · · D O O O · · · E[19]

The process of anchoring in performing such tunes involves not only the melody sequence, but also the encompassing event, with its concomitant body movements and places it implicates. The power of places to anchor varies dynamically according to the flow of events. When enough people have arrived and when all ritual items are in place, the funeral procession takes leave of one anchor point, the site of the bereaved house, and moves centrifugally toward others. Villagers convey the corpse to the cremation ground and send the spirit to the land of the dead.

Some dance tunes, like some funeral tunes, are place-specific. Their performance sets up a time-place-music mutual feedback system that is reinforced calendrically and over the life of a Kota growing up in a particular village. The longer, more elaborate pieces are reserved for performance in the temple area. The simpler, "plain" (*cādā*) *koḷs* are used for dancing on the early days of the festival in the *gagvāl* and for green and dry funeral dances. Being relatively unmarked, they can also be played for demonstrations, for honoring government officials at an inauguration or other municipal event, or for other ad hoc affairs. They fill in gaps; they have no weight; they are not, from this perspective at least, anchors.

God-dance tunes, which are played near the temple, are not used for dancing during funerals. They are special; they give meaning and importance to one period during the year. When Puccan said that at the age of twenty-five he first played on the *pacāl*, he did not merely mean that he played in that place—children practice in that area informally during the festival anyway—he meant that, at the appropriate times, he played the correct dance pieces and the correct god (non-dance) tunes. "I played on the *pacāl* at age twenty-five" means "I knew, at age 25, the pieces that are played on the *pacāl*." During the god ceremony, Kotas focus on the *pacāl* and *guṛyvāl*, believing that at this time of the year god is present and especially responsive to rituals, music, and proper Kota behavior. The god ceremony reinforces village wholeness, solidarity, and identity through its centripetal orientation: Kotas collect all that is important—people, gods, pure food, good music—in the center.

Other kinds of articulations in the calendar year anchor in different ways. The eclipse, one such articulation, provides a tantalizing counterpoint, musically and ritually, to the god ceremony. While both have dedicated musical pieces for the occasion, the god ceremony has many and the eclipse only one. While the god ceremony, in an ideal world, recurs every year, the eclipse should, ideally, never return. The god ceremony anchors the year, the eclipse exerts its effects, largely, over a single day. The god ceremony is centripetally focused and largely concerned with the Kota people; the eclipse is, from the subject's point of view, global.

Music and Eclipses

The song text attached to the melody from which the "eclipse tune" probably originated is in a story that Sulli narrated to Emeneau.[20] A hare approached Koṭērvaykīṇ,[21] the aged grandfather who had been raising hares, only to find that the Kotas were shooting them with bows and arrows and eating them. The hare sang a Kota proverb to the old man which can be paraphrased, "The Kota people seek hares (i.e. fine food for themselves) but do not give food as a mother would to her child; we hares, who mind our own business, have become great like Badagas." (Emeneau suggests this is a Badaga song and story that has been only incompletely Kota-ized.) The old man replied, "next time the hunters come, lead them to me in the forest." Kota hunters customarily set out to hunt at night, their way illuminated by the full moon. On one such occasion, a group of hunters targeted a hare as it hopped off into the forest. Fearing for its life, it ran into the darkness of the trees; the men followed and were spotted by an enormous snake. The snake thought, "Hmm, I'll eat these fellows," and started out after them. But the men managed to escape the snake. Angered, the snake thought, "Well, at least I'll eat that damned hare," and sped up after the hare. The hare ran and ran, finally seeking refuge behind the moon. The snake, rather than wasting its time with a search around the moon, being not merely big but enormous (*kān*), and very hungry at that, began to consume the moon.

As they sat down for supper, the Kotas noticed that the full moon was shrinking and became alarmed. They approached Koṭērvaykīṇ and asked him what was the matter. The aged man replied,

> $_1$Foolish sons! Since that is a hare that I have been rearing with affection and since it is an honest [the word *catyēv*, related to *catym*, is used] hare, it is not fitting for it to be got by your (pl.) bows$_1$, and he said: $_1$Just god did like that. Just god it is who has made so that there must be no way for that enormous snake also to eat that hare and so that (the hare) must go to refuge behind the moon, all of that. Therefore, now we must make the moon to be released from the enormous snake. If we wish to make the moon to be released, all our (inc.) people having been fasting, having made a big fire, having come carrying our (inc.) [*koḷ*, *par*, and *tabaṭk*], all such things, play (pl.) the [*koḷ*] and drums as I say!$_1$

Then Koṭērvaykīṇ dictated the melody orally in the manner we have encountered in other *koḷ* origin stories. He sang it as a song of grief, an *āṭḷ*; the *koḷ* players picked up the melody from his singing, playing it back for him just as he had sung.

Āṭḷ of the snake destroying the moon

kān pāb katygē gōḷō	The enormous snake destroys the moon. Sorrow!
kān pāb katygē gōḷō	The enormous snake destroys the moon. Sorrow!
end ācv āṛy oḍd moltn,	The hare . . . which is my object of affection,
vēṭgārngūḷ $_1$tāvīrkōm$_1$ id̲r,	the hunters, saying: $_1$let us (inc.) kill it!$_1$
moltn ēdyr ōkēdmēl,	when they went chasing the hare,
end cōym, $_1$en moltn kāvkōm$_1$ id̲r,	my god, saying: $_1$let us (inc.) guard his hare!$_1$
vēṭgārngūḷ, kān pāb ēdyr vakcukō.	made the enormous snake come chasing the hunters.
vēṭgārngūḷ, tamd ucrn tapcr vadukō.	The hunters came making their lives to escape.
pābk, peṭyk ilākēd̲mēl,	When the snake did not have its bellyful,
kān pāb, $_1$moltn tinkōm$_1$ id̲r, ōkēd̲mēl,	when the enormous snake went, saying: $_1$let us (inc.) eat the hare!$_1$
molm, $_1$tan tinlk vadū$_1$ id̲r,	the hare, saying: $_1$it is coming to eat me$_1$
$_1$tapcgōm$_1$ id̲r, candr cōymk, moyr iḍgēd̲mēl,	when it made complaint to the Moon-god, saying: $_1$Let us (inc.) make myself to escape!$_1$
candr cōym, gav āḍṭ, tan tak iḍgēd̲mēl,	when the Moon-god, having had pity, put it on his own lap under the cloak,
peṭ īgīpd kān pābak, tigḷōṛ, moltn mingyukō.	the enormous snake, for its part, whose belly had become hungry, swallowed the hare with the moon.
cōym kālk, copnīr viṛtē.	I fall in supplication at god's feet.
tigḷmī, moltnmī viṛcṭ,	Having made the moon and the hare to be released,
kān pābn ēdgē en cōymī	drive away the enormous snake! Oh my god!

The aged ancestor then dictated to the Kotas the ritual by which they should use this *koḷ* to bring an end to the eclipse. While the musicians play, he said, the very small children, the women, and the remainder of the men should clap their hands and say "The enormous snake destroys the moon. Sorrow!" During this time, no one should eat, sleep, or drink anything. Half the women, meanwhile, should make a noise by striking metal eating plates, and the other half of them should balance a four-foot-long pestle in a water-filled metal eating plate. (Duryodhana recalls these rituals from his early childhood.) Such a pestle is said to balance only during an eclipse. As soon as the hare and the moon emerge from the snake's mouth—about an hour—the pestle falls. All this time, they must shout, "God, have pity on us. Return our hare and our moon god!"

The late Isaac Verghese, who conducted research in Ticgāṛ village in the 1960s, recorded a similar ritual (presumably dictated by his informant B.K. Krishna). Fearing "impending danger," a Kota suspecting an eclipse blows the *kob* (or arranges for someone else to) to inform the rest of the village. In response, all, "including mothers with babies, collect in the *kolaval* [temple area] ground and engage in singing bhajana and in folk dances." One of the *mundkānōn*s places a pestle vertically in a bronze plate of water. For as long as it stands on end, the eclipse is believed to continue, "in which case [instrumental] music, bhajan and dances continue until the *elk* (pestle) is separated from the plate and falls down. Music and bhajan, the Kota say, are powerful means of imploring their deities to separate the snake from the moon so that the Goddess of light (moon) would continue to throw light in the lives of the people" (Verghese 1974, 161).

The story Emeneau recorded is probably a shared "folktale" of the period. Certainly widespread is the theme of attributing an eclipse to a voracious snake or serpent, as evidenced in the Indic story of Rāhu, "the huge serpent" who "devour[s] the sun or moon, as the case may be." The eclipse becomes a period for observing pollution restrictions over the "death" of "one of those heavenly bodies" until Rāhu spits it out. "Food and drink taken during an eclipse possess poisonous properties, and people therefore abstain from eating and drinking until the eclipse is over. They bathe at the end of the eclipse, so as to get rid of the pollution" (Panikkar 1983 [1900], 58–9). A great deal can be said of the noise-making, believed to scare the snake away, and of the liminal spacetime that allows an elongated object to stand on end; the Kota practice lies squarely within a larger tradition.

Metvāy's Version

Another story of the eclipse was told to Mandelbaum by Metvāy Kamaṭn, a.k.a. Naṛykēr Kamaṭn, whom we've already encountered as one of

Puccan's gurus. Metvāy explained that the *kān pāb kātd koḷ* ("waiting for the enormous snake tune") was one of the two easiest *koḷs* to play—presumably for its shortness—and was therefore one of the first pieces an aspiring *koḷ* player was able to pick up by listening to his elders. The shortness of the tune also makes it easy to remember—an important attribute for a melody whose performance context is so very rare. As for the ritual, according to Metvāy:

> In former times there were no calendars, so when they saw the sun getting dark the people of each *kēr* would gather in their respective *kēr*, play and sing this tune and the little boys who did not know how to play or sing would get metal plates and beat them and ring bells. It was thought to be a bad sign, that during the year the cattle would die and crops fail. While the eclipse is on we do not do anything, only sing, play and pray that no harm come to us (Mandelbaum, May 11, 1938, p. 1).

Metvāy's story was apparently circulating in the Nilgiris, for a Toda who was present during the interview corroborated the details. In Metvāy's story, a virgin girl was impregnated by the rising sun as she emerged from her house one morning. As her belly enlarged, her father angrily threw her out, assuming her pregnancy was the unintended result of an illicit assignation with a man. She wandered about until taken in by a couple whose daughter was also pregnant. When the two girls gave birth they were blindfolded, as was the custom among these (non-Kota) people. The daughter's son was black and ugly, the girl's, beautiful. The parents took advantage of the girls' temporary incapacity and switched the children.

By some twist of fate, the son grew up and began courting his true mother, who was still young and attractive, having given birth at an early age. Through the mediation of a talking cow—a product of the *catym* of those days—he learned that the woman he desired was his own mother. They confirmed this by a test: if he put his mouth to her breast, milk would issue forth only if he were her son. It did. The boy's friends started to jeer, calling him the son of a dancing girl and whore, for his mother was unwedded. His mother explained the story and the son set off to find his father, the sun.

The sun god took the shape of a man and found his son, who said "If I am your son, I should be like a king's son and have all the things, horses, bungalows, that a king's son should have." The sun-man gave his son a box in which all these things could be found, provided he waited to open it with his mother. Being impatient, the boy naturally opened it up early and found the box empty; then he noticed all of these riches filling the sky. He didn't know what to do.

Fortunately, an enormous snake happened by. The boy asked the snake to help him. The snake agreed on the condition that the boy allow the snake to swallow him on the day of his marriage. Upon receiving the boy's word, the snake shut the box and the riches in the sky disappeared. The boy returned to his mother, explained what happened, opened the box, and started a new life with "all the things that a king's son should have." He forgot about his promise to the snake.

On the boy's wedding day, the snake returned to claim his due. His protective father, the sun, immediately appeared and convinced the snake to swallow him instead of the boy. Metvāy explained: "We say that the sun is allowing himself to be swallowed by the snake and that is why there is an eclipse. If we know of or see an eclipse of the moon, we play that tune, thinking the sun and the moon are the same. But if we don't know about it, we just sleep on. Nowadays we have calendars and watch for it." (Mandelbaum, May 11, 1938, p. 3). In the early part of the century, it was said that Hindus also would play drums to instill fear into the great consumer of the moon. The period is entirely inauspicious, being inappropriate for weddings or important tasks. "More especially is it fatal to women who are pregnant, for the evil will fall upon the unborn babe." (*Madras Weekly Mail*, October 15, quoted in Thurston 1912, 44.)

Metvāy's final comments reflect historical changes in how the eclipse has functioned qualitatively as an anchor: in previous times, the sun and moon were not distinguished (two different anchors were conceived as one), and the onset of the eclipse was rather sudden. The eclipse would presumably have been a more frightening event in the past, one that could not affect the period before its onset (as it can now, with printed calendars providing advance warning), but which would have made a more substantial impact after its onset and occasioned a great sense of relief at its conclusion.

The Temporality of Irregularity

The course of years separating eclipses is the largest-scale Kota musical cycle. Its form is a cycle of melodies with variable gaps in between: some are "free floating," performed according to the whim of the performers; some are consistently anchored in the calendar year, as in *devr*; others are temporally capricious, following the exigencies of funerals.

Traditionally, eclipses may have been feared for reasons that are entirely understandable in a pre-industrial society without a sophisticated system of long-term time reckoning: eclipses could throw into doubt the return of the natural order; threaten the continuity of the productive seasons. But natural phenomena such as the eclipse also serve as potent signs that may not rest on obvious environmental references. Kotas (at the level of "system") regard the entire waning phase of the moon to be inauspicious. It seems a logical extension of this thinking to regard the process of a lunar eclipse as something like the second half of the moon's cycle, sped up from fourteen days to a matter of hours. The formal congruity of these two processes would suggest that the eclipse condenses, and thus intensifies, the negative quality of time over the fourteen-day period. The reverse is also conceivable, namely that the striking and untimely phenomenon of the eclipse serves as a model for understanding the waning moon.

The eclipse is irregular. It fails to register simply within the regularly observable cycles of everyday life. In this, the eclipse shares an aspect of temporality with funerals, and in that sharing can be said to function similarly. Both eclipses (at least before the days of calendars) and human deaths are major events in the flow of human life, events that have the potential to negatively affect—through the proliferation of pollution, fear, grief, and such—the people, the places, and the times (usually reckoned in moon cycles in South India) with which they are associated. Both, as expressions of an uncontrollable agency, suggest that calendars, ritual cycles, and other symbolic representations of temporal order are at best illusory in their ability to actually impose orderliness in human life.

In making use of the anchoring idea, it is important to emphasize the particularity of individual examples in terms both of quality and degree. The weightiness, the ability to affect subjective time, of *devr*, is very different from that in either the funeral or the observance of the eclipse. *Devr* is prepared for in advance; leave must be granted from jobs; wood must be collected, houses cleaned. Musicians brush up on their playing. Excitement fills the air. This affect is replaced by a vacuum, a mild dejection, a feeling of emptiness when the observance is over. The death of an individual is not always unpredictable (and perhaps is more predictable now than it once was), but it nevertheless represents a different qualitative experience of time, leading up to and following the event. Even the flow of ordinary existence lacks predictability: everyday life may be suddenly shattered by the death of a healthy person, just as the unseen onslaught of an eclipse must have instilled fear among those who could neither predict nor understand it.

Both eclipses and funerals bring about concern regarding greater-than-human forces that may be malevolent, and the concomitant wish that the gods observe human suffering and offer some assistance, preventing future deaths, providing healthy children and good crops. This duality, this idea that funerals are polluting and symbolically *anti-god*, and at the same time that they are a ritual way of returning society to a position of godliness, is embodied in some of the ambiguities of the classification of the musical repertoire itself. The eclipse tune too exhibits these ambiguities, as a song of grief, *āṭḷ*, generically associated with the realm of death and originating from an ancestor (as some *āṭḷs* are said to), it is also a melody of supplication to the gods, seeking relief from the dread evil an eclipse represents. The eclipse and its associated rituals and music, like many events and acts that straddle cultural categories, is an anchor of a most special kind.

CHAPTER 6

Affect and Subject

In this chapter and the next I consider in greater depth the ways in which Kotas constitute themselves through their two major ritual complexes of *devr* and funerals (both green and dry), by examining the relationships among acts and practices that connect persons and entities located in different places.[1] Two forms of spacetime, "open" and "closed," are important in both ceremonies and everyday living. These forms are best introduced narratively, for a set of stories whose themes are dislocation and relocation, and the practices Kotas adopt in response to them, provide insights into the larger question what it means for Kotas to remain together or be pulled apart. To bring further spatiotemporal themes of the rituals into relief, five other topics are addressed: (1) travel; (2) transactions; (3) respect; (4) affect; and (5) music and food qualities.

Open Forms of Spacetime

A Ticgāṛ native living in Kurgōj village returned from a local goddess festival carrying the head of a sacrificial goat, which he intended to cook. Kotas customarily leave any such offering to a non-Kota god outside their villages in deference to their own gods. The Ticgāṛ man carelessly dropped the goat's head at the village edge near a spring. The water entering the village became polluted, causing many members of this populous village to become sick or die. The survivors who learned of this believed their father god was angry and had made their village uninhabitable. Some fled to a place called Kavāy. But they found the village unsatisfactory and departed, leaving a pile of stones as a sign that they would never return. To this day, Kota travelers in parts of Kerala and Karnataka return with tales of sighting these lost Kotas. A style of dress, a way of tying the hair, and the shape of a musical instrument have all served as fertile signs for the Kota imagination.

The sense of incompleteness Kurgōj villagers experience knowing these relatives are "out there" leads them to search, imagine, predicate their identities upon little-known, briefly-glimpsed, members of non-Kota communities who live to the west and north. In conducting such searches, or participating in the creation and circulation of legends and sighting of these lost kin, Kotas perform acts of potential closure. The rhythm and directionality of these acts constitute forms of spacetime associated with their reactions to the story. The tempo of these acts is haphazard, depending on neither ritual nor routine, only on the chance perception of resemblances as Kotas go about everyday processes of observing and inquiring. The affective profile of the spacetime these acts produce—which involves yearning, loss, and hope—depends on the fact that one of the intersubjective entities is elusive, separated in location and historical time, and lacking recognizable features of identity.

In a second key narrative, the inhabitants of the original village of Kotagiri, now a bustling Nilgiri town, abandoned their village when faced with a British order to build latrines. For the smell of the latrines was offensive to the Kota gods. In fear, Kotas fled to a place called Āgāl.[2] A land fault made their new home uninhabitable; once again they moved, finally settling in Porgāṛ village, their present location, just outside Kotagiri town. In this story, as in the first, the intermediate place of settlement was physically marked with a sign of separation. In the first case, Kotas marked their separation with a pile of stones. In the second, a fault in the land motivated the Kotas to leave, but the villagers remained together. Today, Porgāṛ villagers perform periodic acts to close the gap which separates them from their generations-old home. On the eighth day of their god ceremony they proceed, with music, to the temple of their original village site, chanting the holy syllables "*a hau kau.*" Only after completing a series of rituals there do they return, once again with *koḷ* music, to perform the temple-opening in their new village (Wolf 1997a, 475).

The departures in these two stories have not been balanced by final returns; the spacetimes associated with these narratives are "open." The choice of villagers to leave their villages has emotional ramifications for those who leave and for those who are left behind. Open forms of spacetime invite actions of closure. In the Kurgōj case, these actions entail searching for lost brethren. In Porgāṛ, attaining closure involves a significant amount of music making. Being periodic, it recapitulates the similar form of temporal closure Kotas seek in the god ceremony, a return to times in which Kotas and gods were as one.

Closed Forms of Spacetime

The events leading to the creation of the *ākēr* exogamous division, where Puccan resided, also revolved around a family departing from the village under duress. An ancestor begat two sons with his first wife and one with his second. Upon the old man's death, the sons quarreled over their shares of his land. The son of the second wife argued for half the land, calculating that each wife was entitled to pass on half of her husband's estate. The two elder brothers countered angrily that the land should be divided into three equal portions; they chased the younger brother out of the village.

That third brother moved to Kalāc village, married, and settled two miles away. His family burgeoned over several generations until a massive storm wiped out all but one mother and her son, who was in his twenties. In Kolmēl, the descendants of the two original brothers heard about this tragedy and invited the mother and son to return. The mother agreed on the condition that the ancestral land be returned and one of their daughters be given in marriage to her son (to ensure his safety). They acceded. The new family was incorporated as a new *kēr* division, *ākēr*. Perhaps it was this very passing of time that enabled Kotas to disregard the prohibition against intermarriage between descendants of brothers and allowed the positive outcome of a village reunited.

The outcome was negative in our earlier story of the *tērkārn*, Kurval, who was stranded in Ceylon, could not return to Kolmēl in time for *devr*, was removed from office, and died soon after. These two Kolmēl village stories articulate "closed" forms of spacetime, in that the separations were balanced by forms of reunion, even though the outcomes were different. The durations separating the departures from the returns contributed to this difference, and they had an impact on the emotions of the actors involved. The period within which Kurval completed his journey was too long from the perspective of his fellow villagers, who needed him to perform his duties as *tērkārn*; they remained angry after he returned and he could not bear his disenfranchisement. The much longer period after which the third brother's family returned to the village made for longing remembrance on the part of the home villagers; it allowed for a dramatic, structural change of kinship organization in the village and the creation of new, corresponding residence patterns.

These four stories are associated with forms of spacetime created by individuals and groups who were motivated to travel—to perform migrations, fleeings, searches, relocations, duty-related comings and goings, and processions. In each case, the spatiotemporal form, the creation of affect, and the effects of both spacetime and emotion on future behavior, were intimately related to the identities of those creating the spacetime. The spatiotemporal processes by which Kotas perform their ceremonies can be viewed from a similar perspective.

Ceremonies and Travel

One of the less obvious differences between god and death ceremonies involves the imperatives for individuals to travel to one another's villages for the purpose of participating in rituals. Funerals are elaborate affairs—whether the initial cremation or the *varldāv* some months or years later. When Kotas die, their relatives and friends from all seven villages are obliged to either attend or send a representative. Kin and affines play specific roles in the ceremony; the gifts they give in honor of the deceased must be returned when the giver dies. This cycle of mutual obligation, in which one form of visit and ritual action or gift "engages the possibility of return," constitutes an intersubjective form of spacetime between (categories of) givers and receivers (see Munn 1986, 9).

Devr, as the central ceremony of god, instigates travel as well by demanding the return of members of the patrilineage to the center: men born to the village must return and stay home if they are not already there. In modern circumstances, Kotas have renegotiated what it means to remain in the village by allowing those who have jobs in Ooty to commute to and from town during the day on all but the most crucial days of the ceremony. But those who live far away in Bombay or Delhi generally take leave from their jobs and travel with their families to be in their villages for a week or two. *Devr* also draws women to their natal villages, sometimes with their husbands; such travel is motivated by emotional and familial attachments rather than by ritual necessity. There is no roll-calling for women as there is for men. Furthermore, since Kotas in most villages celebrate *devr* during the same time period, it is difficult for a family to satisfy its own obligations to village and village deity in one village and then travel to another. Villagers commonly visit one another and participate in one anothers' performances only on the final days of *devr*, at which time participants dance and play, and women sing.

In short, travel associated with funerals creates one form of intersubjective spacetime. Movement is motivated by a consanguineal, kinship, or affective relationship between the mourner and the deceased. And mutual obligations between the deceased's family and the family or village of the visitor are set up and maintained by acts of giving. Travel to god ceremonies creates a different one, which is based primarily upon consanguineal relationships in the male line. God ceremonial spacetime is also distinct in that no rhythm of give and take is created among the participants; rather, humans engage in transactions with the gods, offering foods, music, dance, and various forms of moral behavior in return for divine beneficence.

Spatiotemporal Parameters of Status

The creation and marking of individual status in Kota ritual also involve forms of travel, as well as movement and forms of extension in time and space. Status is expressed in Kota in terms of the kinds of "respect" a person, thing, or deity commands. Kotas use the word *marvādy*, which derives (via Tamil) from the Sanskrit term *maryādā*, meaning "frontier, limit, bounds of morality, and propriety, custom." Crossing my knees in the *guṛyvāl* was considered disrespectful not merely because I was operating within a territorial limit, but because, during the central days of the god ceremony, the spatial frontier for respectful behavior around the *mundkānōn*s was relatively expansive.

Kotas express status, such as the ritual status accorded upper *versus* lower *kēr*s, in terms of (metaphorical and physical) height as well as size. The word *doḍ*, for instance, which means "big" or "great," is applied both to important objects and people. *Mundkānōn*s' houses, certain fires, reserved drinking vessels, and respected male members of the community are all big. Status is also related to fame or renown in the sense of a good name, *pēr*. A dead person's status or "name" is articulated through spatiotemporal extension—the distance persons will travel for a funeral and the length of time over which villagers will perform rituals.

In July of 1991 I attended my first Kota funeral, which was in Mēnāṛ village. Its simplicity was striking. The man, who had been about seventy years old, lay on a cot decorated only by a single umbrella. Few people attended the funeral, and after a relatively short period of funeral melody-making, processioners carried the corpse to the cremation ground. The reason for the small turnout was that the deceased, being unmarried and presumably from a small family, had few kinship attachments with Kotas in other villages. He was also impoverished, a bit of a loner, and mentally unstable or at least off-beat. His lack of status was reflected in the failure of persons from farflung Kota villages to journey to Mēnāṛ to pay their respects; nor was there any family member whatsoever, only village friends, to build and decorate his bier (see also Herzfeld 1996, 157 ff.). The lack of embellishment and size of the canopy were directly related to the fact that the man himself was not regarded as "big."

Kotas usually keep the corpse in the *kavāl* (yard) fronting the bereaved house, where mourners and helpers attend the deceased person, accompanied by funeral music, until all relatives have arrived. Depending on time of death and length of time expected for mourners to arrive, the period in which the corpse rests on the *kavāl* will vary. Thus, for a person with a greater "name," funeral music will be played for a longer time, perhaps even for an additional day. In this respect, length of travel, ritual, and musical time, like the spatial size of the canopy, is a function of the fame or renown of the person (cf. Munn 1986; see also Tambiah 1981). In the old days, this effect was intensified by the fact that Kotas would have had to walk from their villages, arriving in waves whose rhythm was defined not by modern bus schedules (or their delays), but by the synchronization of social groups who undertook the journeys together and by their physical orientation in the Nilgiri Hills.

The Pērn *Ritual*: The practice of welcoming visitors by playing special *pērn koḷ*s further reinforces the link between kinship bonds and the expanse of spacetime in funeral visitation. The etymology of the term *pērn* is ambiguous. One literal meaning of the term is "bullock load;"

this relates to Dravidian verbs meaning "to heap up," "load," or "transport by pack-animal."[3] Historically, according to S. Raman, the deceased's family had to bear the burden of paying for the funerary feast. Later, the *pērn* ritual evolved, in which male relatives through the father (*naṇṭṇ*) donated rice for the funeral. This rice was once placed in a sack and on the back of a pony, which was led around the corpse—thus the relevance of the "pack-animal" or "load" etymology.[4] Via the verbal noun *pēyrd*, the tune can be called the "tune for doing the ritual of circumambulating with rice."[5] Nowadays, men carry rice or other food items on their shoulders and circumambulate the corpse. Duryodhana says they pile up the bags of rice in advance and then circumambulate in a formal ritual so that all those who are giving rice can be identified, honored with music, and later repaid in kind when someone in their family dies.

Young women deceased's family (e.g. female grandchildren, brother and sister's children or grandchildren) line up with baskets of amaranth (*kīr*) which they offer to the deceased. Although only men's actions constitute what is called the *pērn* ritual, men and women's activities are obviously parallel in function as comestible funerary prestations, and during both rituals, so far as I could gather from observation, musicians play the same set of *pērn koḷs*.

The relative social ranking of deceased persons can be "measured" roughly by the expanse of spacetime associated with various aspects of their funerals. By "expanse of spacetime" I mean the relative size, height, or quantity of objects, the duration of actions and the distances their actions cover. The greater the dead person's name, the further those paying respect will travel to attend the funeral. It may take a long time for distant visitors to arive; the procession will be delayed in order to wait for some of them. The funeral of a respected person will draw relatively large numbers. During the funeral, the deceased's status is indexed by the extent of different persons participating. It co-varies in direct proportion with the length of the *pērn* ritual and the material value of foodstuffs the ritual generates.

The ritual is performed for the "name" or "honor" of those who are performing the act of respect as well as for the deceased. As Raman put it (using the English words in quotes), the *pērn koḷ* provides the sort of "power" appropriate for welcoming a "king" or a "general." Through the *pērn* ritual, then, Kotas constitute the status of both the deceased and those who honor the deceased. The mutuality of the ritual is also played out in potentials for the future. By giving grain at one ritual, Kotas set up expectations for return prestations at future rituals. The acts of village males making prestations to the deceased phenomenologically concentrates the value of each individual gift (i.e. an amount of rice) from dispersed givers throughout the village to the single spot where the deceased lies. This sense of concentration is enhanced by the process of circumambulation, led by the musical group. The female prestations concentrate gifts which index wider ties with families in other Kota villages throughout the Nilgiris.[6] Who should place *kīr* at the bier of the deceased is determined by two forms of closeness: *kēr* residence (spatial closeness) and personal affection (*gav*). The *pērn* rituals may also be performed by those who wish to express their friendship with the deceased. The form of giving is related to the value of the gift, what the gift is materially worth. A large and valuable gift, such as a buffalo, will come from one family and be given directly to another. Relatively less-valuable gifts of grain may come from many dispersed sources, but can be concentrated—literally piled or heaped up by the bier.

The *pērn koḷ*s for each village may differ. In Ticgāṛ village, the tune derives from a song (CD 38) in the Badaga language whose lyrics are only partially remembered by Kotas today:

"Sixty cubit buffalo pen"

ārōgē aravate moḷme tōyembā	They say that the female buffalo pen is sixty cubits large
guṇḍgalle mātigā kēṛimbā	Guṇḍgal's son is in danger

The story behind the song, as told by Beḷḷi Mathi, hints at why the tune may be used to honor a personage:

> In Ticgāṛ there was a man named Maḷayṇ, the grandfather of my mother's husband. His father was Guḍlayṇ [referred to as Guṇḍgal in the song]. Guḍlayṇ's father, Kōḍvāyayṇ, built the buffalo pen of sixty cubits in diameter and kept large buffaloes in it. Guḍlayṇ's dog used to roam that area. Whenever a Badaga walked by, the dog would bark angrily and chase the Badaga away. One day, while the buffaloes were out grazing, the dog stayed alone in the empty pen. A Badaga came by and blocked off the

entrance to the pen so that the dog could not come out. The dog made an enormous racket and drew Guḍlayṇ to the scene. Seeing what happened, Guḍlayṇ physically beat the Badaga. It is said that from that time onwards Guḍlayṇ was given respect whenever he happened to pass Badagas in the region.

Too many lyrics of the song and details of the story have been forgotten for me to explicate the meaning further. Why, for instance, is Guḍlayṇ's son in danger? Would the Badaga exact revenge on Guḍlayṇ by harming his son? The important point is that the Kotas found enough in the song and story to appropriate the melody for a *koḷ* that confers honor. The anti-Badaga tone is apparently absent from the melody's abstract meaning, since the tune is also used to honor Badagas when they arrive in the village during the public day of *devr*. The fact that buffaloes and cows are valuable and were once important funeral prestations may also have something to do with the connection of this tune with the ritual.[7]

Funerary Gift-giving: The more general term for prestation in the funerary context is *telac*; in the 1930s such a funeral gift consisted of a cow, a buffalo, or money (Mandelbaum, February 8, 1938, p. 3). Now bovine sacrifices have been eliminated from the green funeral entirely. Elaborate rules dictated who should give such gifts to whom, involving traditional ritual-economic relationships between Kotas and Badagas and Kotas and Todas, as well as kin relationships. According to Raman, if a cow or buffalo were sacrificed in the name of a deceased male, for example, such a prestation would have to be made by his brother-in-law (*ayḷ*) or his daughter's husband (*mōḷāḷn*)—in other words, his classificatory affine in his own generation or the next (defined not by age but by sequential position in a lineage). In this way, the *telac* ritual created an affinal spacetime that linked the deceased, as a member of one *kēr*, either to another *kēr* in the village or to another village entirely, depending on where the sacrificer lived. The time cycle was ongoing, implicating future generations in a complementary fashion, according to the rhythm of deaths. The intersubjectivity of this ritual spacetime is established not only by the mutually constitutive nature of kin relations, but also by the fact that, as Raman put it, "*telac* means 'you are [there] for me; I am [there] for you'" (*telac, nī eṉk oḷī, ān niṉk oḷē ird kaṇk*).

This complex system of interlinkages has largely declined with the removal of bovine sacrifice.

The value of the funeral prestations as well as the wealth of the deceased was and to some extent still is related to the expanse of spacetime created by visitors to the funeral more generally, for if the estate of the deceased—with whatever help from gifts—was unable to pay for feeding the guests arriving from other villages, only a limited number of persons would be called to attend the funeral in the first place. Inasmuch as funerary rituals engage participation of visitors from near or far in direct relation to the deceased's wealth and good name, funerary practices constitute forms of spatiotemporal "extension of the self" (Munn 1986, 11–12).

This is illustrated in a further example. Before dawn on February 4, 1992, the sound of the *kob* announced the death of the former *mundkānōn*, Va. Kamaṭn.[8] Musicians were gathering and began to play funeral tunes; his widow was in the house mourning over the corpse. Later in the morning, several men erected a simple, white *gurykaṭ* (catafalque) over the bier, and waves and waves of mourners arrived from other villages—a dozen or so of them in cars, some of the men dressed smartly in Western clothes. A class of schoolchildren also attended, carrying a placard in honor of Kamaṭn, who had donated money to their school. Normally, for a person of Kamaṭn's wealth and social status, the *gurykaṭ* would have been colorfully decorated and tall. In this case, since Va. Kamaṭn was a former *mundkānōn*, his mortuary accouterments were simple and white.

One Kota present commented cynically during this funeral that one could expect such widespread attendance at a funeral for a man with money and not for one without. This was not simply a matter of the economics of feeding visitors. Va. Kamaṭn had made a point in advance of providing ample food from his own estate for the visitors. The *pērn* ritual was performed, nevertheless. S. Raman carried one bag of rice around the corpse himself.

Emotion and Acts of Memory: To attend the funeral of a great person, one somehow partakes in that person's greatness and finds oneself in the company of those important people who have taken time from their daily affairs to attend. But what carries the most emotional weight is the degree of personal closeness a griever maintained with a dead person. Aspects of a personal relationship such as dislike may also be emotionally significant: one might feel guilty, after a person has died, for treating him badly. In either case, affect is related to memory. The dying Va. Kamaṭn specifically requested of his childhood friend Puccan that he play the *koḷ* "fragrantly" at his funeral (Wolf 2001, 403). Puccan could do so, and Va. Kamaṭn could make the request, because of the memories they shared: running races on the *pacāl*, arguing points in the village council, building a new Hindu-style temple. Puccan's very promise to play served as "the means of moving [his own] mind" to make him remember Va. Kamaṭn (see Munn 1986, 9).

Whereas being close to the deceased may put some in an excellent frame of mind for performing, relatives and friends of the deceased may forbear playing music for a funeral if their relationship to the deceased is too close. Jayachandran, for example, avoided playing *koḷ* for his younger brother Mani's funeral, yielding to Jagganathan, who was visiting from Ticgāṛ village. Along the same lines, Mandelbaum's musical informant, Veln, stated, "There was no objection to my playing [*koḷ* at the funeral], but since it was my sister's husband [who died] and I was supposed to feel very sad I did not play. When the instruments play we are more sad, and we play because we believe that the soul will not reach *amavnāṛ* ["our mother's land," another name for the land of the dead] unless music is played." (Mandelbaum, July 26, 1937, p. 6.) If music is supposed to enhance feelings of sadness, should it not follow that those close to the deceased could mourn more acutely by playing music, thereby embodying the production of that which produces sorrow? This is not how Kotas interpret musical performance. Those who are performing must momentarily separate themselves from their personal sorrow in order to attend mindfully to performing the musical rituals correctly. And yet, a certain degree of heartfelt grief on the part of the performers is believed to add poignance to the music. Kota musicians have told me that they are able recollect the right piece for the right time by immersing themselves in the ritual actions, adopting the appropriate attitude, and embracing the appropriate affect. The aforementioned Jagganathan told me he had trouble remembering funeral tunes until either someone died or the *varldāv* pyre was already burning. The power of affect and mood to aid musical memory is not limited to funerals. Raman remarked that he could not remember *devr koḷ*s without first assuming a devotional attitude, fixing his mind on god. He said in Tamil that it is like plugging in electrical current, "'plug' *pōḍurudu mādiri.*"

Remembrance

What other subjective effects do the deceased—and death-related performances in general—exert on the living? How do funerary participants perform acts of memory and represent their own emotional experiences? Remembrances of many kinds are cardinal in a funeral: remembering the deceased him or herself, remembering the ritual actions (gifts) and the meanings of ritual symbols, calling into play the memorial significance of objects, and musical remembering—the recollection of musical pieces and their associated stories or anecdotes. It is worth distinguishing here between what one actually "remembers" as an event or thought in one's life from the act of "remembrance," in which one actively calls forth information one has learned to associate with the past—whether one actually "remembers" that period in the past or not. Perhaps we need a third term, "recall," for bringing to mind the knowledge needed to complete a task—play a piece, perform the right ritual in the right order.

Hence one can, in a general sense, "remember" individual experiences with a friend, but one might participate in acts of remembrance in the funeral for that friend which are really replicas of others' acts of remembrance. Few Kotas have experience shooting bows and arrows in the forest, but Kotas collectively "commemorate" this kind of activity during the dry funeral because it encapsulates something central to Kota "tribal" identity. They may "recall" the necessity of this ritual when the dry funeral bier is lit and burning; or someone might need to remind them. Puccan's promise to Va. Kamaṭn is an example of how acts of remembrance may be constituted in advance with respect to an anchoring event—here a death; but the phenomenon is similar when one wishes a dear friend, "Bon Voyage."

A form of intersubjective remembrance relevant to our understanding of Kota music is the individual's recollection of specific interactions with the deceased; these feed into the complexity of emotions the subject experiences during funerals and are given concrete form in song texts. When a person composes an *āṭḷ* about another, he may focus on the extreme sadness and loss he feels (and remembers feeling at the time), the dreadfulness of the force (such as Kurumba sorcery) that led to the victim's death, the power of land of the dead and the ancestors, or on their positive memories of experiences with the deceased.[9] The range of possible emotional modes a singer might adopt in her song is an indication of the range of emotions Kotas generally associate with funerals.

When singers sing *āṭḷ*s as aesthetic objects they are performing acts of remembrance; they may not be recalling personal experiences with the person who is the subject of the song. The *āṭḷ* singer strives for musical and dramatic effectiveness, evoking stories or fragments of stories, whether or not they are expressing personal memories. Duryodhana and others have pointed out that *āṭḷ* performances create moods of reminiscence. They stimulate others to sing songs about the dead or simply to talk about missing loved ones.

When I was recording *āṭḷ*s in Kurgōj during one rainy season, a recently widowed woman named Bebi and several others sang a combination of newly composed songs and ones they had learned growing up. In one of the most moving of Bebi's compositions, she had mixed the genres of *āṭḷ* and lullaby (*tālāṭ*) to create a song about her dying husband, which she used to sing to her baby granddaughter. (I had attended the dead husband's funeral some months before this session.) Kunkayn, another woman present, sang an *āṭḷ* about her husband, who had not died, but had decided to go to work at the Deval tea plantation; she warned him off, saying "don't go, it's a bad place, a Kurumba place." Her fearful mood led her to compose the song, and the atmosphere created by the singing session (though, admittedly made somewhat artificial by my presence), brought back the memory.

Singing *āṭḷ*s about those with whom one has no personal connection simulates the reactivation of "memories" once removed—the experience is gone, but the narrative remains in some form, and the genre itself, through musical and conventional textual means, puts singer and listener in the appropriate mood to imaginatively recreate the scenario. The *āṭḷ*s one learns to sing also create a framework—a set of formulaic phrases, terms for address, ways of proceeding— for representing one's own experiences. Playing and listening to instrumental music for funerals, by comparison, may stimulate memories (i.e. acts of remembrance) twice removed, as only a small number of funeral melodies are associated with specific texts, and not all listeners will know those texts. Like *āṭļs*, funeral melodies put listeners in a mood of reminiscence, if they are not already struck by the impact of someone actually dying. This is one of the reasons such melodies should not be played outside of an actual funeral. During the dry funeral, women weep copiously when the funeral music begins. It is not the immediacy of death (since the person may have died months or even ten years before), but music in its ritual context, that contributes significantly to bringing on tears and causing women to remember their loved ones.

The sub-genre of funeral melody called *kēṛ koḷ* deserves reconsideration in this regard. The way Kotas classify such sub-genres is part of how they represent the emotional contour of their mortuary rites and the relationship between memory and continuance.[10] During a recording session after New Year's day in 1991, just out of earshot of the village, Puccan was demonstrating funeral *koḷ*s, identifying them by various criteria. Some, such as the bier-lighting tune (CD 4), are named for their associated rituals; others, such as the "gathering at the land of the dead tunes" (*nāṛgūc koḷs*), refer to actions or metaphysical effects of a melody—in this case, calling spirits of the dead to the funeral ground; Puccan called other melodies (plain) "funeral tunes" (*tāv koḷ*), by which he meant optative tunes which are playable in between contextually specific funeral melodies. And then he played a series of melodies among which he distinguished *kēṛ koḷ*s and *dukt koḷ*s. Duryodhana explained that *dukt koḷ*s are melodies of "full sadness," whereas *kēṛ koḷ*s are melodies associated with both happiness and sadness at the same time.

Whereas it is not difficult to understand why some funeral tunes might evoke "full sadness," the fact that others do not calls for explanation. One reason is that the latter tunes were once performed as part of lively contests among Kota men—and Toda men at Toda funerals—to wrestle down and sacrifice buffaloes. Resonances of agonistic excitement, bravery, and pride have become, for Kotas, "qualities" of the music.[11] Some of these melodies were derived from *āṭļs*, sung either about individuals who had died, or about favorite buffaloes sacrificed in the name of the deceased. These songs expressed affection for the dead person or the buffalo, told stories, presented personal descriptions, and in general represented the person or buffalo in life. As such, these songs and their tunes, became, for Kotas, objects of positive reflection.

Almost exactly ten years after my recording session with Puccan, Raman added that Toda emotional reactions to *kēṛ koḷ*s are different:

Todas weep. This effect may have to do with the particularly strong affection Todas are known to have for their buffaloes; it may also have to do with what remains of memories Todas maintain of their funerals in days when Kotas participated. The sound of Kota funeral music arouses strong feelings of nostalgia in some Todas.

In Kurgōj village, where elements of the buffalo sacrifice are still preserved (although not the public contest), the retired postal supervisor K. Maḷn concurred that for Kotas in his own village the emotional associations of the "buffalo calling" (*im ātd*) ritual and melody are less sad than those associated with *dukt koḷs*, though he found it difficult to express this difference with any linguistic nuance.[12] Duryodhana likened the spirit of *kēr kōḷs* to the energetic, almost optimistic attitude Kotas must adopt, in the face of adversity, to organize and carry out substantial and laborious work for the funeral, not to mention hosting and visiting with mourners. Other Kotas have pointed out that dying is tragic from the perspective of losing a loved one, but positive from the perspective of the deceased joining the world of spirits and becoming closer to god. Kotas have also commented on elements of happiness mixed with sadness associated with funerary dancing. As "Dancing-Ground" Rajan put it, funerary dancing is a *cātrm* (ritual) because it expresses the feeling that the deceased has "won" (Ko. *gel-*), overcome life's difficulties.

Emotional Contour and Texture

Individual Kotas differ in the degree to which they emphasize sadness and various kinds of admixture—e.g. happiness, cool reminiscence, agonistic excitement, pride, or relief—when they talk about their experiences at funerals. Their representations of their emotional experiences vary according to their relationship with the deceased and according to the stage they have reached in the ritual process of a green or dry funeral. We may envision each participant experiencing a ceremony in terms of an "emotional contour," a series of imaginary graphs of contour intensity corresponding to different affects, gross or subtle—one for sorrow, one for cheerful remembrance, one for anger, and so forth. These would change over time during a given ceremony, and would depend on some combination of individual subjectivity and the cultural classification of affect in a ritual frame. A funeral participant may feel the sense of loss to be especially great at some moments, and, as a result, burst into tears. Her sadness may subside at other times, while perhaps she reminisces cheerfully about the deceased with a few friends. Various factors may intensify or subdue each shade of emotion, creating an indeterminate mixing of affective modalities, rather than a set of discrete emotional modes with variable intensity. Collectively, all "emotional contours" of participants intertwine complexly, creating a ceremony's "emotional texture."

The specific content of affective understandings need not be unitary or uniform. Cultural understandings of affect might undergo change as a ritual unfolds. "Emotional texture" is a way of talking about the changing configurations of affective meanings that participants assign to rituals, and these configurations emerge from a tension between individual feelings and experiences and the classification of "emotion" in language and ritual. Emotional texture is neither static in time nor invariant across the population, but it is always conditioned by everyday, agreed-upon understandings of ritual meaning.[13]

Affect is time dependent not only within a given ceremony but also within a given actor's lifespan, as loved ones die and children are born. Affect, like music, may anchor (or be anchored) to particular places or ritual destinations, such as the *nelāgōṛ*, where the widow removes her jewelry and symbolically returns them to the deceased.[14] In this emotionally "intense" place, the widow cries copiously and stirs others in their grief; *koḷ* players mark the location/occasion with a specific piece. Women are anchored to the spot in the peculiar sense that they are not supposed to accompany the procession beyond that village limit.

The spacetime of the funeral, then, takes on "qualities" that can be described in terms of emotional texture. For each individual, places such as the *nelāgōṛ*, and moments, such as when the body is brought from the house to the *kavāl*, are articulations that compose this spacetime. The relative duration of the funeral, the speed at which it is performed, the density of its participants, even the loudness of crying, may be relevant to the "extension" of the deceased's self. In such a spacetime, the specific emotional content—grief, love, repulsion—and the relative degree of intensity to which one emotional component dominates over the others, remain indeterminate. These emotional components may have something to do with the funeral participant's relationship with the deceased; but they may also have to do with the way in which the participant experiences elements of the funeral—the taste of food, the excellence of musical performance and the choice of pieces; a variety of extraneous matters may also play a role, such as rain, drunken unruly men, or monetary concerns. Hence the "emotional texture" of a given funeral performance can in a limited way be regarded as a mode of constructing the deceased in affective terms. But it has at least as much to do with the subjectivity of each individual participating, as against one another and the whole set of cultural institutions that are called into play during a funeral. Kotas agree upon the articulations, the genres, and the categories of emotion, but they needn't agree on exactly how these should fit together in any given situation.

Musical Emotion

Time and place come to be endowed with the quality of sadness, when, for example, Kotas invoke the concept of "bier time." The idea of music possessing emotional qualities such as sadness presents a different problem, which I'll address only briefly here. One way in which people sense that something "sounds sad" is by (subconsciously) comparing that sound to something else, such as the sounds people make when they are sad—crying, moaning, or speaking in a particular manner. Whether these sounds are more or less culturally or biologically determined is irrelevant for the act of comparison. The comparison sound might also be an element associated with sadness in a conventional system of signification, such as a minor key, or for south Indians the *rāgā mukhāri*. The two stages of interpretation are distinct: recognizing similarity between the original sound and the "something else" is an iconic process. Lament "x" may sound like crying, because it shares characteristics such as a particular vocal timbre, shakiness, breathlessness, and so forth. If we interpret "x" as sad, however, we do so indexically through our own bodily experience, interpreting shakiness of voice and so forth as true expressions of an inner emotion.[15]

The problem is that not all Kota musical genres which have particular affective associations can be iconically related to what are understood to be bodily manifestations of emotion. Nor can they be consistently characterized in terms of musical conventions for signification of affect: tempo (such as the association of slow tempo with lugubriousness), intonation, melodic mode, or scale. Instrumental pieces are, for the most part, individually connected with rituals and occasions, and in that sense individually index the ritual, the occasion, and the emotional associations of the occasion. Kotas say, however, that they sense directly, in their hearts and stomachs, the emotional character of their music (Wolf 2001). Virtually everyone with whom I spoke claimed they could recognize a funeral tune even upon hearing it for the first time. In fact, individuals sometimes misidentified such melodies: Raman once identified a historical recording of a god tune from another village as a funeral tune. Some Kotas dispute the classification of certain items of repertoire played during the *varldāv*; still other pieces lie on the border of god and death genres and differ very little in musical content: the grain-offering tunes which are used in the *varldāv* and *devr* are virtually identical. Despite occasionally misreading their "qualities" or disputing their genre affiliation, Kota beliefs that affective qualities exist as musical essences remain unshaken. For Kotas, the affective profile of Kota music is as directly perceivable as is the color red in a ripe, Red Delicious apple to an American.[16]

Even though no systematic feature of Kota instrumental makes a piece "sad" or "blissful," some melodies within the same category tend to resemble one another. Similarly sounding dyads such as the *padneṭ devr ātd koḷ* (CD 26) and the *kunayṇōr koḷ* (CD 39) appear in the sequence of the twelve god tunes in Kolmēl; the bier-lighting tune shares an opening melodic gesture with a well-known *āṭḷ*; and one of the melodies used to send the spirit of the dead to the land of the dead sounds similar to the one used to reconstitute the spirit ritually in the form of *vatm* millet in the *varldāv* (see Wolf 2000/2001). Kotas recognize and point out such similarities; indeed it suits their cultural categorizations of god ceremonial and funerary practices to do so.[17] The network of similarities lends wholeness and distinctiveness to the god and death genres. In this sense, emotional meaning in the major categories of Kota instrumental music is based on iconicity, although to a limited extent, and of a special kind. In the context of language, Alfred Gell terms this "a posteriori iconism": "Once a term [read: musical piece] is ensconced in the language [read: ritual system], sound and meaning, even if arbitrarily conjoined initially, will henceforth be associated, so that new terms [musical pieces] may accrete around the original one, exploiting the same established resonances [ritual associations]." (1979, 59; 1995, 250)

Emotional associations, hence, *become* qualities of music for Kotas, but from an analytic perspective these qualities are different from such directly observable musical qualities as tempo, timbre, and texture.[18] Functionally relevant temporal qualities that are readily observable in Kota music include: (1) length: relatively long pieces tend to be associated with important rituals or themes; (2) duration: the period of time over which a series of pieces is performed may have bearing on the importance of the ritual moment, or the personage being honored; (3) tempo: tunes for men's dances tend to be more rapid than those for women's dances; god tunes and funeral tunes tend, on the whole, to be slower than men's dance tunes; and (4) simultaneity and interlock: unison *koḷ* playing and clearly-interlocked, synchronized drum parts are important criteria for "tasteful" music and are therefore effective means of conveying respect and affection, whether they are for god, the deceased, or patrons in an occasional performance for another community.

Food

Food, which should also be tasty, is at least as important as music in some rituals. Like music, food is a medium for spatiotemporal transactions between Kotas and spirits of the dead or the gods. It also embodies qualities that contribute to the constitution of distinct spiritual and personal identities over the course of lengthy ceremonies. Some such qualities are produced through methods of food preparation—frying, boiling, or dry-roasting—and involve polarized categories, such as the distinction between dry/dessicated (*varl*) and green/fresh/unboiled/uncooked (*pac*). In the *varldāv* (dry funeral), Kotas perform rituals with dry-roasted grains, some of which participants consume, and some of which they throw on the dry funeral pyre as offerings to spirits of the dead. Kotas associate the period over which the ceremony is held, and places in which it is held, with characteristic tastes; in this case the taste of dried-roasted rice and dry-roasted *vatm* millet mixed together with jaggery. The quality of "dryness" serves as an iconic sign, suggesting the dryness of bone relics preserved from the initial cremation, and contributing to the name of the ceremony, the dry funeral (*varldāv*). This dryness contrasts not with wetness but with the quality of being "green" (*pac*), the state of having life fluids coursing through the veins like a plant stalk severed from its root but still retaining color, or the grassy *pacāl*, the focus of play and worship in everyday Kota village life. This quality of greenness is embodied in green plant stalks, which festoon the bier in the *pac tāv*, the "green funeral."

Non-vegetarianness and vegetarianness are also significant qualities of food from a ritual perspective. In both the *varldāv* and *devr* Kotas make offerings of boiled millet, *vatm kū*, in a ritual called *eṛ vecd*. The difference between this ritual in the dry funeral and god ceremony depends on what is served along with the boiled millet: spiced (ideally buffalo) meat stew for the former and salted mung bean stew (*upudk*) for the latter. Kotas offered conflicting responses to the question: "For whom is the offering in the *varldāv eṛ vecd* ritual intended?" Some thought that the food was intended for spirits of the dead; others said it was for the gods.[19]

Those observing the *varldāv* and *devr* are supposed to eat different kinds of food, but it is not clear to what extent this reflects preferences of spirits or gods. I was told that, during *devr*, one eats a stew (*udk*) of mung beans flavored only with salt because Kotas "in the old days" could not forage in the forest for the range of spices they now use in their food. This explanation accords with other Kota interpretations of rituals, which emphasize connections with a primordial past and reify Kota self-identifications as tribal Indians. It does not explain avoidance of meat, however. Since interpretations of such practices, like the practices themselves, are subject to changes over time, the explanation offered to me is probably but one in a line of many interpretations (or for that matter, in an array of possible explanations that exist on the ground today). Mandelbaum's notes on the god ceremony provide another interpretive snapshot, no less valid for its brevity, "intercourse is something bad to the gods . . . meat is also bad and also chili powder." (April 23, 1937, p. ix–31.) It is not clear what "bad" means here, but the notion that meat and chili powder are somehow disturbing to the deity's constitution is at least as reasonable an explanation as the idea that in the old days there was no red chili.

Kota patterns of food consumption, along with the full range of practices in a given ritual category, invite comparisons (brief here) with those in the wider Hindu Indian context. By eating vegetarian, spiceless food, and claiming such food preferences for their gods, Kotas contribute to the larger *devr* category, which also includes values of goodness, truth, and purity and a centripetal form of cohesion. This category corresponds rather well with the Hindu "quality or disposition" (*guṇa*) of *sattva*.[20] For Kotas, buffalo meat stands for the *varldāv* in the same way that salted mung bean stew, *upudk*, stands for *devr*. By (once) performing aggressive animal sacrifices and consuming those sacrifices in spicy food preparations for funerals (green or dry), Kotas created a contrast with *devr* that is parallel to the contrast between the *guṇa*s *raja*s and *tama*s taken together, and *sattva*. *Raja*s applies to the aggressive and competitive disposition of those participating in the animal sacrifice, and by extension, those consuming it. *Tamas*'s associations with death, inactivity, and dissolution in this case apply to both the animal sacrifice and the funerary context.[21]

Although I have limited my scope to the larger ceremonies, it is worth describing some of the commensal and gustatory aspects of one of the smaller ones, *pabm*, short for *doḍpabm*, meaning "big pabm," or *puḷ ācd pabm*, meaning "tipcat-playing pabm." These adjectives distinguish this ceremony from the other (smaller) *pabm*s devoted to sowing and reaping. The Kota word *pabm* is derived from Sanskrit *parvan*, which means festival (DBIA 256). As a "festival" this ceremony is more celebratory, slightly less reverent than *devr*. The central acts of *pabm* involve eating and playing two forms of a game known in English as tipcat (Ko. *puḷ*). A player uses a stick to fling a short length of wood up into the air and then hits it again to knock it forward (see Emeneau 1937–8). The game is competitive, the score kept with a pile of stones. The location of the game and the stones serve as anchor points for a set of ritual ambulations during *devr* (see Map 6: 18, 19).

Pabm is celebrated the month after the god ceremony in Kolmēl. Though less elaborate than *devr*, it belongs in the same "god" ceremonial class, involves some of the same activities of playing, music-making, and dancing, and requires similar purity restrictions and uses of space. During *pabm*, Kotas place special fried cakes (*piṭāṛ*) on the right side of the hearth (*talēl*) to offer them to the household deity. Then, over the course of the day, each Kota eats at least a little bit of rice, *vatm kū* (boiled millet) and *udk* (bean stew) off a communal plate in each house of the village—and then more substantial amounts of food, including ordinary rice, in the houses of close kin. The offering to god, a flat pancake-like *piṭāṛ* made of millet (*āminj*), is slightly different from *piṭāṛ*s made for ordinary guests, which are smaller, more plump, and made of wheat flour. Like Americans during Halloween, Kotas, children especially, walk from house to house, bag in hand, and hoard the sweet cakes for later consumption.

The status of this central food as a fried sweet—a heavy food which tends to cause lethargy—distinguishes it from any food used in *devr* or the *varldāv*. Dr Varadharajan rationalized that one *pabm* ritual is meant to help Kotas digest these oily cakes: in the evening, young men and boys walk back and forth three times across the *pacāl*, chanting "*a hau kau.*" The form of the food as well as its style of consumption support the ceremonial purpose of inviting the deity into the home. As a dessert-like food, the offering engages the deity's gustatory sense. As a heavy, oily food, *piṭāṛ* would tend to make the consumer, god, lethargic and less likely to move away from the house.[22] Through sharing food off the same plate, Kota perform their values of unity and equality in each and every house. Whereas in the god ceremony Kotas attract god to the *guṛyvāl* by locating their performances of unity largely in the village center, during *pabm* Kotas attract god to the household by replicating acts of commensality in each locale.

Let us briefly compare the structure of Kota eating practices to the wider caste context in South India. Depending on their orthodoxy, Hindus in South India consider plates off which food has been eaten or glasses that have been touched by lips to be defiling (Ta. *eccil*). But within a family, a woman should eat off her husband's plate (or leaf). Hence Hindus construct both hierarchy (husband before wife) and mutuality through the medium of *eccil.*[23] A similar principle of hierarchy pertains to the *mundkānōn*, who must drink from a larger vessel than ordinary Kotas. Since Kotas store water in larger vessels and pour them into smaller ones for drinking, the *mundkānōn* prevents himself from being defiled by the *ecl* (spittle—a cognate of *eccil*) of ordinary Kotas by drinking from the larger vessel. This practice also reinforces the spatial extension of the *mundkānōn* as someone who is "big." Kota household members, who are, through their familial closeness, personal extensions of one another, eat off the same plate. Kotas consciously represent this act as an expression of family affection. By formally doing the same in every house of the village, they expand the compass of family or household to incorporate the whole village.

The spatiotemporal unity of this aspect of the ceremony is created by interlocking, the formal joining of complementary components, rather than by centripetal action. Here the complementary components are rather atomized, consisting of each and every village member, rather than, say, affines, or representatives of particular *kērs*. *Pabm* food rituals create unity without centripetence. The other rituals of *pabm*, such as playing *puḷ* (tipcat) in the *guṛyvāl* (temple area), and dancing, however, are centripetal. The domestic rituals in conjunction with the *pacāl* rituals are what give this ceremony spatiotemporal distinctiveness.

Shifting Sands

Pabm provides another case for the study of shift in points of anchor. In the view of the ritual specialist Angārn, of Mēnāṛ, the *kēṛ* that lingers in the village after a year of deaths is not completely removed until Kotas perform *pabm* rituals. Most Kotas tell me the *varldāv* is supposed to perform this very function. Yet Angārn's statement makes historical sense. The sowing ceremony traditionally followed *pabm* in the ritual calendar. In the period in which the sowing ceremony constituted the New Year, *pabm* and not the *varldāv* would have been the final ceremony in the annual cycle and consequently would have been the final opportunity for Kotas to stem the flow of *kēṛ* from one year to the next. So *pabm* once stood in the same relationship to the sowing ceremony as the *varldāv* now does to *devr*. Moreover, Kotas feel the need to remove any lingering animosity and unresolved disputes between individuals in order to prepare for a fecund new year. In addition to actually resolving such differences, Kotas use rituals of commensality to symbolically mediate personal differences. *Pabm*'s extensive rituals of eating together provide a form of closure to the the "open" spacetime of the annual cycle.

The *varldāv*, which has been in considerable flux since it was first described in detail (Mandelbaum 1954), has also provided a form of closure to the annual cycle. Our discussion of food is relevant to the *varldāv*'s changes. The omission of animal sacrifice fueled a new theory of what happens to the soul. The souls of the dead were represented as making a spiritual journey to a place near god where they didn't need buffaloes, rather than making a journey to the land of the dead and living as Kotas do when they are alive (i.e. maintaining herds of cattle). The *varldāv* began to reflect this change through the medium of vegetarian food; Kotas began serving beans rather than meat at *varldāv* feasts.

Affect and Subject

Kota subjectivity can be described in terms of various "spacetimes." Open spacetimes may be suggested by a story's lack of acceptable social resolution or the incompleteness of an action cycle. In either case, open spacetimes invite Kota action to create closure. Such acts of closure may activate feelings of togetherness, satisfaction and purification, or they may precipitate further frustration; they may or may not involve musical acts (and obviously, musical structures themselves may also embody aspects of openness and closure); and they may or may not extend the spatiotemporal compass, or draw attention to the status, of individual or group. Closed spacetimes do not invite acts in quite the same way. When the story is complete, it is merely retold, left for the listener to draw his or her own conclusion. A well-anchored melody can be repeated again, or not; deciding when a piece is finished may require a subtle act of intuition. Kotas begin rituals constituting the yearly cycle once again after a cycle is complete; they do this not because they have to (as one must cope with death) but because they can.[24] Beginning again, "making god," (*devr gicd*) stimulates what Kotas refer to as "bliss" (*ānandm*). This is not fun-and-games but a great deal of hard work, involving physical hardships during the cold season and abstention from easy pleasures of drink and sex. Kotas consciously recreate themselves during the god ceremony; this is a very serious matter indeed.

The next chapter explores the many details of form and symbolism in god ceremonies and funerals which endure despite traceable changes in Kota rituals over the past fifty to seventy years.

CHAPTER 7

Ceremonializing the Self

Kotas, in performing transformative acts in god ceremonial and funerary ceremonies, reconstitute themselves, their gods, and their spirits of the dead. Such transformative acts involve making fire, participating in music and dance, and offering food, gold and silver tokens, and music. Fire holds properties that are ideal for rituals, especially those connected with Kota spiritual ideas, in that it is capable of combining things of different sources (fuel for flames or the flames themselves) into a single entity; and conversely, it can replicate itself (any number of flames) without becoming divided. Most ritually-important fires are made by churning one piece of *vag* root against another, a method called *neyjkōl* (indicated by "nk" in the following ritual descriptions). Matches are used in comparatively less "sacred" instances. Fire is central to the first rituals of the god ceremony, performed on the first Monday after the waxing crescent moon in December–January. Ritual locations marked (+) appear in Map 4; those marked (‡) appear in Map 6 below.

Devr: The Kota God Ceremony

Day 1 (Monday) "Passing of the waxing crescent moon day" (per gayc nāḷ): The ceremony always begins on a Monday, a day reserved for god. Each of the two *mundkānōns* produces fire (nk) in his house and uses it to light a more substantial fire in the center of the nearby raised circle of stones, called *tondiṭ* (+). Using a torch from the *tondiṭ* fire, each then lights his kitchen hearth and bows to worship the divine part of it (the *talēl*). This new, god-ceremonial fire is used to cook all the food consumed by *mundkānōns* in their houses during the ceremony. The *mundkānōns* then ritually clean and sanctify their houses using special plants (see Wolf 1997a).

Map 6: Kolmēl Village, Areas of Central Importance During *Devr*

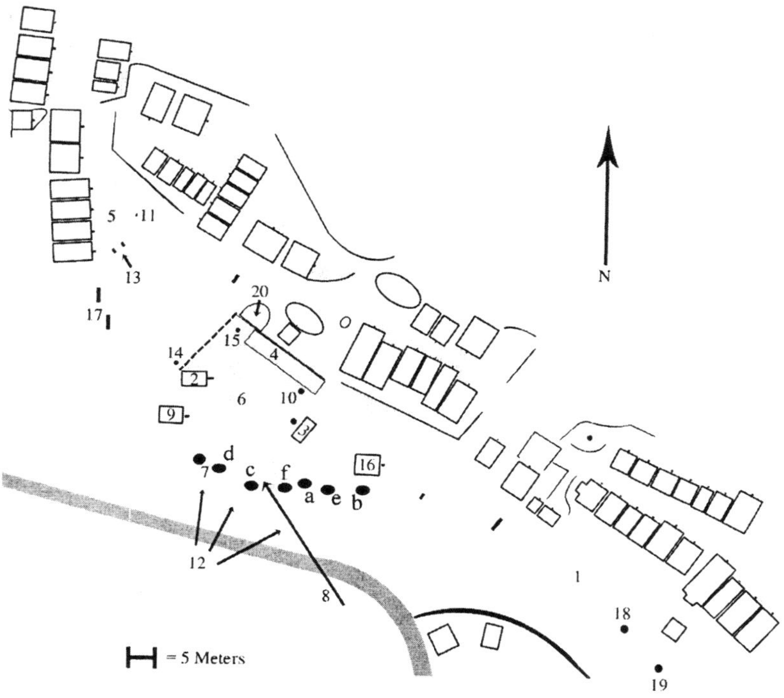

1. *ākēr pacāl*, eastern part of *pacāl* above *ākēr*
2. *amnōr* temple
3. *aṛcāyḷ* for *mundkānōns*, with fire in front
4. *aṛcāyḷ* for ordinary villagers
5. bonfire in center of *gagvāl*
6. bonfire in temple area (*guṛyvāl*)
7. bonfire southeast of *doḍaynōr* temple
8. cane and bamboo (*vet* and *vedyr*) ritual: three men enter village from fields in direction of arrow; then all men, in order of seniority, face east and bow before the cane and bamboo
9. *doḍaynōr* temple
10. *doḍ tic* ("big fire") also called *devr* (god)
11. fire at edge of *gagvāl*
12. food preparation areas: (a) common area for *udk* (stew), one clay pot per family; (b) *vatm* millet for *ākēr* except Puccan's family; (c) *vatm* millet for *gagēr*; (d) *mundkānōns*' and *tērkārns*' food; (e) *vatm* for Puccan's family; (f) *vatm* for *korykēr*
13. *gagvāl* entrance
14. heap where procession of women deposits firewood
15. house of erected post fire (*kab iṭ pay tic* or *kun tic*), near *tak* tree
16. *kunaynōr* temple
17. *naṭkal* (meeting stones)
18. *puḷ ācd eṛm* (place for playing game of *puḷ*)
19. stones for keeping score when playing *puḷ* during *pabm*
20. *tak* tree

The rest of the villagers clean and purify their houses using branches from the *tak* tree (‡) near the *pacāl* and light their hearths using the *tondiṭ* flame nearest their houses. These fires trace their source to *mundkānōns*' houses and embody corresponding village deities, which inhabit stick-bundles in a back room called the *kakuy*. With god now present in each home, villagers are prohibited from engaging in sex or consuming meat or alcohol for the ceremony's duration. Out of respect for god, and to prevent contact with defilement, *mundkānōns* and *tērkārns* are enjoined from leaving the village; other villagers may leave only to collect provisions (or, if necessary, to attend their jobs).

Following this fire ritual, Kotas would formerly have begun forging new iron temple ornaments in a primitive smithy located in each temple, but by 1958 they had shifted this activity to their blacksmith shops. Now the temples are permanent and so are the ornaments affixed atop (see photo section). The memory of the primitive smithy is now represented in each temple by three stones, the only objects in a Kota temple other than an oil lamp. No activity other than lamp-lighting and praying (briefly) takes place in the temple nowadays, and at that, only once a year during the god ceremony.

Day 3 (*Wednesday*) "*Fire-lighting day*" (tic iṭ nāḷ): At about 8:00 p.m. the village men assemble at the *gagvāl*. A man living in the "house of the erected post" (*kab iṭ pay* +) produces a flame in his house. This man, who is ordinarily a direct descendant of the village founder, uses this flame to build a small fire at the edge (‡) of the *gagvāl*, and then transfers the flame to a location near the *pacāl tak* tree where he builds a third fire, called the "small fire" (*kun tic*) or the "house of the erected post fire" (*kab iṭ pay tic*) (‡). This fire, made with matches, does not contain, or serve as a conduit for, divinity.

Next, while women remain in their houses and refrain from watching, men gather at the *doḍmundkānōn*'s house. He carries out a twig-bundle (*kaṇk*) torch, lit from his hearth (still burning from Monday's ritual). This flame is the medium through which, Kotas say, "god comes." Walking carefully around the village (he may not travel on common footpaths now) he carries the flame to a special spot on the *pacāl*, near the place a canopy (*aṛcāyḷ* ‡) will later be erected for men to sleep. Here he lights a new fire, called the "big fire" (*doḍtic* ‡) or simply "god" (*devr*). The actual size of the fire is small, however. Out of respect for god, the fire should remain attended by at least one of the *mundkānōn*s throughout the ceremony. Communal praying in the temple area follows. Ideally, the *tērkārn* will "shake [as a] vehicle [of god]" (*tēr oṛto*): "god comes" (*dēr vadṭo*) to him and gives divine words (*vākm*). A man then takes a flame from the "house of the erected post fire" (*kab iṭ pay tic*), which is still burning in the temple area, to start a new bonfire in the center (‡) of the *gagvāl*. Once the fire is lit, men play *ōmayṇ*, loudly sounding all instruments at once, and then dance.

Neighboring villagers know from the sound not to enter Kolmēl at night during the ceremony and that they are invited to the penultimate "dance day." The dance *koḷ*s played on the *gagvāl* are short and contextually unmarked in that they can be performed for virtually any ceremony or demonstration. They contrast with the special dance tunes played later in the ceremony on the *pacāl*. These tunes are generally longer and are not supposed to be played in any other context. The first three dances, *kālgūcāṭ*, *tiruganāṭ*, and *koynāṭ*, do not vary in form. The melody accompanying the dance varies according to whether it is played in the *gagvāl* or the *pacāl*. The "leg joining dance" (*kālgūcāṭ*) is danced first in any sequence, perhaps because it helps synchronize the dancers.

Since *mundkānōn*s cannot dance in the *gagvāl*, they stand or kneel with the *tērkārn*s to the left of the *gagvāl* entrance (‡) and watch. If the *tērkārn* gets possessed he will join in dancing and *koḷ* players will take this as a cue to play the *temāng* melody, said to be one of the gods' favorites. Men, in turn, bare their chests and dance, tying their shawls (*varāṛ*s) around their waists. Stereotypically, the possessed *tērkārn* will use his bare hands to pick up hot coals from the fire and strew them about.

After dancing, men discuss village issues, attempt to resolve conflicts, assign tasks among themselves and divide up expenses for the ceremony. This night ritual constitutes a firm sense of "beginning": from this day forward men are not supposed to clean their own plates after eating—women must do so. As the ceremony deepens, gender roles become intensified and men must avoid all forms of defilement because they are now closer to god—even their own leftover food becomes polluting.

Day 4 (Thursday): Rituals are performed much as the evening before.

This night, the *naṛykēr mundkānōn* takes fire from his house, accompanied by village men and out of women's sight. He adds this flame to the "big" fire on the *pacāl*, thus reinforcing the connection between the three village gods, the village center, the two *mundkānōn*s' houses and hearths, and the hearths of every household in the village. Men build the *gagvāl* bonfire once again using the "house of the erected post fire" (*kab iṭ pay tic*) which is still burning in the temple area. On this night women also dance on the *pacāl*, following the men.

Day 5 (*Friday*): During the day, older women perform menstrual seclusion for "ritual's sake" (*cātrtk*) in the lower part of the village (+) so that they can, in name, participate in the *pacāl* rituals beginning on Sunday. The ritual of fire-lighting and dancing on the *gagvāl* takes place as it did the night before.

Day 6 (*Saturday*): Younger women perform the seclusion ritual until evening when they hear the *kob*, which the men use to announce they've completed their "channel-clearing" ritual of bathing, clearing debris from the water channel, and offering a ring to the river goddess. While on procession, musicians play the *aṇviṛcd koḷ* or "channel-clearing tune," made up of sections from the temple-opening tune. At the water channel, men invite god by uttering "*ōḷy ōḷy*." Then they collect *valāry* (*Dodonea viscosa*) stalks for cleaning their yards later. Returning to the village, they chant "*a hau kau*." Since the *toḍbāl* tree is on the processional route, the men stop to pray there as well.

Upon their return, men (except the *mundkānōn*s and *tērkārn*s) dance the three first ritual dances in the *gagvāl* and then go home, placing the *valāry* stalks they had just collected in a raised place, so as not to touch the ground. After eating dinner, men and women proceed to the *gagvāl* and dance late into the night.

If the village is in need of a *tērkārn* or *munkānōn* post to be filled, the men will be particularly fastidious in their adherence to their ritual prescriptions: growing their hair a bit, bathing in the icy water during the channel-cleaning. God might, they know, choose them. One Saturday evening of the god ceremony I sat hunched at the edge of the grassy *pacāl* with S. Raman. Though Raman belongs to the *tērkārn kuyt* (the family from which one of the *tērkārn*s is selected), he did not expect to be summoned as *tērkārn*. "God knows," Raman said, "the village needs me to play *koḷ*." The *mundkānōn*s and *tērkārn*s are not supposed to play musical instruments.

Day 7 (Sunday) Temple-Opening Day (guṛy terdd nāḷ): The rituals of this day are extensive and complex. The *mundkānōns*, followed by the rest of the villagers, clean their *kavāls* (packed mud yards) using dung water and *valāry* stalks collected the day before. All gather at the temples and, in descending rank, men wash themselves and a few coin-shaped precious metal offerings at the nearby, more ritually pure tap (+). They offer units of three such "coins" (*paṇm*). Outsiders follow suit.

Then follows one of the most important ritual sequences. Men walk silently to the *pevāy* (+), where spring water once entered the village from the hill channels cleaned the day before (now water enters through pipes). Men shoo away passers-by on the nearby road; women stay out of sight. Each *mundkānōn* then ties a knot in his forehair. This knot, called *vāraṇm* or *mumuṛy*, is said to contain god. Out of respect for god, the *mundkānōns* and those nearby speak softly and refrain from making noise (except for musical offerings) for the remainder of the ceremony.

With god brought to the *pacāl* via the fires and the *mundkānōns*' hair, the *mundkānōns* unbolt the iron gates of each temple in turn, *doḍayṇōr*, *kunayṇōr*, and *amnōr* (‡). For each, the men stand in front (some women watch from a distance) and pray fervently. The *mundkānōns* ask if everyone has "joined;" the men respond in the affirmative. They hope that a *tērkārn* will speak or that god will pick a new medium. The *mundkānōns* at this time (and earlier, when coins were being offered) intone the following in alternation

(1) oṭḷkōm cōymgūḷ devr dēvāydgūḷ	We will do [the needful, i.e. rituals etc., even though we may have erred in the past], gods!
(2) kaṭḷkōm cōymgūḷ devr dēvāydgūḷ	We will learn [and obey], gods!

At times the utterances are short. The *mundkānōns* simply say "oṭḷkōm cōymgūḷ" and the men repeat with intensity; or one man spontaneously leads with this phrase and the rest answer. In the midst of this, a *tērkārn* may tremble, then run and place his hands on one of the stone pillars fronting the temple. Kotas used to rethatch the temple around these more lasting, anchoring pillars.[1] Now, since the temples are permanent, the special status of these pillars emerges only at key ritual moments. In preparation for the god ceremony, the *tērkārn*, or would-be *tērkārn*, grows his hair long enough to tie it with a strand of thread, inserting a small ball called *ceṇḍ*.[2] "True" possession occurs when the shaking person agitates the ball out of his now-loosed hair and speaks the words (*vākm*) of god. In the old days each man kept a *ceṇḍ* in his tuft; now most wear short hair and keep a *ceṇḍ* on a thread underneath their shirts. In about 2000, when the present *tērkārn*, Sivakumaran, first began to shake with the power of god, he silently motioned for someone to tie a *ceṇḍ* for him. Duryodhana, standing nearby, took a *ceṇḍ* from B. Murugan and tied it tightly in the short growth on the back of Sivakumaran's head.

The sequence of temple-opening, prayer, and possession is repeated at each temple, then a new fire is made (nk) on the *pacāl*; a flame from it is transported with a torch of *kaṇk* twigs to light a bonfire just southeast of the *doḍaynōr* temple (‡). The instrumentalists now gather; the *mundkānōn*s first face east and ask, "Shall I beat the *ērdabaṭk?*" After the men respond affirmatively, *mundkānōn*s begin to strike it, *koḷ* players play the temple-opening tune, and other men sound the *kob* loudly in cascading pairs. The dramatic verbal lead-up, and the intermittent drum and *kob* articulations, help constitute the *ōmayṇ* as a significant, high-level anchor in the ceremony: it makes audible the fact that the god ceremony has proceeded into the next major structural section. The actions that follow further articulate this anchoring moment. Male members of the village step up in order of seniority and beat the *ērdabaṭk*; *mundkānōn*s chase away evil forces and impurities from the temples by waving censers in front of them.[3] Meanwhile, women, who have cleaned the *vatm* millet to be consumed during the ceremony, have begun boiling water in their houses. As soon as they hear the *kob*, they drop the millet into the boiling water.[4]

Then the *mundkānōn*s, with men following behind, paste dung on the right pillar of each temple. The dung comes from the special "god given" cow (iconic of the *kārāv*), which the *mundkānōn*s keep in their private pen/milking sheds. On each dung-patty they paste flat, coin-shaped, precious-metal offerings called *paṭm*. The "coin-offering tune" (*paṭm kac koḷ*), underscores this action. Together, the activities surrounding the temple pillar (*kab*) structurally replicate, intensify and make centripetal, the earlier activities at the "house of the erected post"—the site of another pillar, which is, mentally, at least, also permanent.

Following this, men enter the temples one by one for only a few seconds—the only time anyone enters the temples all year. *Koḷ* players play the temple-opening tune and, processing from one temple to the other, lead the men who chant "*ōḷy ōḷy*." The music stops at about noon. Until about 5:00 p.m., villagers perform ceremonial chores: cleaning the remaining ornaments and arranging them on the dung-patties; spreading out boiled millet to dry; and erecting two canopies (*aṛcāyḷ*), one for the *mundkānōns* and one for the rest of the people (‡). Villagers who have not had the time to eat do so now. In this period of unscheduled time, the less-experienced may pound on drums and practice appropriate *koḷs*.

Three specially selected men start out for the forest, where they collect cane and bamboo (*vet* and *vedyr*) to memorialize the bygone practice of temple-rethatching. Although the temple-opening tune is sometimes used to usher the men back into the village (e.g. as in 2001, see CD 1), the *aṇviṛcd koḷ* ("channel-clearing tune") is supposed to be played, according to Puccan. Either way, the *koḷ* players create a musical link among the rituals of temple opening, temple rethatching, and channel cleaning. The "post-cutting tune" (*kab ercd koḷ*) was once played for the ritual as well, according to Puccan, since a wooden post is also brought back with the cane and bamboo.[5] Now the post-cutting tune is played as one of the twelve *devr koḷs*. The three men return to the village and lay the cane and bamboo in a row on the grass; all men, in order of seniority, worship before them (‡). All the men then perform the first dances—at least three of them—in the temple area (*guṛyvāl*); the first dance, *kāl gūc āṭ*, is accompanied by a special *koḷ* for that place and time. For the first time, *mundkānōns* and *tērkārns* dance together with the men.

If this simple ritual telescopes the primary, and most arduous, task the men once had to fulfill for the god ceremony in former times—the annual rebuilding of the temple—the ritual that follows stereotypes women's roles in Kota society generally as attractive mates and providers of cooking fuel. In this "depositing wood-loads ritual," women carry heavy loads of specially collected firewood for the following days' feasts in a procession (north-west across the *guṛyvāl*) and deposit them behind the *amnōr* (goddess) temple in a heap (‡). Older women, who visibly strain under the weight, are helped along by kind male relatives or friends. The *aṇviṛcd koḷ* is once again the preferred melody for this ritual, according to Puccan. Following this, women tie their white clothing in a special manner (knot on shoulder and waist tied tight) and dance their first dances on the *guṛyvāl*, once again three dances at a minimum, to special *koḷs* for this occasion. Kotas sometimes invite friends to witness this much acclaimed dance. Women must don precious jewelry, even if they have to borrow it from neighbors and relatives, for the aim is to please god with a beautiful "show." Ideally this ritual is completed before dark (by 6:00 or 7:00 p.m.) so that its beauty is visible in daylight.

Again accompanied by *koḷ* players, who perform the temple–opening tune, *mundkānōns* round the three temples, this time going to the side together and throwing thatch on each temple roof. At these moments *koḷ* players insert the high-tessitura Section G of the temple-opening tune. Whereas the earlier ritual of entering the village with cane and bamboo recalled the collection of materials for temple rebuilding, this ritual signifies the rebuilding process itself. This is virtually the only instance in which the physical and moral dimensions of height are signified iconically by the high tessitura of a melody. The moment is clearly an important one.

Another period of unscheduled activity, which includes eating dinner, follows. Boys of twelve to sixteen years old make a cacophonous racket by practicing any suitable *koḷ* as they form a procession and demand at least five bundles of firewood from each household for the dancing-bonfire later at night. At about 9:00 p.m., some assemble near the public *aṛcāyḷ* (‡) to listen to the suite of twelve *devr koḷs*. Puccan used to play these god tunes in order and call out their names.[6] Playing them as a suite draws together their indexically related associations with stories, rituals and deities, and brings Kotas closer to their gods, whom they believe are present, listening.

An elder sitting in the *aṛcāyḷ* calls roll of all the adult male members of the village. Following this, the oldest man in the family/lineage (*kuyt*) to which Duryodhana belongs takes a flame from the *doḍtic* and uses it to make a bonfire in the temple area (‡). Dancing, which goes on late into the night, begins now—men followed by women (who tie their dress in a different manner, now with the waist loose). At around 2:00 a.m. the women retire to their houses and able-bodied men sleep outside under the canopy.

Day 8 (Monday): Many of Sunday's rituals are repeated: tossing thatch atop the temples, pasting "coins" on the temple pillars, worshiping at each temple (women do so as well on this day). Following the *ōmayṇ* (using the temple-opening tune), men and women dance with their respective ritual leaders. The first morning men's dance is performed to a melody reserved for this occasion.

Much of the day is spent preparing ritual meals, called *ūṭm*. The spatial orientation of the food preparation reflects kinship and ritual hierarchy: each *kuyt* (family/lineage) prepares boiled millet (*vatm kū*) in its own designated cooking spot; these spots are further organized by *kēr*. Hence the millet-preparation areas for the *kuyts* of Puccan and S. Raman/ Duryodhana are right next to one another, just as their respective rows of houses are organized in *talkēr* (‡). The salted bean stew (*udk*) is prepared in a common area for all *kēr*s. The *mundkānōn*s and *tērkārn*s prepare their own millet and stew in a separate area (‡). The measures of millet that were cleaned, boiled, and threshed in each house individually are cooked in their respective cooking areas and then mixed together in a large heap under a small tent (*aḍguy*) erected near the *mundkānōn*s' "big" *arcāyḷ*. When the cooked millet is dumped together in a heap, the *koḷ* players must play the "offering tune" (*eṛ vecd koḷ*), and the *kob*s play loudly.

Then all the villagers make offerings to god via the *mundkānōn*s and walk to each temple to pray (*parcvd*). While walking they intone "*ōḷy ōḷy*" and the musicians play the temple-opening tune. As soon as everyone has finished praying at the three temples, young men and boys chant "*a hau kau*" and walk three times back and forth between the meeting stones (*naṭkal* +‡) and the location of the ritual game of tipcat played at the *pabm* festival (*puḷ ācd eṛm* ‡) at opposite ends of the *pacāl*; younger ones circle around a clump of stones used to keep score in that game (‡); and still others race.

Following these activities, the specially-prepared millet for the ritualists is served to the principal male and female ritualists (*mundkānōn*s, *mundakānōḷ*s, *tērkārns*, *tērkārc*s) and their young children; and later to elders and important men of the village. Next a serving of cooked millet is offered to god on a type of leaf called *giviṇḍ el*, said to be the Kota plate in days of yore. The musicians play the "offering tune" (*eṛ vecd koḷ*) once again. The millet for the rest of the village, having all been mixed together, is then redistributed to a woman from each household; the women sit in lines, waiting with large baskets used for this purpose.

The importance of the food preparation and serving is marked by its formality: the "grain mixers" belong to one family (*kuyt*), that of Raman and Duryodhana, the "grain servers" belong to another, that which lives on *korykēr*, the "grain carriers" who transport the grain from the common heap to the serving area belong to another family, that of Puccan, and those who ladle out the stew belong to yet another family, the "big" *mundkānōn*'s family, which lives on *gagēr*. Thus the entire process of preparing and serving food at the god ceremony is a complex one in which the various divisions of family, residence, and ritual office interlock.

The "offering tune" is played while the grain from all the families is mixed together and redistributed. Many villagers then sit on the temple grounds and eat off of banana leaves (formerly *giviṇḍ el*). Others eat in their houses. The grain taken home is eaten for other meals as well.

Later, musicians begin to play the twelve *devr koḷ*s and the rest of the villagers begin to assemble. Men build a bonfire, then men and women dance into the night. If the feast is three days long, the events are repeated. On the third night (or this night if it is a one-day feast[7]), the dancing ends with a special women's dance, accompanied by the "coin removing tune" (*paṭm erykd koḷ*), which is considered both a god tune and a sad tune because it signals the ceremony's end. While this tune is being performed, the *mundkānōn*s remove precious metal offerings and dung from the temple pillars and rub the pillars with clarified butter. They do this in darkness, reflecting the sadness of the occasion, the idea that the gods are departing. The term *erykd*, used for the action of removing, actually means "to take down a heavy load." Using this verb rather than such descriptively more accurate ones as "take off" or "unstick" reflects the seriousness of the action: the precious metal offerings are symbolically "heavy" and "high up." The importance of the ritual as a whole combined with the genre-boundary status of the associated tune contribute to making this ritual a high-level anchor within the god ceremony.

Day 9 or 11 (*Tuesday or Thursday*) *"Dance Day"* (āṭ nāḷ): In the morning, as villagers begin to assemble in the eastern part of the *pacāl* above *ākēr* (+‡), *koḷ* players play the *devr koḷ*s perfunctorily, a minimum of three. Dancing begins and visitors arrive from other villages. The Badagas from the nearby village Sogatore, with whom Kota continue to maintain close relations, and other special visitors, such as the Collector of Ooty, are welcomed into the village formally with *pērn koḷ*s. The dancing ground opens up and at least one dance consists largely of Badagas. Kotas then dance a few special dances in which young men take turns wearing a few fancy-dance dresses (*āṭkupāc*; see photo section) then they change to street clothes and dance again, which signals the beginning of one of the final structural sections. Women conclude the *ākēr pacāl* activities by performing god songs—men nowadays tend to accompany them on cymbals and drums. Afterward, villagers proceed westward toward the temple area led by the musicians, who play several "canopy-disassembling tunes" (*aṛcāyḷ piṛcd koḷ*). Men play the *kob*, chant "*a hau kau*," energetically take down the canopies, and head to the *gagvāl* for a final set of dances.

Day 10 or 12 (Wednesday or Friday) "Song day" (pāṭ nāḷ): In the afternoon, women gather in the *gagvāl* to sing songs for three to four hours; then they play games and tell jokes. The ceremony formally ends when several young people dress up in ferns and dance around, allegedly to ward off evil influence. Nowadays, Kotas broadcast recorded music, act in skits and perform dances into the evening. These activities are perhaps transformations of earlier practices of burlesquing Toda buffalo fights (Emeneau 1944-46: IV, 294–5).

Following this, in earlier times, the men secretly used to take the god-infused bundles of shafts, silver arrowheads and bamboo bows from the *mundkānōns*' *kakuys* and wash them at the *toḍbāl*. They would then shoot an arrow north to commemorate the still earlier practice of shooting a bison, which, according to Kota belief, the gods used to send to the *toḍbāl* every year at this time. All these rituals were once accompanied by the "hunting-god tune" (*vēṭkār cōym koḷ*). This tune, part of the twelve *devr koḷ* suite, now commemorates both bygone practices and bygone commemorations. It also, in a more diffuse way, indexes tribalness through the "hunting" theme.

Music and Spacetime in the God Ceremony

To summarize our main points:[8] Special musical pieces, forms of significant sound, and silences of various lengths qualitatively highlight the ceremony's structural sections, which are both spatiotemporal and social. The progression from male to female, found at macro and micro levels of the god ceremony, reflects the order of most complex Kota ceremonies and articulates a more general hierarchy of the genders in time and three-dimensional space.

Activities gradually move from the domestic periphery of the village to the divinely saturated center, and then back out again. Kotas experience this inward movement as emotional and devotional intensification. Movement toward the center is accompanied by increased kinship differentiation through the assignment of ritual tasks; this spatiotemporal interlocking generates a kind of organic solidarity. A unity of what Kotas understand to constitute sameness—mechanical solidarity—is also important in drawing together those who are not ritual leaders; it is articulated by the use of identical forms of dress (for each gender), the eating of identical food, dancing communally, and the sharing of fire.

Intensification involves a qualitative and quantitative change in musical repertoire from common, relatively context-free (or little-marked) dance pieces, most of which are short in length, to ritually-specific pieces used for particular actions or sets of related actions or for dances defined by time and place rather than by style. The more important among these are often longer and considered "big," like the divine fire and respected personages. Silence too is marked as compared with ordinary noises of talking, singing, or playing the radio or tv. Although the logical property of silence is absence of sound, silence in contexts I have discussed is performed as a ritual act and is associated with presence (god) rather than absence.

Movement toward the center involves divinity in several ways: calling gods to the center by playing the twelve *devr koḷ*s; transporting fire from *mundkānōn*s' houses; villagers and outsiders making offerings in the temple area; and Kota men and women ushering-in forest products. The status of such flora is ambiguous when the plants are still a part of the forest. The forest is a place of death and uncertainty as well as a place where god originally helped Kotas by teaching them "tribal" survival skills. The ambiguity is clarified by the context in which these products are used in ritual and by the musical piece that ushers and announces the arrival of these products into the village.

The temple rebuilding is emphasized musically in two other contexts (both repeated several times): throwing thatch on the temple roofs and performing the "post-cutting tune" in the twelve *devr koḷ* suite. This process of converting ambiguous forest products into a house for the divine instantiates the ceremony's central function of making god (*dev gicd*).

Centripetence on a larger, moral scale, follows from the idea that god is hidden, absent, and away in the fields (while paradoxically residing in *mundkānōn*s' houses) during most of the year and returns to the village center during the god ceremony. The return of all villagers to the village and their commitment to remain there and demonstrate unity both constitutes divinity (in a rather Durkheimian fashion) and attracts god toward the center. The spacetime created in the god ceremony is intersubjective through the form of Kota actions and the transactions that Kotas make corporately or individually with their gods. Human togetherness or unity is both a form of action and an offering to god. God ceremonial spacetime is thus a model for everyday life. Because Kotas (like all humans) experience arguments, dishonesty, and distress, they "perform" a periodic societal reharmonization each time they "make god."[9]

In the 1990s, the center of the village was cordoned off, the temples locked and empty, and the god tunes avoided during non-god ceremonial times of the year. (Minor exceptions were the rain ceremony and Kōjkāl *devr*, which are similar in spirit to *devr*.) At such times, the center becomes a void, a vacuum that, desiring filling, animates time and space and focuses group identity. The absence of god in the center thus generates a potential for centripetal spacetime—an open spacetime—every hour of every day, no matter what the ritual status of the village with regard to the number of *mundkānōn*s or *tērkārn*s, the advent of death and defilement, or the disunity created by interpersonal disagreements. In this respect, the empty center is situationally equivalent to the old Kotagiri village and lost Kurgōj villagers: in each case, Kotas satisfy perennial yearnings by traveling and/or conducting rituals.

Pac Tāv and Varldāv: The Green and Dry Funerals

Kotas expel three things from the village in their funerary ceremonies: the corpse, the defilement and ill effects of death, and the soul. Kota movement patterns, music-making, ways of using fire, and ways of processing and consuming food in funerals all contribute to a broadly centrifugal form of spacetime characteristic of funerals. In funerals, unlike in god ceremonies, Kotas pay a great deal of attention to the identity of the individual (deceased). This is a correlate of centrifugality. Seen in this way, as Kotas move away from the center, they become individualized. At the conclusions of both the *pac tāv* (green funeral, i.e. initial cremation) and *varldāv* (dry funeral), however, Kotas phenomenologically and morally reverse direction in order to return to normalcy:

villagers must eventually return to their villages and re-establish their communities as wholes. Another correlate of individuation is the spatiotemporal process of interlock: as individuals and categories of individuals are articulated, they are simultaneously reintegrated as parts of a complementary whole. The *pac tāv* illustrates most of these points and is presented in some detail first. The *varldāv*, which is far longer and more complicated, will then be summarized briefly, with attention devoted to thematic and musical relationships between the two ceremonies.[10]

The *Pac Tāv*

In the 1990s and 2000s, all the green funeral ceremonies have generally been completed within a day or two of a death. The rituals begin in the moments preceding death, during which the dying person will be brought to the central room (*kuḍl*) to die. At the moment of death, a small gold coin called "mouth money" and a small amount of husked millet are placed in the mouth. This practice is transformative in that it "must cause life to go" (*jiv ōkcrbōṛo*), in the words of K. Caḷn; some have said that it provides the soul food and money for safe passage to the other world. Duryodhana thought it a token of respect for the deceased. A small amount of barley broth (*kaj*) may be given to those in their final agonies, for it is believed to help them die.[11]

Villagers prepare the corpse for removal from the house by shutting its eyes, stretching the arms along the body, and tying the jaw shut. Clothing and adornments of the corpse have varied historically, often reflecting a spirit of celebration. Important now are a set of cloths laid on the dressed corpse: a new white cloak (*varāṛ*), a red- or green-colored shawl, a loosely woven cloth, and a black-and-white striped cloth (*ārakm*). The death is announced only after the corpse is dressed. Men begin entering the house and bowing to pay their respects to it.

A man of no special qualification bares his right shoulder, faces east, and beats the *ērdabaṭk* with two thin sticks to formally announce the death. Two men then sound the *kob* to proclaim the death more loudly. A man brings a firebrand from the deceased person's hearth to the *kavāl* (packed mud yard fronting the house) and builds a fire. This fire mediates the sustenance of life in the home and the destruction of the corpse after death; it is structurally (but not in meaning) analogous to the fire on the *tondiṭ* carried from the *mundkānōn*'s hearth at the beginning of the god ceremony. After the drummers tauten the heads of the *par* and *tabaṭk* near the fire, all the musicians begin to perform, sometimes sitting or standing outside, other times sitting in the verandah of the bereaved house.

Individuals will set out to inform other villages, sometimes by telephone. In the old days, if an important person died, fellow villagers would have been waiting up to three days for mourners to arrive from other villages. Someone would remain beside the corpse with a lit oil lamp keeping vigil the whole time. The spacetime of arrival, which was connected to the status of the deceased, has for obvious reasons contracted in modern times. The spatiotemporal structure of the event has remained: three successive kinds of call (drum, horn, *koḷ* ensemble), one short and not extending into surrounding space, the second short and extensive, the third ongoing and extensive. This is followed by physical and electronic forms of extension. In response to the appropriate call, mourners arrive gradually, first from nearby and then from further away.

A few men take the corpse out of the house during the daytime after enough mourners have arrived. Before this, however, a bier and catafalque (*gurykaṭ*) must be constructed and elaborated in proportion to the status of the deceased. *Gurykaṭ*s are shorter, with fewer "stories" (*kōl*) than they once had because their height presents a serious hazard with electrical wires. A group of men hoists the corpse and carries it out the door to the bier, which is then positioned under the catafalque. The musicians play the "corpse crossing-over tune" (*tāv kaṛtd koḷ*) at this important moment of transition. The tune is common to all Kota villages. As the corpse is taken out, the "fire-grasping boy" (*tic pac mog*) ritually cleans its path using a ball of cow dung inserted with an odd number of *nakarg* grass (*Andropogon foulkesii*) blades.[12] He then discards the ball away from human contact.

The body and bier are brought to a ritually "high" part of the *kēr*, the *gagvāl* in *gagēr*, or the area in front of Puccan's house in *ākēr*. The musicians will then play a minimum of three dance melodies, which are selected from the relatively context-free repertoire of short dance tunes, not from the ritually-specific repertoire used for the *pacāl*. Men dance around the bier. Some Kotas find the dances sad; others see them as expressions of respect; and still others see them as joyful, embodying a cheerful reminiscence of the deceased person's dancing when he or she was alive (Wolf 2001). In former times, men then selected buffaloes for sacrifice. Musicians played a "buffalo-calling tune" (*im āt koḷ*) to calm the buffaloes while another man called each sacrificial buffalo by its own personal name; the appropriate buffalo would come when called and its horns were marked with clarified butter (Wolf 1997a, 250).

Following this, without musical accompaniment, women wash the corpse behind a canopy. At about the same time, if the deceased is a man, the widow's female relatives feed her freshly prepared homemade rice on a new clay plate (*pat*) and assist her as she walks out of the house, washes herself, and breaks the plate. This ritual now signifies the end of dietary mourning restrictions.

Throughout the funeral, mourners pay respect to the deceased by bowing over the corpse and touching their heads to the colored cloths placed upon it. Women generally huddle around the corpse and near its head, weeping copiously. Men come and go, but tend to show their emotions less.

On the *kavāl*, some men shout "*a hau kau*" encouragingly. *Koḷ* players render *pērn koḷ*s for the men's *pērn* ritual of rice offering; women perform the ritual of delivering baskets of roasted grains. The grain, emptied into baskets under the bier, is burned with other items which are believed to be useful to the deceased in and on the way to the other world; and which, more basically, reinforce the idea that such a world exists. Grain cremated with the corpse references for Kotas a former way of life and a bygone set of agricultural methods that encode "tradition." The broader range of foodstuffs includes: two kinds of barley, amaranth, raw sugar, fried, sweet wheat cakes, and any other favorite food (e.g. Milk Bikis biscuits) of the deceased. Later, dry-roasted millet (*pacayk*) is tied into the right corner of the *varāṛ*.

The practice of cremating the corpse with a favorite food is part of a larger pattern of identity differentiation in funerary ritual. Metonymic items of male everyday life are found under a man's bier, for example a walking stick, ax, knife, cattle-driving stick, *bugīr*, or *pulāng*. The *koḷ*, which is passed down materially from generation to generation, is not cremated with the corpse. For a woman, cremated items include a pestle, winnowing basket, rice measure, and favorite jewelry. These materials index aspects of the dead person's uniqueness, gender, or status in the community. Once all these items are in place, and enough mourners have arrived the funeral procession is ready to begin.

An odd-numbered group of men lifts the bier and proceeds behind the musicians. The fire-grasping boy carries coals in a clay pot tied to the end of a short pole. He had collected these symbolically important coals from the *kavāl* fire, which originated from the dead person's hearth. Women, carrying items from under the bier, trail behind. Male relatives carry the widow but a widower is expected to walk. The *koḷ* for removing the corpse from the house is played again when the bier is lifted. Then musicians audibly mark the beginning of a new ritual stage by playing the "corpse lifting and going tune" (*tāv tuykr ōybd koḷ*) when the procession starts.

Men carry the corpse to an intermediate place, the *nelāgōṛ* (+), at the edge of Kolmēl village, beyond which women do not continue in the funeral. While the widow and several men perform rituals, the musicians play a special *koḷ* named for this place as well as others according to their tastes. The fire-grasping boy dispassionately ties together the big toes of the deceased (later, on the funeral ground, he cuts them free with a knife). Meanwhile, a significant display of sadness prevails as the male relatives of the mourning widow strip her of her jewelry, which is symbolically returned to the dead spouse. The widow leaves her hair untied. Although subject to a variety of interpretations, the form of these rituals strongly suggests the release of bonds, both those of marriage and of mortal existence itself.

Bovine Sacrifices

The cow sacrifice, discontinued in the late 1930s or early 1940s, once fulfilled a similar function. One Kota interpretation was that the sacrificial cow absorbed the sins of its owner.

The fire-grasping boy ritually initiated the sacrifice, but a more experienced man actually killed the cow, thereby releasing the soul from the weight of the ill deeds the person may have performed when alive. The formal principle of ritually initiating an action and then carrying it out more effectively—as when the *ērdabaṭk*'s soft sound is followed by the penetrating sound of the *kob*—is shot through Kota ceremonial life. The deliberateness with which Kotas sometimes begin actions marks those beginnings as anchor points.

The fire-grasping boy then placed an *ārakm* cloth on the cow's belly. This kind of black-and-white cloth, which had also been placed on the corpse, served as a sign vehicle for the identity relationship between the cow and the deceased. In the vocabulary of ritual eating, the cow was distinguished from the buffalo. The Kotas could not eat themselves, so to speak, so the cow carcass was given to Scheduled Caste persons. Kotas ate the meat only of the sacrificial buffaloes. In the vocabulary of ritual music, the two were not distinguished: the same "buffalo-calling tune" used for both the cow and buffalo sacrifice served a generically "bovine-sacrificial" function.

Sulli fought to discontinue bovine sacrifices in the late 1930s when David Mandelbaum and Murray Emeneau were conducting research. The cow sacrifice was abandoned first because the cow became increasingly identified with god, as it is in Hindu traditions. Yet the cow could also be interpreted as a vehicle for divinity rather than an embodiment of it. The sacrificial cow that absorbed the sins of its owner, then, complemented the *mundkānōn*'s cow, which was then as it is now a sign of village fecundity, providing milk for the milk ceremony (see Emeneau 1944–6: IV, 300 ff.) and reminding villagers of the primordial black cow.

The removal of the cow ritual at the end of the funeral collapsed the dimension of Kota spacetime which concerned the span of individual life in relation to the emergence of the Kota community as a whole, and the many individual cycles of birth and death over the centuries. The cow, via the footprint and milking stories, had served as a sign of communal beginnings in the Kota village, the *kōkāl*. In connection with the sacrifice, the cow was an index of individual endings, the passing of the soul to the other world. As a reminder of some things most Kotas would like to forget, the sacrifice itself, the cow now instigates what Michael Herzfeld calls "cultural intimacy" (Herzfeld 1997). For, every time a Kota instantiates the identity between Kotas and cows, he potentially activates an embarrassment about a ritual that the surrounding Hindu population could never understand, and which modernizing Kotas would no longer accept.

The possible "meanings" of the cow for the Kotas are now more narrow: the cow is regarded with the reverence of a god (and by some, regarded as divinity incarnate). Nationalism and its connection with Gandhi's emphasis on non-violence cannot be ignored as catalysts for this process; according to Paul Hockings, "Gandhi visited the nearby town of Coonoor at about the time of David G. Mandelbaum's first visit" (pers. com. July 2002).

Kotas once performed a ritual involving bulls carrying millet for the deceased, the millet being distributed to the poor. This shared a formal redundancy with the cow sacrifice and was similar to other rituals on the subcontinent in which the deceased's *karma*, and the inauspiciousness of death generally, is transfered onto an other of less status (see Raheja 1988; O'Flaherty, ed. 1983). In another ritual, men competed to catch and wrestle buffaloes, and then sacrificed them. The performance of *kēṛ koḷs*, including the "buffalo-calling tune," added stimulus to the energy and excitement. As Kotas recollect their history now, they were at one time so strong as to be able to wrestle down a large, semi-wild buffalo (*kāṛim*) singlehanded. As generations of Kotas became weaker and weaker, as their *catym* diminished, it took more and more people to accomplish the job: two, then four, then eight men for a single buffalo. The place of buffalo sacrifice, whether in the village or near the cremation ground, was not important, but the spot on which the cow was sacrificed was: this spatial constraint reinforced Kota identification with cows as opposed to buffaloes (the important animal for Todas).

At the Cremation Ground

At the time of writing, Kotas are not performing any of these bovine-related rituals. The next significant action is for the funeral processors to approach the cremation area, *tāv nāṛ*, and respectfully remove their shoes. An older man leads the fire-grasping boy around the cremation site in rehearsal for the actual fire-lighting ritual. Wood of two kinds, bundles of thin branches and large logs, is piled on the appropriate cremation spot (*dū*). The funeral ground is meticulously laid out with fixed locations for each ritual, object, and class of ritual agent. In Kolmēl, *ākēr* and *īkēr* corpses are incinerated in one spot, reflecting the historical kinship of these two affinal divisions, and those from *naṛykēr* in another, reflecting the idea of miscegenation.[13] The directional orientation varies from village to village and does not seem to be of systematic importance, although the corpse should supposedly point east, the direction in which houses face and that in which the *ērdabaṭk* is supposed to be played.

Using the coals he has carried, the fire-grasping boy makes a small fire in the *doḍ dū*, the "big" or "great" cremation spot, named for its importance rather than its size. The much larger site for the funeral pyre, which is ritually less important, is called the *kun dū*, or "small cremation spot."[14] The men carefully remove everything from the vicinity of the corpse except for clothing and, without allowing it to touch ground, carefully place it on the pyre's wood. Large logs are then placed around the pyre in the shape of a tipi and bundles of kindling wedged in the gaps. As before, the fire-grasping boy is guided by an older man while he performs the ritual of lighting the fire. He first draws the flame from the fire on the "big" cremation spot and, facing east away from the corpse, throws the firebrand behind him onto the pyre; he performs the same action facing away from the pyre in the opposite direction. This ritualized lighting has little practical effect, so the men will then unceremoniously continue to light the bier until it is burning substantially. The "bier-lighting tune" (*tic iṭ koḷ*) is supposed to be played the moment the bier is lit, but musicians tend to be more casual about the exact timing than they are in the case of the two *koḷ*s played for the movement of the corpse from the house to the *kavāl* and from the *kavāl* out of the village.

Fire in the funeral links the continuity of life with transitions from life to death. The former continuity, based on transformation of food, is anchored in the hearth. The transitions are both physical—fire transforms the body from "fresh" (*pac*) to "dry" (*varl*) bones—and eschatological—fire also creates a "vapor" (*āyv*), the form in which the soul begins its journey to the other world. Significantly, a young person from the deceased's own *kēr* (the "fire-grasping boy"), embodying the principal of genealogical succession in a place, is the agent of these transformations through fire. Noteworthy also, kin-place relations of the village *kēr*s are maintained in the cremation spots on the green and dry funeral ground.

The green funeral's conclusion is soteriologically ambiguous because, being dead, the deceased person has for all intents and purposes already completed the process of becoming a fullfledged spirit of the dead, or "resident of that land" (*ānāṭōr*). Some, however, believe that the dead person's spirit lingers by the cremation ground until the village performs the *varldāv* (or some substitute for it), which ritual helps bridge the soul's transition from earth to *ānāṛ* and/or to the abode of the gods.

The men leave silently and respectfully as the pyre burns, then bathe in a special water source using the suds formed by *veky* plant bark (*Pouzolzia bennettiana*). The power of this soap-bark tree to remove defilement seems to derive from its status as a "traditional" soap from ancient times. It also iterates the idea that natural forest products contain a form of moral power (here, to undo the contagious, ill effects of death) that cannot be obtained from commercial products: Kotas do, after all, use store-bought soap for ordinary bathing. Back in the village, visitors continue to pay condolence visits and the fire-grasping boy stays overnight in the bereaved house. In former times, all-night wakes were performed after the cremation. Men would play the *bugīr*, said to induce the *pēnpacōḷ* to become possessed and convey the words of the spirits of the dead (and not necessarily the person who had just died).

Early in the morning a few men check on the progress of the fire and other men, especially those of the deceased's *kēr*, begin preparing the stew. In the days of the buffalo sacrifice, meat would be cooked; now *udk* (stew) is made from beans. Women cook rice in the household as they did millet during *devr*. After the funeral pyre has extinguished itself, the fire-grasping boy and a group of other men perform a set of rituals at the cremation ground collectively called *karm ītd*, "charcoal-clearing," in which the ashes are cleaned up. Important here, in preparation for the dry funeral (or a substitute ritual), the fire-grasping boy or his instructor selects a piece of skull bone, wraps it in fern and puts it in a crevice with an emblem of the deceased (like a ring) for identification. Then men wash with *veky* and return to the village, where they are partake of the meal first.

Following the feast, villagers collectively bathe with *veky* bark at a water source called *nōmbnīr*, "[funerary] austerity water." In earlier times, close relatives of the deceased continued to observe mourning austerities for a week or until the next new moon. The green funeral then concludes when the fire-grasping boy rubs clarified butter into his hair after this bathing ritual.[15] The jewelry removed at the *nelāgōṛ* is purified by exposure to fire and returned to the widow. (This same procedure is repeated later in the *varldāv*.)

THE *VARLDĀV*

The green (*pac*) and dry funerals (*varldāv*) share similar themes. Rituals in the dry funeral, which are performed for all the people who have died over a stretch of time, tend to exhibit the themes of individuation in intensified form, for in the dry funeral all the brightly decorated biers are lined up, *kēr* by *kēr*, complete with photographs, garlands, and umbrellas of different heights (see photo section). Many of the *tāv koḷs* (funeral melodies) can be played according to the will of the players at either ceremony; but the subtleties of the classification system, and the series of equivalences set up by melodic parallelisms, deserve as much attention here as they did in the god ceremony.

If the green funeral spans a full night, musicians perform the four *nāṛ gūc koḷs*, "gathering at the land of the dead tunes" at the break of dawn (CD 5). These are categorized as *varldāv koḷs* even though they can be played in this green funereal context. The *ānāṭōr*, "residents of that land" (i.e. souls of the dead), are especially attracted to the funeral by these tunes and come to welcome the deceased into their midst.[16] The transition from darkness to light, which in both cases signifies the completion of the soul's spiritual journey, gives rise to an alternative name for one of the four melodies: "country-becomes-clear" tune ("*nāṛ terdd koḷ*"). The tune indexes the appearance of the planet Venus in the early morning sky. The word *nāṛ*'s multivalence lends an additional meaning: as the "country" (*nāṛ*) becomes clear/light, so does the "land of the dead" (*nāṛ*) become clear or manifest to spirits (*āyv*) of the dead. Spirits of the dead gather at the funeral ground and the spirit of the newly deceased joins them.

This aspect of dry-funerary spacetime is symmetric, then, with that in the god ceremony, where village residents strive for unity to attract god. In the *varldāv*, Kotas perform musical and other rituals for the sake of the deceased in order to foster a form of unity among the ancestors. The use of *nāṛ gūc koḷs* at green and dry funerals reflects a slippage between the idea that once a person has died he or she almost immediately, and automatically, becomes a resident of "that land," and the idea that the *varldāv* is necessary to effect that transition. All the *nāṛ gūc koḷs* are considered to be the most poignant funeral melodies. The final push of the spirit to the other world is effected emotionally. Mourners feel their pain acutely with the awareness that the deceased is, at that moment, really going to another place.

Two examples of similarities among *varldāv* melodies point to parallels in associations with their ritual referents. The *manḏ ākicd koḷ* ("funeral ground clearing tune"), which musicians play as part of a ritual in which men clear vegetation, debris and feces from the path connecting the village to the dry funeral ground, is similar to the tune accompanying the procession of villagers carrying cooking pots to the dry funeral ground later in the ceremony (see also Wolf 1997a, 301–20). The similarity between the two comes to be associated more generally with travel between village and dry-funeral ground. These tunes are convenient for processions because they are short and simple; this is true of many Kota tunes used for fairly long periods of walking (e.g. thirty minutes or more).

The second example is the musical similarity between one of the *nāṛ gūc koḷ*s and the millet-pouring-tune (*koṭanm iṭd koḷ*) played at the beginning of the *varldāv*. A man pours *vatm* millet (provided by the households of the deceased) in front of the houses of all those who have died since the last such ceremony was performed—a period of a year or more (see photo section).

Each person in the village touches a bit of the millet to his or her head as a form of respect. Kotas say that the millet, called *koṭanm*—the "food which is given" for the sake of the deceased—is literally the *tāv* (corpse/dead person). This metaphysical transformation occurs through a set of ritual actions: preparing millet, cleaning the target area on the *kavāl* (packed mud yard), and musicians' playing the millet-pouring-tune "thunderingly."[17] As in other cases, this melody's similarity to another one suggests the possibility of correspondences among their extra-musical referents. The *koṭanm koḷ* (millet-pouring tune), which reconstitutes the spirit in the millet, resembles one *nāṛgūc koḷ* in Kolmēl, which effects the transformation of the spirit from the body to the community of the ancestors.

Over its course, the ceremony calls for other foods and other millets, but the fate of this particular millet is to be dry-roasted, placed under a highly decorated chair (standing for a bier), and cremated with a variety of symbolic items and with bone relics of the corpse. The millet, then—as a stand-in for the corpse—is the medium undergoing transformation from "green" to "dry." The actual bone relics are added to the "bier" only during the procession to the *varldāv nāṛ* (dry funeral ground).

Bond-breaking

A key to the significance of the transformation from green to dry in the funeral complex may lie in the cross-cultural theme of bond-breaking: bonds inhibit motion, including passage to the land of the dead. One might employ the metaphor of weight for the inertial capacities of "sin," which keeps the individual anchored to the village, unless said deeds are transferred to the cow (as in the past) or released through the ritual of cutting toe strings. The metaphor of sin as weight is attractive because some Kotas (since the 1930s) have envisioned the journey to the land of the dead as one in which the spirit of the dead becomes a "vapor" (*āyv*), which is virtually weightless. The spirit proceeds on foot to places of higher elevation crossing various known landmarks but must ultimately cross a "thread bridge" before entering the land of the dead. If the deceased had been evil in life, he or she would be metaphorically too "heavy" to cross this fragile thread bridge.

In a broader soteriological sense, then, in the funerary process, various physical, social, and moral forces that would inhibit the soul from making its journey upward and over the thread bridge are palliated—bonds are broken, that which is heavy is made light. From a physical perspective, the transforming of *pac* to *varl* also converts heaviness to lightness. Fire then makes the final transformation in two ways. First, it makes the deceased even lighter: the word *āyv* means not only "soul," or "vapor," but also "breath" and "steam": fire turns bones, millet, bier and all its accoutrements to dust and air. And second, it purifies (and/or breaks the bonds of attachment of) the deceased, just as it does the jewelry of the widow or widower. Because the bones and the millet, both of which are embodiments of the soul in different ways during the *varldāv*, have been effectively made "dry" (and of course more flammable), the final incineration is not only material but also of critical worth in that it helps the deceased reach the final goal of communion with the ancestors.

Rituals similar to those of the *pac tāv* (green funeral) take place on the *kavāl* (yard) up to the point where the bones are added to the dry funeral biers. The symbolic items placed on or under the *varldāv* bier are larger in number and more dramatic in their articulation of individual status, age, gender, tastes, and personal qualities—a photo of the deceased, for example (see photo section). The procession begins grandly, with decorated poles and umbrellas, crêpe paper, and sometimes dozens of biers. The attendance is significant and the music forceful.

The biers are set down in a special place near a stream in order of seniority, deceased males followed by females, and a group of men dispatched to the green funeral ground to retrieve the bone relics (*nelm*). In former times, bovine sacrifices took place at this time. Shortly after the bones are collected, an elder places on each bier an old silver coin wrapped up in a thorny plant. He then sprinkles water mixed with cow dung on the bier three times while a specially selected set of *mel pac mog*, "breast-clutching boys" (i.e. chief mourners) ring bells.[18] Maḷn of Kurgōj interpreted the bell-ringing as a call for "liberation, absolution from sin" (Ta. *vimōcaṉam*) and to grab the attention of god, asking him to come and "give goodness" (*oḷyd tā*).

As these bier-carriers cross the very pure water (called *kargaṇnīr*, "pupil water") the soul too is seen to cross over into the other world. Immediately upon crossing the stream, bier carriers touch the bier legs to particular stones and sacrificial cows, one set for *ākēr* and *īkēr*, one set for *naṛykēr*. (The touching to stones is still done in Kolmēl, but not the sacrifice.) Then a specially appointed ritualist called *koḷytāḷ* used to sacrifice the two cows with the blunt butt of an ax. The ritualist from *ākēr* struck the *naṛykēr* cow and the *naṛykēr* ritualist delivered the blow to the *ākēr-īkēr* cow (Mandelbaum, April 7, 1938, p. 7).[19] The heads of the cows were then laid on the corresponding stones (but not decapitated). This bygone sacrificial practice exhibited a social complementarity that Kotas represented in explicitly spatial terms. This too was a kind of "interlocking" deployed in the interest of community togetherness.

Among the important rituals that follow the stream-crossing are smearing the bone relics with clarified butter, a jewelry-removal ritual much like that in the green funeral, and a fire-lighting ritual (formerly done by a *mundkānōn* in Kolmēl, nk) for the incineration of the "biers," the bones, and the ritual items associated with each person who died. During the incineration ritual, a man will shoot an arrow from a small bow (in honor of a deceased man). Like the cow sacrifice, which completes a cosmic time span beginning with the village-founding, the shooting of the bow and arrow recapitulates the image of *ayṇōr* shooting the bow and arrow to protect the Kotas as they made their way to Kolmēl village. It also resonates with the bygone practice of shooting a bison after the god ceremony, as if the actions of hunting were somehow auspicious for an ending. The bow and arrow is also more broadly used by Kotas as an emblem of their identity, especially as "tribals" (see image on rear of van, photo section).

This final fire is also used to signify the end of marriage bonds by transforming the jewelry of the widow: the jewelry is waved before the flames.[20] Those present will then remain in a designated area of the *varldāv* ground for the entire night listening to *dukt koḷs*. Formerly (according to one of Mandelbaum's informants, Kākākamaṭn), the *pēnpacōḷ* would become possessed and report on whether the rituals were all performed correctly. She would not act as the mouthpiece of those who had just died, but rather speak in the persona of an earlier ancestor. Before the break of dawn, the planet Venus becomes visible and *koḷ* players perform the *nāṛgūc koḷs*. In the 1930s, at the sight of Venus, the *koḷytāḷs* would chop off the cows' horns and place them on the corresponding stones (Mandelbaum, April 7, 1938, p. 4).

Thereafter follow dancing, cooking, and feasting. Meal preparations, offerings, orders of precedence and use of space are all as complex as those connected with the god ceremony. In one important "interlocking" ritual, *jādykū* ("community-cooked-grain"), classificatory affines from visiting villages eat in male–female pairs, each pair sharing a banana leaf. This affirms the unity of the entire tribe (not just the village) and also implicates symbolism of fecundity and rebirth.

Sulli, in describing the events of the all-night musical ceremony on the dry cremation ground, emphasized the sexual activities of the young people. That such activity might have taken place informally is difficult to doubt, but Sulli's descriptions seemed to imply more than this, and in part reflected his own prurient interests. The ceremony was and still is a context for young men and women from different Kota villages to get to know one another. This lies in marked contrast with the god ceremony, whose scheduling makes it difficult to attend in more than one village, and whose ritual imperatives demand celibacy. In the *varldāv*, by contrast, the contest to catch and subdue buffaloes was a particularly opportune moment for young men to show off their manliness and in doing so, to invite physical attraction of the opposite sex.

Following the feasts and dances, a series of rituals culminates with each *mel pac mog* (chief mourner) spilling and then dashing a clay pot of clarified butter on his respective cremation site and running back to the village without looking back. (The widows and widowers return along a different path to the village.) The *mel pac mog koḷ* for this ritual is associated with the text, *ākērōne īkērōne*, meaning, "residents of that *kēr*, residents of this *kēr*," and presages a mild competition in which members of each *kēr* strive to be the first to light a friction fire (nk) and start dancing. It encodes a wake-up call, "hey you people here, you people there, get ready, the *mel pac mog* is coming."

When the fire is produced in one *kēr*, the corresponding *mel pac mog* draws a flame using a piece of cloth and starts his own small fire. He boils a small amount of *vatm* in a clay pot (*kuck*), which he rests on a plaform of three stones, and then completes the ritual by throwing the pot out beyond the edge of the *kēr*. S. Raman interpreted this ritual as one that feeds the spirits of the deceased infants (*pot guy mog*), who remained nameless when born and who were buried rather than cremated. This interpretation is, in an odd way, a musical one. Since the melody is called the *pot guy mog koḷ* (in Kolmēl) and not *mel pac mog koḷ*, the ritual must originally, he reasoned, have been for the *pot guy mog*.

Following this, music and gay dancing take place in each *kēr* in which there was a death. In the "interlocking" *jādy kupāc* ("community dressing gown") ritual, a male representative of each of the seven villages dances wearing the type of dance costume used during the god ceremony. This parallels in name and function the *jādykū* ("community-cooked-grain") ritual of eating in classificatory affinal pairs, but it does so with men only. Rituals and dancing continue on the next day as well, which is named the *āṭ nāḷ*, "dance day," comparable to that at the end of the god ceremony. The dry funeral ends on the following day, the *pāṭ nāḷ*, "song day," with the performance of women's songs and games, paralleling the god ceremony and encoding gender values: women's activities are at once auspicious endings and appropriately take place after men's activities.

Conclusion: Models, Objects, and Mutability

Kotas constitute themselves through the god ceremonial and funerary complexes in ways that exhibit parameters of relationality: directionality (inward and outward), distance (intravillage, intervillage), succession (including order of musical pieces), spatiotemporal specificity, duration, and degrees of regularity. Different transactions between human and non-human entities engage these parameters variably, since the moral home of "god" is in the village and that of the spirits of the dead is away from it. Aspects of status and ritual intensity are directly related to spatiotemporal dimensions: as the god ceremony gradually approaches its peak, villagers focus their activities centrally.

Remembrance registers multiply in both god ceremonies and funerals. Important differences lie in the degree to which such memories are shared. A theme in all Kota rituals is remembrance of "traditional" things and activities. The formal recollection of practices such as using soap bark (*veky*) confers, in the ritual context, forms of power—"power" is one of the common English words Kotas use; in this case power is linke to *catym*. An example of such power is the ability of soap bark to re move not only dirt, but also defilement. Only in funerals, however, i commemoration geared towards the individual. One simple formulatio of how "Kotas constitute themselves" ceremonially could then rea "Kotas constitute themselves as a unified whole, living in the presen faithful to the past" in god ceremonies; "Kotas constitute the decease as an individual, living on in the land of the dead and in memory" i funerals.

Kotas generate forms of spacetime in these two complexes throug their ways of manipulating music, food, and fire. In the god ceremony each of the energetic and loud musical beginnings (*ōmayṇs*) follows significant making of fire: on the *gagvāl*, the returning of the "house o the erected post fire" from the *pacāl* to initiate dancing; in the templ area, the new creation of a bonfire (nk) which is used to heat the cen sers. The important fires are like light being refracted and absorbe Men carry them from either the *mundkānōn*'s houses or the "house o the erected post" to either individual houses (on the first day) or com munal places, where they serve as bases for further fires around whic the community dances.

Mixing, offering, and redistribution of grain are similarly lent em phasis by the performance of a dedicated melody. Kotas combine grai contributions from each house in a *kēr*. They cook the grain in thre separate areas, one for each *kēr*. Then they mix these separately cooke pots of grain together before distributing the grain to the whole village.[2] Like a light filtering through a magnifying glass, grain focuses in on direction to a point; and then, like light diffusing from a single source the grain is redistributed to individuals.

Specific spatiotemporal forms differ in part because fire and foo are essentially different kinds of substances, used ritually for differen purposes: fire is essentially of god (and transforms the raw to the cook ed); food is being made and offered to god. Both have the capacity to b combined into seamless wholes and divided into parts without becom ing fragments. They model well for the diverse formulations of "unity" so important to Kota rituals and especially god ceremonies.

Agents, both human and non-human, savor music and food as the consume them. People interacting with musical performances and in volving themselves in activities in a particular place and time generat a complex affective texture: happiness tinged with sadness at the end of the god ceremony; sadness mixed with excitement and sentimental recollection during the funeral.

For the Kotas, the god ceremony is a "model . . . of timeless perfection."[22] Through it, Kotas seek to recapture a sense of the time when god and man were one—before any Kota had died, when people behaved as they were supposed to, and when *catym* was maximal. But the god ceremony is not itself "timeless," despite Kota affirmations of its enduring moral essence, because its meaning relies upon the recognition that the "present" (in whatever historical period) has been severed from a utopian past. Ever since the Kotas emerged from their ideal world, the god ceremony (in all the representations currently available to us) has been concerned with recreating a primordial sense of a divine, collective self—in Kota terms, "making god." In the process, *devr* incorporated into itself rituals referenced by secondary rituals, and so on recursively to a degree that is ultimately unrecoverable.

Kotas recognize that individual rituals have changed in the god ceremony; but for them the overall meaning of the ceremony has not altered. Puccan used to emphasize the significance of changes only in the funerary realm and downplay changes in individual *devr* rituals. "Our *pacāl* has remained the same," he said. "Centripetence" is metaphorically apt in describing the continued, if guarded, incorporation of practices into an immutable center. The god ceremony models, for Kotas, communal continuity in everyday life: Kotas legitimize themselves as being "the same" even though, in the context of the *kūṭm* (village council), individuals such as Dr Varadharajan continually raise new issues of Kota self-comportment, in continually changing social, economic and political contexts.

Kota funerals, in contrast, do not provide a static model of the past—or for that matter, for the future either.[23] While they share a strong theme of persistence with all Kota rituals, Kota mortuary ceremonies have historically been subjects of heated debates. Kota cultural sensitivities (especially in the public eye) have centered on cow sacrifice, buffalo sacrifice, meat eating, expense, sexual conduct, and the appropriateness of celebration and revelry in the context of a funeral. When considering that the funeral is a process of many kinds of removal, the possibility that this may be socially problematic is not difficult to entertain: put simply, the difficulties of saying goodbye to the deceased (and attempting to expel all that is considered negative with respect to death) could serve to stimulate or generate complex emotional behaviors. They may also tacitly justify "letting go," since, as some Kotas put it, the funeral is like a going-away party: a person is honored in this way once.

This is not to say that emotion and emotive behaviors are not culturally conditioned—although the debate between cultural constructionists and biological determinists remains strong on this issue—but merely to point out that death and its accompaniments do not provide a blueprint for all apparently "emotional" behavior. Furthermore, as William M. Reddy has convincingly argued, certain kinds of expressive behaviors (especially, for him, verbal statements made by the experiencer of an emotion describing the emotional state) have a "self-altering effect" (Reddy 2001, 101; see also Wolf 2001). And to return to a more general point, individual mortuary rituals—such as animal sacrifice, musical performance, or dancing—will tend to have an emotional impact on those who are ostensibly "mourning" quite apart from the impact of the death itself. Taking this point further: historical changes in funerary practice, such as the ban on cow sacrifice, have not only raised emotional issues, but also necessitated cultural (and soteriological) justification or instigated broader-scale reforms.

Why is it, then, that Kotas recognize (or accept) change as such more readily in the funerary complex than in the god ceremony? One possible (if psychologically simplistic) answer is that death and all the rituals connected with it stand as irrefutable evidence that the world in fact does change. This is not in every way true, of course, because funerary rituals often seek to reunite communities and suggest symbolically that life will go on as before. Nevertheless, the very need for such rituals betrays a certain recognition of change.

Another way of approaching the problem is to examine what *could* change in both ceremonies. Consider, for instance, the different points of departure for referencing "pastness." Funerals do not hark back to a primordial beginning in the way that god ceremonies do, if we take one "beginning" as a time before death, when man and god were "as one." Kota funerals, then, exist not because of timeless beginnings, but because of timely (or untimely) endings, and their constituent rituals refer back in time in at least three ways. One, which funerals share with god ceremonies, is an emphasis on certain kinds of bygone practice generally. In both, for instance, Kotas place importance on consuming a type of millet no longer part of an everyday diet; both also make use of musical pieces that remind Kotas of activities or stories. The common theme is that the Kotas continue as a community, with a historical memory. The second way of indexing the past is through reference to the community of ancestors in general, through practices or beliefs that posit these ancestors as agents, or through practices that ascribe material existence to the land of the dead. The third is the capacity for the funeral either to represent the deceased or to cause participants to reflect upon the life of the person who just died.

As for mutability of these aspects of pastness, Kotas could potentially construe "the Kota community" and "the ancestors" as "timeless" objects, even though Kotas no longer strongly affirm the realm of the ancestors via female spirit-mediums (*pēnpacōḷs*). The third point of departure, "the life of the deceased," however, will always remain contingent on individuals and therefore be variable.[24] As long as Kota funerals remain focused on individual identity—although we recognize all the while that this identity is constituted by membership in overlapping groups or social categories (gender, age, residence)—they contain within their form at least one model for internal historical change. The most simple articulation of this principle is in a recent compromise in Kolmēl over the dry funeral: those who wish to have their remains recremated in the dry funeral have the choice to do so; those who do not, as Va. Kamaṭn did not, have an alternative.

A message that emerges from the form of funerals is not only: "We may change on the surface, but we remain Kotas," but also: "Each of us lived a distinct life." Beyond this is the suggestion of an eschatological identity: "Even in the land of the dead we remain Kotas." The question raised by some of the more substantial changes in mortuary practice, the discontinuance of the dry funeral, is whether indeed Kotas are still Kotas after they die. The rituals that replace the dry funeral are ones that suggest the souls of dead Kotas are akin to some among many Hindu souls that, through the agency of Brahmans or the association of local streams with the Ganges river, merge with a more unitary image of divinity (see Wolf 2000/2001b). The fact that ritual change in the funeral is connected with soteriological change, and that views on both are not settled, suggests possibility for change in the moral underpinnings of the funeral complex that is not really present in the god ceremony: the question of the fate of the soul. Whereas the *pacāl* and its equivalent in other Kota villages are places symbolic of communal continuity, the land of the dead is not. At one point in time considered a physical geographical place, it is now abstracted: it is simply "not here." If Kotas use the god ceremony as a static spatiotemporal model of what is true, and literally central, they are able, through funerals, to work out cultural matters that are more ambiguous and mutable.

CHAPTER 8

Conclusion: Dancing where their Ancestors Danced

Critical aspects of music's cultural meaning within and beyond the Kota context may be discovered by examining phenomena that are non-musical, or not directly musical. Musical processes participate in some of the same forms of cultural and social production as do performances of ritual, calendrical time reckoning, and everyday movements and speech. One common denominator is a set of spatiotemporal forms and representations, which serve as maps or traces of the processes by which groups constitute their identity and individual subjectivities. Kotas generate and act out their own forms of subjectivity through developing personal musical styles, swinging rhythms or intoning in distinctive ways, enacting preferences for eating or dressing, or giving voice to interpretations. Kotas also strive for group identity through embracing generalized experiences, merging with others. Whether Kotas choose to sing or play the *koḷ* in unison, to wear matching clothes, or to affirm shared values verbally, they perform one of their central modes of "being" by explicitly yielding their individuality for the sake of the group.[1]

Sameness and Difference

From a social psychological point of view, the two broad processes of differentiation, "a movement toward uniqueness," and integration, "union with other people," contribute more generally to the complexity of human subjectivities (Csikszentmihalyi 1991). These processes appear in different forms, with different names, and serve different purposes from society to society. The Beng of Ivory Coast, for example, describe these "two quite distinct [and compatible] visions of how the world can be structured" with two phrases in their language, which mean "we are different" and "we are all one" (Gottlieb 1992, 14–15). The *Kapok* tree in Beng society is a powerful, ambivalent symbol of "the oscillation" between the disjunctions and the connections "that together define the relationship between human-occupied village and spirit-occupied forest" (Gottlieb 1992, 43–4). "Integration" and "differentiation" may exist as (or in) many kinds of culturally constructed units. They may be expressed as concepts, as in the Beng "we are all one," or in interactive verbal performances, as in the Kota "Are we all joined?" . . . "We're joined;" they may be subtly embedded in categories of action, such as the Kota ceremonial complexes of *devr* and *tāv*; and they may involve projections of sameness and difference onto spatial categories, as in both Beng and Kota cases.

To represent certain god ceremonial activities as "centripetal" and funerary activities as "centrifugal" is to describe forms of integration and differentiation in particular spatial terms. Yet the articulation of these two principles is more complicated than this. Kotas gradually mediate between processes of differentiation and integration in their dry funeral. They also integrate through differentiation: they "interlock" at the dry funeral by eating in affinal pairs and dancing as representatives of each of the seven villages. Musically, Kotas perform interlocking drum patterns, creating complementary social categories—players of one drum or another—which are temporary, limited to the musical event. Spatially, this interlocking is an extension of the physical motion of producing musical sounds and of the musicians' standing next to one another. Another form of interlock is found in Porgāṛ, where one *koḷ* player from each of three *kērs* formally participates in the opening musical fanfare (*ōmayṇ*) of the god ceremony. Musically, the *koḷ* players perform in unison; socially, they interlock, bringing together the musical forces from distinct kin-residence groups.

Projected longitudinally, "sameness" and "difference" become "continuity" and "change," which are also registered in local categories and practices.[2] The Kota *devr-tāv* pairing captures something of this contrast, but the opposition is not mutually exclusive. Continuity always implies a devaluation of change; the seeming permanence of physical locations in the landscape helps individuals emphasize continuity. The *pacāl* and the "house of the erected post" during the god ceremony not only remind Kotas what endures, but also provide platforms upon which

Kotas recurrently perform what is "traditional" (*māmūl*), even while they recognize that they do not replicate every movement and gesture of their ancestors.

If being the "same" does not entail being exactly the same, neither do departures from the status quo necessarily threaten the continuity of the community. At some level, however, death is evidence that the world does change. Mortuary rituals provide Kotas means for mediation as they transcend the ongoing cycle of deaths; as in many parts of the world, mourning and mortuary rituals foster reintegration of the living. Kotas have also constructed local soteriologies in accordance with changing ritual practices, which point to two possible destinations (anchor points) for the soul. The earthly land of the dead geographically registers the idea that Kotas remain Kotas after they die, that they live on, side by side with their ancestors in a world parallel to that of the living. A place for the souls of the dead somewhere in the sky indexes the contrasting idea that dead Kotas spiritually travel to the abode of the gods, which "god" is shared by Hindus. Kotas seem not to experience cognitive dissonance in holding some combination of these two views, although, in the absence of major social upheaval, they will likely move from a focus on the former to a focus on the latter.

Culturally-specific conceptions of identity and difference, continuity and change, are embedded in the ways Kotas organize and execute musical and other actions in time and space. Forms of action in music, ritual, and various arenas of everyday life are all components of inchoate indigenous models, theories that are never completely articulated in words.[3] Much like the stories and emotions to which some mourning songs (*āṭḷs*) allude, Kota verbalizations are "approximate expressions rather than exact explanations of experience" (Jackson 1996, 10). Hence Kota explanations about how and why actions are accomplished or what they mean should not outweigh detailed, phenomenological considerations of the actions themselves, whether such actions are music-making and listening, figuring out when to perform a ritual, or struggling to complete preparations for a cremation before sundown.

Spatiotemporal Forms of Identity

The table below consolidates our discussion of relationships among identity, action class, spatiotemporal form, place, and musical genre. The table reads from left to right and from top to bottom, and proceeds

Table 2: Spatiotemporal Forms of Identity (expanded version)

A. identity descriptor	B. additional details of identity or subjectivity	C. class of ceremony	D. ceremony or action type(s)	E. spatio-temporal form	F. places of action	G. objects of spacetime	H. musical and dance genres
1. wholeness	community of sameness at village level	*devr* (god)	*devr* (the god ceremony)	centripetal	village & environs	locations of divinity	god tunes, god songs, dancing
2. wholeness	complementary inter-connectedness at village level	*devr*	*doḍpabm*	interlocking & centripetal	homes & village center	hearth	dancing, god songs
3. wholeness	complementary inter-connectedness of entire Kota community	*devr* and *tāv*	dry funeral (especially toward end)	interlocking	village & dry funeral ground	land of dead	dancing, god songs
4. individuality	characteristics of individual remembered by community	*tāv*	green and dry funerals, singing	centrifugal	funeral ground & homes	land of the dead, forest	funeral tunes, *āṭḷ*
5. community distinctiveness	tribalness: self-sufficiency, artisanship, domesticator of wild	(modernist)	intertribal gatherings displays	(ideationally centripetal)	public, spheres	village forest	all, esp. songs on tribal identity
6. community distinctiveness	calendrical routine: emphasis on days Kotas do special rituals	scheduled rituals	god rituals, dry funeral, agricultural	anchoring	village, fields, & dry funeral ground	dates of the year	all ritual repertoires

Table 2 (*contd.*)

7. emergent aesthetic individuality	musicianship: standing out by manipulation of time and pitch, merging with group	(instrumental music events)	*koḷ*, *dobar*, and *tabaṭk* especially	anchoring	multiple	pitch location; drum strike	all instrumental music
8. emergent affective sense of place	relationship of an individual or group to important religious or memorial sites	(many)	processions and pilgrimages	anchoring	multiple	sites of gods, spirits, purity, pollution	some god tunes, dancing, songs of places
9. extension of self	measures of the reputation of the deceased or the power of past Kotas	funerals and god ceremonies	arrival distance, prestation value, performance length, loudness	centrifugal, centripetal	village	visitors, prestations, fire, musicians, listeners	all instrumental genres (potentially)

very roughly from general to specific. Column A presents identity descriptors, beginning with "wholeness" and "individuality." "Community distinctiveness" comes next as a slightly more focused term; finally, "emergent aesthetic individuality," "emergent affective sense of place," and "extensions of self" are quite specific descriptors. Column B fleshes out the meaning of each identity descriptor. The three kinds of wholeness, for example, depend on whether that wholeness is created by "sameness" or by "difference," and whether the unit of analysis is the village or the whole community. The reasons for these distinctions appear further to the right: different kinds of wholeness are emphasized in different ceremonies. While the wholeness of Rows 1 and 2 are related at the ceremonial-class level (god), for instance, they are distinguished by different ceremonies. In the "god ceremony" Kotas emphasize a community of sameness, while at "*doḍpabm*" they articulate complementarity by eating in one anothers' houses.

The ceremonial class category is not always applicable, as in Row 5, where "community distinctiveness" is labeled "modernist," since it involves self-awareness. This consciousness of self is articulated in contexts in which the modern political entity of the "tribe" in India is significant. Row 6, by contrast, could be summarized as "community distinctiveness by virtue of *having* a local calendar." All ceremonies and constituent rituals that can be located in the calendar, i.e. that are planned, constitute a temporal cycle distinctive to the community.

Spatiotemporal forms, in Column E, refer to the forms of several kinds of processes. In Row 1, centripetal motion applies to physical movements of people to the center as well as to moral notions of centeredness, of being near the gods. In Rows 2 and 3, interlocking refers often to the formal joining of classificatory affines, but also to the drum parts in any instrumental musical performance. In Row 6, the patterning of calendrical activities is a spatiotemporal form. Anchoring here refers to the shaping, the active constructing of the calendar, planning one event in relation to the other. Anchoring also describes how Kotas lay claim to particular positions in the calendar year as definitive, in some respect, of the collectivity—as in the statement, "this is our new year."

Anchoring in Row 7 concerns the way an individual *koḷ* player aligns his melody with the drum ostinato—what I call "emergent aesthetic individuality." In Row 8, it refers to the power of places to "pull" Kotas in, whether those places are temples, abodes of the souls of the dead, or mythically important sites. Kota relationships with such places creates an "emergent affective sense of place." "Extension of self" in Row 9 refers to the centripetal motion of, for instance, funeral attendees—the more the attendees and the further they travel, the greater the deceased's status. It also refers to the centrifugal extension of the village when the blast of the *kob* reaches the heavens, or a distant village. Temporally, this is associated with a past when Kotas lived righteously and were more "powerful." They could play louder and their music project over longer distances.

Column F, "places of (ritual) action," designates the physical place where Kotas carry out the actions to which Columns C and D refer. Column G, "objects of spacetime," refers to moments or locations relevant to the creation of the spacetimes in Column E. The hearth is the center of activity in offering food to the household deity during *doḍpabm*, and the social focus of activity when each Kota eats in every other's house. The "land of the dead" is a metaphysical goal of centrifugality in funerals and the forest is an evoked locale in mourning songs (*āṭḷ*). These locations, in turn, bear on distinguishing the "individuality" of the subject as remembered or represented by the community (Row 4). The "village" and the "forest" (Row 5) are sometimes evoked as "tribal" kinds of places when Kotas perform their "community distinctiveness" for outsiders.[4]

The final column, H, refers to the dance and musical genres associated with the "specific type of ceremony or action." One can move between music and dance genre and Columns A and B, the details of identity and subjectivity, only by taking into account at least some of the information in Columns C–F. Extra-musical data helps elucidate music's cultural meaning. Thinking back to my concentric model from the introduction, what "logic of relations" may this phenomenology of Kota music and ritual life share with various "theories of time and space"?

Philosophical Distinctions and Real-world Articulations

A number of writers in the Western world have drawn attention to two "kinds" of time: "external" time, spatialized, measured, clock time which is divided into chunks; and "inner" or "subjective" time, represented as fluid, flowing and non-homogeneous (not divided into units of the same length). The French philosopher Henri Bergson (1859–1941) authored one version of this distinction. He represented the former "kind" of time as quantitative and spatialized and the latter, which he called "duration," as qualitative.[5] For Bergson, quantified time is spatial because to quantify time is to divide a period into like units and count them. To visualize these divided units, for Bergson, is to project time into space. Duration, in contrast, lacks articulation and is not spatialized:

> A melody to which we listen with our eyes closed, heeding it along, comes close to coinciding with this time which is the very fluidity of our inner life; but it still has too many qualities, too much definition, and we must first efface the difference among the sounds, then do away with the distinctive features of sound itself, retaining of it only the continuation of what precedes into what follows and the uninterrupted transition, multiplicity without divisibility and succession without separation, in order finally to rediscover basic time (Bergson 1965, 44; see also 49).

For Bergson and many others music gets at a world beyond words, approximating closer the inner experience of the individual, before it is reflected upon, theorized. The social theorist Alfred Schutz (1899–1959) distinguished between the "outer time" of realized performance and the subject's "inner time" (modeled on Bergson's "duration"). He used the intimate musical communication among members of a string quartet to evoke the "tuning-in relationship, the experience of the 'We,' which is at the foundation of all possible communication." For Schutz, music was a means through which inner time could be socially shared, a form of "living through a vivid present in common" (1977, 115). The listener's awareness of measurement, punctuation and segment may be backgrounded as he or she focuses on overall flow and sense of sequence.[6]

The two categories Bergson and Schutz articulate philosophically may be approximated by a number of complementary adjectival pairs: segmented *versus* flowing, homogeneous *versus* heterogeneous, or quantitative *versus* qualitative. Leaving the more esoteric aspects of the philosophies aside, let us consider the adjectives as descriptions of distinctions we make in our everyday experiences of the world. You are standing in between cars on a commuter train, hearing the proverbial "clickety clack" of the wheels rolling across the gaps between tracks; the number of "clicks and clacks" between two train stops remains constant each time the same journey is made. The articulations are clearly demarcated on the landscape through segments of track, switches, and train stops. Envisage, by contrast, a leisurely trip in a row-boat, the regularity of the creaking oars broken up by the sound of water swishing along the sides; you stop rowing for a while and glide. You cannot find a clear imprint of passing time intervals in the patterns of the water or the objects floating by.

It has become a habit among some writers on time to describe the terms of such distinctions as different "kinds of time," when more properly they are contrastive categories through which individuals have proposed differences in human experience.[7] Subjective ideas about temporal experience probably derive from individuals observing and meditating upon the patterns of real world events—their own melodies, boat rides, and train trips. From this perspective, Bergson may have erred in asking the listener to "efface the difference among the sounds." What agents experience of time is based on their perceptions of real-world phenomena, which have articulations of different kinds and degrees.

Durkheim and his associates developed their theories of time along similarly inductive lines. For Durkheim, temporal categories derived from "the rhythm of social life" and spatial categories materially emerged from "the territory occupied by the society." The categories, thus derived, "reach out to all reality" (Durkheim 1915, 488). One of his influential colleagues, Henri Hubert, asserted in the introduction to his published lectures on time that a "religious notion of time . . . presided over the development of calendars." Hubert explained how a sequence of events creates a "rhythm" whose reality exists independently of the content of those events. This rhythm of articulations, once established, tends to perpetuate itself. Cultural or religious meanings connected with a date are gradually lost, or diminish in significance. Then members of societies graft new meanings onto it. Halloween, wherein the Celtic *Samhain* influenced the later Christian All Hallow's Eve, is such an example in America.

Bergson considered this process by which events were emptied of their content—what he called qualities—as the first step in the spatialization of time. Emptied of their content, events become mere articulations, each like the other, homogeneous and countable. Hubert differed theoretically from Bergson, but he nevertheless adapted Bergson's notion of quality when he wrote that a period's constitutive acts "contaminate" the entirety (Hubert 1905, 14). A Kota funeral makes the period between the death of a person and the funerary feast into "bier time."

"Anchoring" dovetails with Hubert's "rhythm." Not only do "myths" get "rejuvenated," as Hubert put it, by the superimposition of new holidays on old, but even nearby days are given prominence. If the Friday after the Thursday of Thanksgiving in America tends to become a holiday by default, Labor Day brings to mind, for many Americans, the beginning of the school year, which often begins one day later. Dates or moments become anchors to which surrounding events gravitate, in actual scheduling or by mental association, just as the Kota seed-sowing ceremony became grafted on to the end of a calendrical, religious ritual after losing its mooring to the seasons.

Kota melodic positions, which acquire importance as anchors when they coincide with structural drum strokes, also create their own "rhythms." The performer can maintain these anchor points, dynamically slowing down or speeding up the melody to maintain the correct convergences. Alternatively, owing to lack of care or ability, he may line up the melody differently in some or all cycles; or, the performer may settle on a new point of anchor, perhaps as he alters or misremembers a tune.

The settling on anchor points in a Kota melody and the giving of relative importance to dates, while different, share important underlying constitutive features with respect to how humans orient themselves in time. Actors first create articulations in time. Then certain of these articulations seem to take on lives of their own. Their lasting character is determined by the ways in which future actors place events in relation to these earlier articulations. This creates both a hierarchy of articulations, as well as the possibility of qualitative differentiation among them, as in colored points on a line or in space. Memory is involved when any cycle needs to be reiterated, and "retention" is necessary as a musician keeps track of the meter while playing.[8]

"Anchoring," then, is available to actors in many cultural contexts. Products of Kota action are, in a trivial sense "culturally specific," but they are not culturally specific as a collective. Kotas don't organize calendrical or musical processes according to a larger cultural entity, "Kota" time, which can be contrasted with another collective other, such as "Western" or "Japanese" time.

Foundations of Spatiotemporal Thought

The shifting of anchor points—either in the long term (calendrical or musical), or in the short term as a Kota musician negotiates a difficult tune—exemplifies the idea that orientation in time is itself a temporal project. It may not be arguable that "basic cultural assumptions about time and the organization of events [affect] rhythmic perception,"[9] for the notion of "basic cultural assumptions" presumes that the choices have already been made. Actions in time and space often require navigating through more than one structure (a solar and lunar calendar; two roughly drawn road maps). Musical performances may entail making choices among such alternatives, at different times along the way, just as, in Harris Berger's apt words in the context of Heavy Metal and Jazz, "different performers see different members of the rhythmic section as the rhythmic foundation" (1997, 483) and may choose one or another, accordingly, at different moments (1997, *passim*).[10]

Actors make spatiotemporal distinctions that relate both to their verbalized concepts of time and space and to their embodied practices. Sometimes actors strategically use music, one of these embodied practices, to describe more abstract ideas or theories. These strategies are "poetic" ones in that they are rhetorical attempts to evoke something evasive—such as "consciousness"—by emphasizing the iconicity of selected features.[11] Bergson's likening the flow of melody to the "fluidity of our inner life" is but one prominent example.[12] Through such associations, some reflective writers begin to draw connections between the inner world of the individual and ideas of flow or continuity. Having thereby downplayed the force of articulations that subdivide experience, some writers take the further step of bringing these ideas into relation with that of transcending categorical distinctions more generally.

Music-making, particular kinds of melodies, and ways of thinking about such melodies have become so closely associated with discussions of time and space, in many discourses, that it becomes very easy to accept music as a sign of temporal or spatial relations. It doesn't require much of a leap of faith to move from considering music as a sign of inner time to considering it as an index and agent of authentic and transcendent spiritual experiences. Steven Friedson, in his study of kaleidoscopically polymetric drumming and trance healing in Malawi, suggests that "Music shapes both spiritual and human energy into the same modal pattern. Drumming in the *vimbuza* mode constructs a time so deeply felt that its flow can become the flow of inner time—that which Bergson calls *durée*" (Friedson 1996, 161–2).

Writing on Sufi *qawwālī* performances, Regula Qureshi relates musical temporality to listeners' transcendence in a different way: "the musical idiom . . . acts as a catalyst for the separate, yet simultaneous apprehension of different kinds of time into a synthesis that can be profoundly moving" (1994, 526). The different "kinds of time" to which Qureshi refers include simple patterns of musical articulation (regular, drummed musical metric patterns and non-metric verbal rhythms), longer term musical processes (the sequential use of three different kinds of musical-textual repetitions), and Sufi philosophical concepts of "annihilation," *fanā*, and "sustenance," *baqā* (1994; 513, 518, 504). Rather than explain the concepts of "annihilation" and "sustenance" in terms of their iconic relationship with embodied musical processes (as Bergson does in his explanation of duration), she implies that *qawwālī*'s temporal multiplicity itself emotionally "moves" the Sufi subject to transcend existential dualities.[13]

Friedson and Qureshi link concrete musical characteristics to forms of transcendence and implicate one or another broader theory of time. A few characteristics of Kota music, such as the ethereal timbre of the *bugīr* and the shortness of a few possession tunes, may seem to relate to transcendence, but the relationship remains ambiguous, for the same musical qualities pertain to quite ordinary pieces. The same problem obtains when trying to find the musical basis of Kota affective categories. More concretely, Kota music indexically grounds the listener and player in particular dances, locations, rituals, and processional paths. If it is possible to accept music as a sign of temporal or spatial relations in the Kota case, it is because Kotas draw attention to analogies between traveling by foot and making music, sometimes through language and sometimes through other forms of action.

Footprints and Anchoring

Kotas, like other Nilgiri natives, indexically relate paths to music by assigning instrumental pieces to sections of significant movement. They iconically inscribe paths in songs, as singers invite the listener to move through the song, retracing the steps of the protagonist. Anchor points bend, shape, and mark paths. Kotas morally inflect paths and musical pieces in various ways, and in degrees "high" or "low." Some of the destinations of those paths, and the genres and pieces of said music, are gendered. One may choose a long or short route and one may have to alter one's path according to the ceremonial time. Musicians and walkers can make melodies and paths longer or shorter depending on how they decide to reach Point B from Point A.

Kotas conceive a melodic step (*meṭ*) as a single articulation, or as a set of articulations. Kotas link melodies, conceived as series' of note-articulations, to paths, conceived as series' of temporary destinations, in terms of their mutual flexibility relative to fixed endpoints (A and B).[14] Kotas recognize an essential difference between the ways in which they bend and stretch *koḷ* melodies such as the temple-opening tune and the gridlike precision with which they must articulate the foundational strokes on the drums. Some of these foundational strokes are made to correspond with fixed melodic endpoints (A and B) through "anchoring."

When comparing melodies to paths, Kotas theorize music and spatiotemporality together. The distinction between fixity and flexibility which Kotas implicate in playing music and explicate in speaking about music shares a logic of relations with the distinction that Bergson and other philosophers have drawn between kinds of time. The significance of the analogy rests not on "inner time" or any other "kind of time" as a universal category, but on the role that articulations of different rates, flexibilities, and kinds play in the ways humans form categories—whether in the minds of individuals, in the explicit collective representations of groups, or the implicit knowledge actors use in their daily lives.

Through performance, Kotas give dynamic, spatiotemporal form to the deep truths which they associate with some of their places. John Cleese's character may have been right when he said, "The first step to knowing who we are, is knowing *where* we are, and *when* we are," but in Kota words of god, mention of "where" is enough: "when" and "who" follows.[15] The diviners of Kolmēl village were known to speak formulaic words of god, treated as enduring truths no less fresh for their repetition. The diviner, Maṭa Kamaṭn, chanted this assonant pair of phrases metrically,

tal	ā	jārm	tāl	ā	jārm
1	·	· ·	2	·	· ·

Literally "that which is at the top of the tree [should stay] at the top; that which is at the bottom of the tree [should stay] at the bottom," this principle of vertical hierarchy is evident in such varied domains as gender, generations, dry funeral umbrellas, places of musical performance, and paths.[16] For the gods to function, for Kotas to have *catym*, "up should remain up" and "down should remain down" in all domains of Kota life. In the horizontal dimension, Kotas project temporal continuity onto the image of walking forward and leaving behind a recognizable stamp, "following in one's footsteps," a trace of individuality:

ajk aj ("print to print")	Put your footprints in the footprints [of the ancestors],
meṭk meṭ ("step to step")	Place your foot where the [ancestors] placed their feet

The diviner Maṭa Kamaṭn used to stamp his feet to emphasize and embody this phrase (bold indicates foot stamps):

aj	je	ke	**aj**	je		**meṭ**	ṭe	ke	**meṭ**	ṭe	
1	2	3	4	5	6	1	2	3	4	5	6

Moving about in the landscape, vertically or horizontally, then, provides Kotas a set of "root metaphors" with which they describe other aspects of experience.[17] "Aj" (imprint) and "meṭ" (step) invoke both "place" and "placement." Kotas imprint their feet in their ancestors' place by dancing in front of the "house of the erected post" where the primordial black cow left its footprint (*aj*). The black cow's footprint returns as an anchor in many Kota "paths." Perhaps the most widely-shared god song (CD 37) is "bacāna bacavanīlo, bacavana pādike caraṇa caraṇame," "we take refuge in the foot of Bacavan, Bacavan who is a cow"—a multiply resonant reference to sustenance which, in the song, connects the milk-bearing black cow to the beast of burden in the harvest and anchors today's fecundity to the footprint of the ancient bovine.[18] As the Kotas dance where their ancestors danced, singing where their ancestors sang, they embody the principle of following in their ancestors' footsteps (*meṭ*). This density of linguistic, physical, and visual imagery, grounded in the iconic relationship among various semiotic sets, emphasizes worship as an action and divinity as a presence in a particular place at a special time.

APPENDIX

A Musical Census of Kolmēl Village

To overview a few villages statistically and create a context for conversing with as many Kotas as possible, I spent about four months in 1991–2 collecting genealogies; these included both male and female lines and in as many generations as my interviewees could remember. I noted educational and professional information as well. Most Kotas provided such without my asking, being quite familiar with the word and concept of "census." I was the first census-taker to include musical questions, however; in speaking with a large number of men and women I identified musically-interested persons and determined that to some extent musical abilities/interests ran in families. Brief interviews frequently led to impromptu singing demonstrations, especially among women; lively recording sessions happily interrupted my mundane task, allowing me to ask more detailed questions about specific performances.

I intended eventually to link all the genealogies together, but tracing the multiple ways in which families connected with one another proved difficult: the core husband and wife of a household may each have had several previous marriages; men were sometimes married to two wives at the same time. Furthermore, I learned that what constituted "marriage" was not a single ritual, but several rituals, so the question of how many times a person had really been married was not always possible to determine. It was also difficult to determine who were the proper residents of a house. Families in which one or another working-age adult was employed in Ooty (or further away) might reside in the village only sporadically; some men and women commuted on a daily basis; others did not. Older women, widows whose children lived in several villages, often visited one or another child for weeks or months at a time. It would have been arbitrary to classify such a woman as a member of one household and not another.

There were 228 residents in Kolmēl village according to my estimation—this included some but probably not all those who lived most of the year outside of the village and returned for important occasions such as the god ceremony. Most Kotas practiced agriculture and continue to do so—noted here are those who specifically mentioned agriculture as an occupation. The category "occupation" allowed subjects more than a single choice. A man may be simultaneously a carpenter, blacksmith, and agriculturalist, for example. These figures are only intended to give a rough idea of what I in fact intended to count; they do indicate, of course, the many problems with census categories of any kind.

The age group of those up to eighteen years of age comprised 45 per cent of the village population: 51 males and 51 females, almost all of whom (of the appropriate age) were or had been studying in school. The age group 19–25 composed 15 per cent of the village population, again evenly split between males and females (17 each). Here the education level clustered in the range spanning from the 9th standard to a Bachelor's degree for men and from 7th standard to 11th standard for women. Occupations of men in this group, when mentioned, were: 1 HPF (Hindustan Photo Films), 1 Cordite Factory, 3 agriculturalists, 3 carpenters, 1 postal employee, 1 blacksmith, 1 *mundkānōn* (a ritual leader), and 1 other.

The age group 26–40 (21 per cent of the village) was once again very closely split between men (25) and women (22). Education for men spanned from the 5th standard (1) to a Bachelor's degree (3), with a cluster in the 8th–10th standard range. For women, education spanned 4th–6th and 9th–11th, with the largest number completing their education after the 6th standard (8 women). In this age group, for men, the occupations were: 6 HPF, 2 Cordite Factory, 9 agriculturalists, 1 carpenter, 1 blacksmith, 1 *mundkānōn*, and 4 others. In the age group above 40 gender demographics diverge: 19 men (8 per cent) versus 26 women (11 per cent). 17 of the 19 men had at least had some education, with clusters at the 5th (6) and 8th (4) standards. Dr P. Varadharajan, MBBS (graduate of a Medical School), was the only one in his age group to study beyond the 10th standard. Only 6 women of the 26 had had any education; only one had studied up to the 3rd standard. If we define a literate person as one who has studied up to the third standard as a minimum, such women over 40 in Kolmēl village (23 per cent) well exceeded the average literacy rate of Scheduled Tribal women living in rural areas in India generally (16.02 per cent according to the census of 1991) and nearly attained that of the total Scheduled Tribal population, male and female (27.38 per cent)—this is particularly striking in light of the fact that literacy rates nationally are calculated among those who are fifteen years of age and older. In fact Kota literacy overall (if Kolmēl is any indication) well exceeds the Indian national average of 54 per cent.

As for musical statistics, among boys up to the age of 18, four reported ability to play the the cylinder-drum, *par* (they didn't distinguish between the deeper sounding, *dobar*, and the higher, *kiṇvar*), with one of these also able to play the frame drum, *tabaṭk*, and idioglottal clarinet, *pulāng* (this was Kaṇṇan, now one of the top young *koḷ* players). In the 19–25 range: 9 *par* players (4 *dobar* only, 1 *tabaṭk* and *dobar*, 1 all instruments), 3 *tabaṭk* players (one of them mentioned only *tabaṭk*), and one *koḷ* player (the one who plays all instruments: this was Duryodhana). In the 26–40 age range there were 13 *par* players (3 *dobar* only; 2 *tabaṭk* also), no exclusively *kiṇvar* or *tabaṭk* players, and no *koḷ* players. Of the men above 40, there were 10 *par* players (2 *dobar* alone; 2 *tabaṭk* and *par*; 1 *tabaṭk* and *kiṇvar*; 1 *kiṇvar* alone; 2 all instruments), 6 *tabaṭk* players (those mentioned, plus one exclusively *tabaṭk* player), and 2 *koḷ* players (all instruments: Raman and Puccan). Altogether, 12 men mentioned ability to play the valveless trumpet, *kob* (this instrument is not considered particularly musical, however). One mentioned ability to play the *mridangam* (a barrel drum used largely in Karnatak music).

In viewing these statistics I noted that not all those who might be seen playing an instrument during a festival or a funeral described themselves (or were described by others) as instrumentalists for this survey. There were only three *koḷ* players, Puccan, Raman, and his son Duryodhana, for example. Although these three were indeed considered the best at the time, several others used to attempt to play along as well. The idea that the *kiṇvar* requires special ability is reinforced by the ways in which people responded to the survey: only two responded naming the *kiṇvar* as a specialty in comparison with 10 who mentioned *dobar* specifically. Overall, this means that 34 per cent of all the males in the village (all ages) perform musical instruments (*kob* not included). Although I did ask women about their singing abilities, I did not include this information in my survey because such musicianship is not discrete: all women and girls participate in communal god songs. Among these, certain individuals stand out and compose their own songs, others are repositories of old traditional songs. I learned about the talents of some of these women gradually over several years; a few of their stories and a number of their songs are presented in this book.

Glossary

(#) = number of DEDR entry

[#] = number of DEDR entry to which item probably belongs

[-] = no entry in Emeneau's works or notes

"x" = Emeneau's definition of term (my own, if different, is not in quotes)

'x' = quotation or literal translation

verb- = verb stem (used in future constructions)

(verb)- = simple present and past stem

English Terms

Anchor a value-laden point of reference that affects events or places surrounding it

Spacetime a definable pattern with respect to both time and space within which a set of related events are performed or, in the case of natural events, are perceived to occur

Kota and Other Indian-language Terms

ādivāsī "original inhabitant," tribal

āminj *Eleusine coracana*, commonly known as *rāgī*, a staple millet in several parts of the subcontinent

ānāṭōr (*ā* + *nāṛ* + *ōr*) 'people of that land'; spirits of the dead, ancestors

aṇviṛcd koḷ tune, similar to the temple-opening tune, played at the channel-cleaning and other rituals during the god ceremony

aṛcāyḷ tent or canopy under which Kotas sleep during god ceremony or dry funeral

 238

*aṛcāyḷ koḷ*s	twelve *devr koḷ*s which are played while men sit under or near the *aṛcāyḷ* during the god ceremony
āṭ	dance
āṭ koḷ	dance melody, instrumental
āṭḷ	song of grief or mourning
ayṇōr	Kota father god
āyv	(393) "soul, steam, vapor"
bugīr	five- or six-holed bamboo trumpet
cādā	plain, ordinary
cādā dāk	'plain type' of rhythmic pattern, a kind of compound duple
catym	(< S. *satya*) truth, genuineness, or virtuousness and the power attendant on possessing such qualities
cātrm	(< S. *śāstra*) ritual
ceṇḍ	[-] a ball made of cow dung, *nakarg* grass, *pacāl pūdy* (ash from the *doḍtic* at *devr*), gold, copper, iron, brass, and silver; worn around men's necks or in their hair
cōlai	(Ta.) a type of forest (Badaga, *sōle*, Ko. *tēl*)
dāk	kind, type; rhythmic pattern; melody
daṛv	(3024) path, way
dayṇ	(< S. *dhvani*) voice quality
devr	The god ceremony
devr/devrgūḷ	god/gods
devr koḷ	'god tune'; melody played at the god ceremony and related ceremonies
devr pāṭ	god song
dobar	deeper-sounding, sometimes louder type of double-headed cylinder drum
doḍ	big, important
doḍayṇōr	'big father god'; the main deity at Kolmēl
doḍ tic	the 'big fire', or main fire which is supposed to contain god and must remain lit throughout the god ceremony
doḍ pabm	'big festival' of food, ritual games, and dancing in February–March. Also called *puḷ pabm*
dū/dūv	cremation area of funeral ground

dukt koḷ	sad instrumental pieces, usually from the funeral repertoire
dukt pāṭ	sad song (*āṭḷ*)
ēkaḷc- (ēkaḷc-)	(879 reads *ēkalc*) "to shout to someone from a distance"; shouting "eh" to someone without saying their name. Toda style of shouting "*a hau kau*" in their dance songs. Way of calling cattle. Ringing sound made on *kiṇvar*, with fingers splayed
elkāl	hearth, woodfire stove in kitchen for cooking
eṛ	(< S. *iḍā*, offering [EVS]) food as offering
ērdabaṭk	Kota kettle drum
eṛm	(434) place
et- (eyt-)	(796) "to take (by picking up and carrying), take off (cloak), raise (as legs to the sky when one is knocked down), join (hands in salutation), open (eyes in amazement), build (house)"; heed (words), render (song instrumentally or vocally). Often pronounced īt- (īt-)
	vākm et- — for *mundkānōns* to utter prayers
	jōṛ et- — to play musical instruments
	koḷ et- — to play the koḷ
gag	the syllable Kotas use to represent the lowest pitch on a wind instrument; serves as a pedal tone
gagarcd	warming up on the *koḷ*, making the *gag* sound (with all holes covered) clearly
gagvāl	dancing area in front of *kab iṭ pay* in *īkēr* of Kolmēl village
guṛy	(1655) temple
guṛykaṭ	catafalque canopy erected above bier in Kota funerals
guṛyterdd koḷ	the temple opening tune (also called *ōlāgūc koḷ*)
guṛyvāl	protected area around Kota temples
iḍ- (iṭ-)	(442) "to put, fix," plant (seeds or larger items); shoot with bow and arrow or gun; light (fire)
iḍ- (iṭ-)	(443) "to beat" (in Kolmēl dialect); clap hands in *kummi*, place finger on hole of wind instrument.
	koḷvar iṭo — the musicians play
iḷv- (iḷt-)	(504) "to drag on ground (intr.); drag (tr.)"; produce fire by twirling; prolong note on the *koḷ*

irp- (irpy-)	(751) "to blow through (tube, wind instrument)"; *cīl pacṯ irpkōṟo*, one must blow into the *koḷ* by taking in air, i.e. by circular breathing. This is the verb for 'blowing' into the *koḷ, pulāng, kob*, and *bugīr* and 'playing' the *pījl*. To 'play' the *koḷ* is to 'render', et- (eyt-)
jālrāv	(< S. *jha*) hand cymbals
kab iṭ pay	'house of the erected post': house lying on site of first house in village or exogamous division. See also *iḍ-*
kakuy	sanctified inner chamber of *mundkānōn*'s house
kāl gūc āṭ	'leg joining dance'; always played/danced first in a sequence of dance tunes/dances
kaṇ	note, eye, words to a song, joint of bamboo
kanjar	the bell/mouth of the *koḷ*
kāṟ	(1438) "jungle without trees, uncultivated ground, unfenced field"
kāṟ	[1438] (jungle or not) place without people
kāṟ-kar	(1293) farming land
kaṭ	(1147) "knot, caste custom; case of which decision has been given"
kaṭ- (kac-)	(1147) "to tie, build, manage (house), be equal"; compose song or melody
kaṭḷ	cot, bedframe, bier
kār āv	'black cow'; the divine black cow that originally led Kotas to their village sites
kavāl	grassless yard, area of tightly packed earth or cement in front of a house or row of houses
kavāl condm	[-] 'yard relations': members of family sharing a line of houses (i.e. smaller division than *kēr*, determined by space as well as *kuty*); non-blood relatives may become yard relations by moving next door
kēr	row or cluster of houses, the three largest units of which, *ākēr, īkēr, naṟykēr*, house exogamous groups in Kolmēl village
kēṟ	(1942) "harm, danger, loss, funeral, corpse;" death pollution
kēṟ koḷ	type of funeral melody associated with buffalo sacrifice

	and with sad emotion tempered by excitement and mild joy; tunes played for Toda funeral
kiṇvar	higher pitched, sometimes smaller type of double-headed cylinder drum
kō	cow
kob	(2115) "branch, horn of an animal. . . tusk;" pillar; curved, brass, valveless trumpet
Kōjkāl	temple to the god *rangrayṇ* (Ko.), or *rankanātar* (Ta.), on the site of a former *kōj* tree
Kōjkāl devr	annual festival at the Kōjkāl temple
kōkāl	Kota village
koḷ	a shawm (double-reed instrument with conical bore); a tune played on the *koḷ, bugīr*, or *pulāng*
koḷ arcd	warming up the *koḷ*, getting in tune, etc.
kōv	Kota ethnonym
kummi	circle dance form practiced by women of Tamilnadu and Kerala which resembles that practiced by Kotas. Involves singing, clapping the hands and stepping rhythmically
kunayṇōr	'small father god;' the god in Kolmēl said to have originated from Porgāṛ
kun tic	'small fire' near *tak* tree during *devr*
kuty or *kuyt*	family, lineage
kūṛ- (kūc-)	(1882) "to join, gather, meet, assemble"
kūṭ- (kūc-)	(1882) "to make to join, summon (a meeting), gather (tr.), shut in (cattle);" enclose, lock up, block entrance; *kūcd*, joining
kūṭm	(1882) village council meeting
man tāv	a dry funeral celebrated on a small scale with local participants (contrast with *ūr tāv*)
marvādy	respect
māmūl	tradition, longstanding custom
mel pac mog	'breast clutching boy' (i.e. chief mourner): child or young man who serves as an officiant during the dry funeral

meṭ	(5057) footstep
meṭ	melody; e.g. cinema meṭ: film melody
mumuṛy	(4921) knot tied in front of *mundkānōn*'s head, said to contain god (same as *vāraṇam*)
mundkānōḷ	wife of *mundkānōn*; leads women in god-related ritual activities
mundkānōn	leader in all village rituals relating to god
nakarg	sp. grass (*Andropogon foulkesii*) stuck in a dung ball and used for various purificatory or protective purposes
naṇṭṇ	male relatives through the father
neyjkōl	firesticks, fire by friction
nērl	sp. *Ligustrum lucidum* (Emeneau 1944-46, II: 361) or *Eugenia arnottiana* (DEDR 2917). Type of ritually significant tree; tree at toḍbāl
nīdy	justice, truth
ōlāgūc koḷ	temple opening tune (also called *guṛy terdd koḷ*), tune for saying "*ōḷy ōḷy*"
ōḷy	sacred sound Kota men utter during central moments of the god ceremony
ōmayṇ	[-] sound of all musical instruments playing at once
oy- (oc-)	(4534) "to beat (percussion instrument);" to play all instruments
ōynāṛ	(4572) path
pac	green, fresh
pacāl	grassy area near the temples in Kolmēl associated closely with divinity and the god ceremony
pac tāv	'green funeral'; funerary rituals and cremation following shortly after a death
par	double-headed cylinder drum played with the hands (see *dobar* and *kiṇvar*)
pāṭ	song, piece on the *pījl*
pay	(3984) house
payvāl	verandah
pēnpacōḷ	female medium of spirits of the dead

pēr	(4410) name
pērn	(EVS: bullock load) ritual of circumambulating and offering rice at funeral; see *pēr- (pēyr-)*
pēr- (pēyr-)	the action of carrying bags of rice and playing the *koḷ* for those rice carriers offering ritual gifts to the deceased. *Pērn* is used in the phrase *pērn koḷ*; can also say *pēyrd koḷ*
pījl	bamboo Jew's harp
piṭāṛ	(EVS) "fried cake of wheat flour and jaggery water, about 3 inches across, fried with hole in centre where implement was stuck in removing the cake"
pul	grass, reed
puḷ	a ritual game (tipcat) played during *doḍpabm*
pulāng/pīk	(Ta. *pullānkuḻal*, bamboo tubular instrument, *pīkkai*, that which is delicate or thin?) [4097] Kota bamboo idioglottal clarinet with downcut reed
rāgam	melodic "mode" in Indian classical music; melody, more generally, in Kota and Tamil
shola	see *tēl* and *cōlai*
stānm	(< S. *sthāna*) place (robustly established)
tabaṭk	frame drum played with sticks
tak	(3096) a purple ellipsoidal berry that grows on a thorny stem (*Berberis tinctoria*); the thorny branches from this plant are used for ritual purificatory purposes
tāḷam	rhythmic framework in Karnatak music; rhythm more generally for the Kotas
talēl	the sacredmost part of the hearth
tāv	death, funeral, corpse
tāv koḷ	funeral tunes, generally
tāvnāṛ	funeral/cremation ground (*pac tāv nāṛ* and *varldāv nāṛ*, green and dry funeral grounds)
tēl	(2891) "forest, menstrual blood"
telac	ceremonial gift
tērkārn	diviner
tērkārc	wife of diviner

tic	(1514) fire
tic pac mog	'fire-holding-boy'; child who symbolically lights funeral pyre and acts as officiant at green funeral
tiruganāṭ	Kota 'turning dance' and accompanying simple-duple rhythmic pattern
tīṭ	Kota: pollution from menstruation or childbirth; Tamil: (*tīṭṭu*) pollution from menstruation, childbirth, or death
toḍbāl	sacred tree area 'gaur place' in Kolmēl and other villages
tondiṭ	raised circular areas surrounded by stones in Kolmēl village where first fire is placed at the commencement of the god ceremony
uḷī/uḷīḷ/uḷīv	kitchen
ūr	village, town, city
ūr tāv	large-scale celebration of dry funeral (contrast with *man tāv*)
valāry	*Dodonea viscosa*
ūṭm	(600) "meal paid to god at god ceremony"
vag	*Salix tetrasperma,* wood used to make *koḷ*s and churned to make fire
vākm	"prayer, promise, god's words" (EVS)
vāraṇm	foreknot in *mundkānōn*'s hair during *devr*; said to contain god
varāṛ	traditional Kota white cloak
varldāv	(*varl* + *tāv*) 'dry funeral,' the Kota secondary mortuary ceremony
vatm	*Panicum miliare*, a type of millet
veky	plant (*Pouzolzia bennettiana*) whose thin bark is rubbed with water to produce washing suds
veḷk	oil lamp
vet-vedyr	cane and bamboo (used to symbolically rethatch temple)

Notes

Chapter 1

1. "Forms of spacetime" are compatible with what Munn terms "spatiotemporal processes," "modes of spacetime," and "spatiotemporal forms" (Munn 1986, 10, 11).
2. Although forms two and four resemble Durkheim's mechanical and organic solidarity respectively (Durkheim 1933), I do not wish to imply that the coexistence of both processes has evolutionary significance.
3. See Pollock (1989, 18) on the word *śāstra* in ancient India. In South India, the stipulated action itself, the "ritual," is often termed a *śāstra*, as is a book prescribing such rituals or rules. See Asad (1993, 58) for parallels in the historical development of the English term ritual.
4. Lit. "one [who acts as] vehicle of god;" see related Tamil word for temple chariot, *tēr* (DEDR 3459).
5. Emeneau's etymology for *kōv* links it to the Tamil term for potter (DEDR 1762). Only Kota women have traditionally practiced pottery.
6. Rajan and Angarn spoke to me in Tamil and Kota, inserting the English words indicated in quotes.
7. This consultant strikes to the heart of Toda culture, the dairy, in his first reference to dependence on the Kotas.
8. Brief discussion of such time and space theories appears in Chapter 8.
9. By a "phenomenological" I mean an approach drawing from the philosophical tradition that German philosopher Edmund Husserl (1859–1938) is credited with founding, which focuses on the direct objects, or "phenomena," of experience. In some social-cultural anthropological and ethnomusicological writings, including the present work, this involves exploring how subjects constitute their worlds through action; often a phenomenological attitude questions the epistemological priority of language. Some ethnomusicologists have used ideas from the phenomenological tradition to explain how their own experiences of learning to perform music inform their explanations of their subjects' musical understandings (cf. Bakan 1999, 292ff.; Rice 1984, 72 and *passim*). Certain kinds of musical insight can be obtained only through such

sustained, critical learning of performance; however, I am not convinced that the language of phenomenology is always necessary to convey that point.

10. The term originated from the Sanskrit *satya*, "true, real," and entered Kota through Tamil, *catyam*.
11. This conveys a casualness inappropriate before someone for whom it is important to show respect. One leg over the other also suggests a hierarchy that implicitly challenges the social one. Kota women must sit at an equal or lower level than men, and *mundkānōns* or *tērkārns* (types of ritual specialists) must never sit at an elevation below that of anyone else. By crossing one leg over the other, one risks having one's leg elevated above that of the ritually elevated personage across from whom one is sitting. A similar taboo is observed in Ghana when an ordinary person sits before an Ashanti chief. I suspect this form of repose suggests hierarchy in a variety of societies, as do a number of bodily comportments (see Douglas 1970, 70).
12. Ethnologue.com provides a population figure of 2,000 in 1992.
13. This is established by Emeneau primarily on the basis of a palatalization of proto-Dravidian *k*- before front vowels in Tamil/Malayalam, which does not occur in Kota or Toda (Emeneau 1967, 367).
14. It is also possible that they were sufficiently isolated from the mainstream on the plains—perhaps for social reasons—to develop their own dialect of pre-Tamil, if not a distinct language, before they migrated. It is not necessary to have total isolation from a parent language group in order for a new language to break off; but some sort of boundary should exist, whether social or geographic.

Chapter 2

1. See comparative table of Nilgiri instruments in Wolf (*ca*. 2006).
2. For the construction of Irula musical instruments, for instance, see Zvelebil (1979–82, pt. III: 185).
3. In "*gag*," the [a] is short, sounding like the [u] in the English word "gun."
4. It also refers to the Toda dance song style, which sounds very much like a form of religious calling-out Kotas perform with the syllables "*a hau kau*."
5. The *ḍhol* in this ensemble is usually a cylinder drum; the *tāshā* is a shallow kettle drum; cymbals called *jhāñjh* are often included as well. These ensembles perform for weddings, Muḥarram, and a variety of other occasions in many parts of the Indian subcontinent.
6. For description of tribal music in such terms, see Knight (1983; 1993), Dournon (1980), Wade (1980, 153), Powers (1980), and Babiracki (1991).
7. This paragraph quotes from and paraphrases my fuller treatment of these issues in Wolf (2000/2001a).

8. Wade (2000, 307) notes that the drone does not appear iconographically until the 1500s. But the underlying musical reason for a drone, the "conceptual change moving towards the notion of a single system tonic," was probably earlier, perhaps "well under way during the last centuries of the ancient period," i.e. twelfth to thirteenth centuries (Powers 1980, 79).
9. On taxonomic anomaly, see Douglas (1999). On taxonomic overlap, see Tambiah (1986b).
10. The binary idea is tricky with respect to the 3 + 2 + 2 + 3 pattern, because while the *tabaṭk* pattern, at minimum, divides the pattern in half, the cymbals, I have noticed, sometimes emphasize **3** + **2** + **2** + 3; other times they emphasize **3** + 2 + **2** + 3.
11. Compare CD 15, Raman alone on the *koḷ* playing the temple-opening tune with drummed accompaniment, with CD 16, Raman playing the same tune unaccompanied on the *pulāng*.
12. Kotas in the 1990s told me that five-hole *bugīr*s were the norm, but some Kotas make them with six holes and I recently learned of six-hole instruments that have survived from earlier generations. Jagor (1914) found six- as well as five-hole *bugīr*s at the turn of the twentieth century. See Fig. 9.
13. See Herzfeld's discussion of *disemia* (1997, 14).
14. Gurkhas are ethnic Nepalis known for their wiry robustness, who made up many of the ranks of the army, the police, and watchmen under the British.
15. See Gell (1992, 54) and Jackson (1996, 6) on the cultural significance of categorical differences.
16. Cīrmuk, "lice-egg nose," is a nickname referring to the smallness of his nose. Since Kamaṭn is a common name, such nicknames are used to distinguish one Kamaṭn from another.
17. The historical memory the god ceremony now evokes is, for the most part, one in which the Kotas have already settled in the Nilgiris. What this central ceremony might have been in an even earlier age, before there was a Kota village in the Nilgiris, is hard to imagine. This song's interpreters would suggest that it consisted of a ritual leader, a knot on the forehead containing god, and some activity with a cow.
18. The composer of this piece is not known. Syllable elongations due to singing are not shown here, except in the last word of a line. Vocalizations on "la" and "le" have also been omitted. Stanzas and lines are divided according to melodic criteria.
19. Its root is *sthā*: according to Monier-Williams "to stand, stand firmly, station one's self." *Sthāna* means "place, location, spot, station," and more importantly "home, abode" (TL s.v. *tā̱nam*). The place where milk is ritually placed is an *eṛm* (e.g. a *pāl vecd eṛm,* milk-keeping place); what a new location becomes in performing this act is a *stānm*, with an implication of permanence, continuity in time.

The importance of milk as a ritual element in making a place a home is also reflected in the Tamil custom of boiling milk in a house just prior to or immediately upon moving in.

20. It is possible that the interpretation of the cow as potentially a form of god—as virtually any being or object could be, if god chooses to enter it—eventually evolved for some to a view of the cow *as* god, inherently a form of a mother goddess as in some Hindu belief systems. This would logically intermesh with the outcry against bovine sacrifice in the period of accelerated assimilation in the 1930s and 1940s.
21. This is a common phenomenon in origin stories of Hindu temples, see e.g. Eichinger Ferro-Luzzi (1987).

Chapter 3

1. Roll is not called for women, who stay in their houses or return to their natal villages at this time.
2. Cf. Mines' analysis of the Tamil *ūr* as a political entity (1995, 209).
3. Tamil terms *nāṭu* and *ūr* "derive their meaning from the contextually shifting spatial orientation of the person" (Daniel 1984, 70). Through the soil, the Tamil village (as an *ūr*) comes to embody inhabitants' waste as well as the fruits of their productive labor; likewise, the village soil constitutes residents' bodies through the foodstuff produced from it (Daniel 1984; cf. Toren 1995, 170).
4. In Kolmēl, the temples are within optimal reach of all houses. In Kurgōj, stones mark the central place in which the temples once stood. The temples were moved to an area above the village, probably to create a buffer zone from mundane activity and to make room for more houses.
5. See Gell's discussion of "physical time" or "temporal territory" (1992, 240).
6. See Casey's criticism of the concept of "place" as a particularization of undifferentiated "space" and space as a "neutral, pre-given medium, a tabula rasa onto which the particularities of culture and history come to be inscribed" (Casey 1996, 14). I cannot avoid using the word "space" in a conventional, descriptive sense to refer to where objects and actions are located in physical terms; but I will avoid, for both theoretical and ethnographic reasons, using the term "space" to refer to this tabula rasa.
7. My usage of the term "space" closely parallels that of Michel de Certeau, in that it "takes into consideration vectors of direction, velocities, and time variables . . . [and] is composed of intersections of mobile elements" (Certeau 1984, 117). But space in my usage is not merely "actuated by the ensemble of movements deployed within it," for I would argue that places themselves are associated with motion. To say that "space is a practiced place" (ibid.)

implies that there are places that are not practiced; from my perspective, no such place exists.

8. For village, forest, and other categories of place in Sanskrit literature, see also Feldhaus (1995; 1990) and Bakker ed. (1990).
9. See also Raymond Williams (1973), who, in another context, argues that it is "outsiders" who "entertain an objective concept" of landscape (Hirsch 1995, 13).
10. The poems are said to be "realistic [portrayals of] the actual customs of the people and the actual state of the landscape" (Thani Nayagam 1966, 87); they characteristically lack abstraction, accomplishing their "most complex thinking . . . in terms of physical detail" (Ramanujan 1985, 287). These "objective landscapes" become what Ramanujan calls "interior landscapes" when the Tamil poet, in the "interior" or *akam* genre, uses these synthetic topoi to evoke five types or phases of love.
11. An inscription of the Hoysala general Punisa in 1117 CE is the first written mention of the Nilgiris and the Todas. His army had "frightened the Toda, driven the Kongas underground, slaughtered the Poluvas, and put to death the Maleyalas, terrified king Kala, and entering into Nila mountain offered up its peak to the Lakshmi of Victory" (Francis 1908, 91–2). According to C. Hayavadana Rao, "The title 'Subduer of the Nilagiri' (*Nilagiri-sadaran*) seems indeed to have been borne hereditarily for long afterward by the Hoysalas and their successors. Perhaps one reason why they gloried in it was that the Nilgiris were holy hills" (Francis 1908, 92).
12. "Verticality" is significant cross-culturally as a phenomenological dimension of rulership. Humphrey, in her study of landscape in Mongolia, argues for a "chiefly mode" of social action in which "the aim is reaching upwards, the making of a link between earth and sky" (Humphrey 1995, 142).
13. The ritual protectivity of thorny plants relies on the physical ability of thorns to pierce the skin, and hence to ward off physical intrusion. Hence the form of this sign vehicle "is intrinsic to the message carried" (Munn 1974, 580).
14. *Tēl* is a cognate of *shola* (DEDR 2891).
15. Duryodhana, for instance, showed me a patch of *pul* from which *koḷ* reeds are made, telling me he keeps the location secret for fear of losing his source. Good *pul* is hard to find around Kolmēl.
16. This *āṭḷ* is transcribed as sung. The transcription includes vowels at the end of words and in between consonants. These would not normally be included in speech. The parenthetical (a) sounds are glottal articulations characteristic of the genre; they are said to signal sadness (*dukm*).
17. From this point onward in the song the words appear to be forced into the pattern of the song. Here redundancy seems to have occurred by mistake.
18. Literally, "I poured unconsciousness medicine into her body."

19. There is here a split between what would in Tamil society be seen as two sides of the same coin. Malevolent spirits of the dead in Tamil society can become *pēy* or *picācu* (demons) which may, among other things, be attracted to the odor of female sexual activity; men, however, are not subject to the same danger (Ram 1991, 90). Among the Kotas, it is the libidinous qualities of other people, especially those who possess supernatural powers, that are potentially harmful. The spirits of the dead are still Kotas, in a sense, and thus are protective.
20. See also Toren's Fijian study, in which "the passing of time" is remarked upon "in terms of places and landmarks that function as reference points for the succession of events" (Toren 1995, 163).
21. One difference is that no such time category exists in Kota culture; since Kotas do not believe that all places and place-names were fixed at a particular point in time, it is always possible for new places to be named, discovered, and given representation in ritual and song. Another difference is that the paths mentioned in *āṭḷs* do not trace out regions that guide the ways in which particular clans should behave or understand their "spiritual identity" (see Morphy 1995, 205).
22. God songs bear similarity with Australian aboriginal songs in that they pertain to the "spiritual identity" of Kota villages as wholes. See previous note.
23. For a different version of the text, see Wolf (1997a, 342–3).
24. The *mundkānōḷ* and *mundkānōn* are interlinked in that they must be one another's first spouses, and if one dies the other loses office.
25. See Babb (1981) on "visual interaction" and Eck (1998) on *darśan*.
26. Occasionally, speakers will collapse both semantic fields into the word *tīṭ*, whose Tamil form, *tīṭṭu*, refers to both kinds of defilement. This Dravidian term (e.g. Ta. *tīṇṭu-*) concerns relationships of proximity: to touch, feel, come in contact with (DEDR 3274). Defilement is transmitted by touch, or by physical proximity.
27. Hunting societies cross-culturally maintain more acute menstrual restrictions than do non-hunters. For theories on why, see Buckley and Gottlieb (1988, 21–3).
28. After a funeral or a dry funeral, jewelry removed as a part of mortuary ritual is restored after purification by exposure to fire. See photo in Wolf 2001 (407). The quintessential Hindu example of "trial by fire" is Sita's entrance into a bonfire to demonstrate her chastity after being rescued from the hands of the demon Ravana by her husband Rama.
29. According to Mandelbaum's and Emeneau's notes, the upper *kēr* of *īkēr* was called *gagēr* in the 1930s. Now *gagēr* commonly refers to the lines of houses collinear with the *gagvāl*. I am using the current terminology.
30. "*Ōmayṉ jāyct dārāḷm oyḷām pacandāyṟ oḷd.*"

31. During the early 1990s, when I began my fieldwork, up through 2002, Kotas kept the *guṛyvāl* fenced off to prevent entry. They later decided to remove the fence, since "traditionally" no such fence was used. However, the restrictions on entering the area remain in force.
32. I obtained this list of directional terms from M.B. Emeneau's notes (EVS) and confirmed their meanings with Duryodhana. The term *mārnmūl* refers, according to Duryodhana, only to the setting of the sun. However, in the context of the other terms, where the postfix "n" signifies the back of the body part, *mārn* could well have once meant the upper back, that is, the back of the "chest" (*mār*).
33. Michael Herzfeld discusses fireplaces as sites of both "reconstituted rurality" and "intimations of primitive, 'un-European' living," whose "functionally small value . . . has been displaced by their display value and by their objectification as the loci of nostalgia" in Rethemnos, Crete (1991, 62; 143; 231). One may surmise that fireplaces are maintained as important foci of local meaning, even in changing functional and technological contexts, because of their former centrality in family life. In the Kota case important symbolic associations connect fire with divinity; the hearth as a point of social gravitation and as a site of bodily constitution (through cooked food) is a phenomenologically prominent one that deserves comparative investigation.

Chapter 4

1. Translation condensed from about three minutes of speech recorded in 1991.
2. I excerpted segments of our recorded conversations for the quotations that follow, editing slightly to remove repetition or clarify a point. The irregular English usages are a combination of Varadharajan's own personal speech style and habits of English usage common to many local speakers of English who did not have the benefit of studying in English-medium schools. The same comments apply to my quotations of Jayachandran, who spoke with me in English.
3. Now that Puccan is dead, *koḷ* players in Kolmēl are learning and practicing using recordings of Puccan. See photo section.
4. The Kota entry in Thurston and Rangachari's *Castes and Tribes of Southern India* (1909) includes a description of a funeral in Kotagiri, which suggests the two of them had visited this village on at least one occasion.
5. The temple opening tune is also called the *ōlāguc koḷ* because of its association with the intoning of "*ōḷy ōḷy*" during the god ceremony.
6. See EVS (s.v. *dayṇ*) and Monier-Williams 1990 (s.v. *dhvani*).
7. She said, in Kota, "*nenciṯ unciṯ rāgm ēyk ēyk enm iṭām pacandāyṛ ikvo iḏr pāṭ etkōḍo*," "thinking, considering, where where [in the] melody, how if [we] set [the words] it will be beautiful, thus it is necessary to render a song."

8. I defined *et-* as "render" because it applies to a variety of spoken, sung, and played forms. Although excessive emphasis should not be placed on the other meanings of the verb as a key to the concept of musical variation, the full range of meanings is: "to take (by picking up and carrying), take off (cloak), raise (as legs to the sky when one is knocked down), join (hands in salutation), open (eyes in amazement), build (house)" (from DEDR 796). I recorded, additionally, "heed (words), render (song instrumentally or vocally); *kaṇ et-*, to render '*a hau kau*' with words, *vākm et-*, for *mundkānōn*s to utter prayers, *jōṛ et-* to play *koḷ, par, tabaṭk, kob. Koḷ et-*, to render a *koḷ*." Often pronounced *īt-*.
9. Cēlkāl means "area around the Cēl [type of fig] tree." This place name is found in several villages.
10. Literally "middle raised area," a place Kurgōj residents would recognize as part of their local topography.
11. I have notated the motive on the slightly flat E as a pickup note, but something like it is often squeezed into the return to Measure 1 from Measure 10.
12. The first time he plays this phrase on the recording, Mundan employs an artful ornament on the slightly flat F-sharp, as notated in Measure 5. Subsequent returns to this section begin as in Measure 8, directly on G.
13. Examples are reordered for presentation here.
14. In South India, diarrhoea and purulent skin eruptions are believed to be caused by excess heat in the body and are commonly attributed to local goddesses or *amman*s.

Chapter 5

1. The question remains open whether "tendency tones," as they are known in the Western classical tradition, are perceived as such by Kotas in their music. Although I can analytically describe melodic directionality and infer tonal functions, I have yet to devise a satisfactory methodology for gaining insight into how Kotas understand the function of pitches in melodies. They do not have a vocabulary for such matters.

   Bharucha's concept of "mental representation" is congruent with the "interpretant" in a Peircian framework. In the tonal tradition Bharucha analyses, a non-chord tone is a pointer (an index) toward the tone to which it will resolve; this tone of resolution remains an "object" as long as the non-chord tone remains unresolved. Just as signs may have multiple "objects," unstable tones and rhythmically fluid melodies have many potential anchors.
2. See Munn (1992, 102), Hallowell (1955 [1937]) and Hanks (1990, 295–351).
3. See also Bourdieu who writes, "practice unfolds in time . . . Its temporal structure . . . is constitutive of its meaning" (1990, 81).

4. OED online s.v. "quality" 7a.
5. The use of the body to "map" some aspect of society is common cross-culturally. In the Indic context, the most striking example is the primeval man, Purusha, who, in the Vedas, was the object of sacrifice. His body parts were conceptualized as parts of the universe and the four *varṇas* (ritual and occupational divisions of ancient Hindu society).
6. I present the text here as normally pronounced, not as it is sung, with syllables somewhat deformed; my purpose here is to discuss the text, not the performance. "Mother" is a term of endearment for the girl.
7. I am regarding Christmas here as a holiday on a fixed date, not as a commemoration of the historical event.
8. Historically, Sunday was important as the day of Christ's resurrection, but individual churches argued as to whether Easter should be celebrated on a Sunday or on the appropriate date in the Jewish lunar calendar. Those who opposed reliance on a calendar regulated by "Jewish priests," beginning in the third century, decided on a new "anchor date," in the words of David Duncan: they linked "Christ's resurrection to the solar year and to Ceasar's calendar by using the spring equinox as a fixed astronomic date to determine Easter." Hence, "a formula could be devised to correlate the equinox with the phases of the moon and the weekly cycle of Sundays" (1998, 52–3).
9. Calendrical and certain musical systems "represent closure" in that they structure human experiences of beginnings, middles and ends, whether these experiences are framed within a recurrent cycle, or within an ongoing unfolding of events whose final articulations may or may not be predictable. Barbara Herrnstein Smith, in her landmark study *Poetic Closure*, drew sustained comparisons between poetry and music and focused on what makes the reader of a poem feel "cessation is also conclusion" (1968, 5). The ways in which various systems for organizing time create the experience of structured conclusion make comparisons between music and poetry, or music and time reckoning, especially compelling. Smith's discussion of closure as "a modification of structure that makes *stasis*, or the absence of further continuation, the most probable succeeding event" (34) is somewhat limiting, in that it does not apply well to structures which recur indefinitely (or forever, as in the cycle of months making up a year), but which, at a local level, exhibit forms of closure (the new year). More to the point is her assertion that "whenever a poetic [read: musical] form repeats at its conclusion a formal unit with which it began, closure will be thereby strengthened" (27).
10. I thank Michael Herzfeld for this turn of phrase.
11. This melody is also called the *ōlāguc koḷ* because of its performance when men intone "*ōḷy ōḷy.*"
12. I have about twelve different recordings of the instrumental version of the

temple-opening tune, each about three to twenty minutes long. Only short excerpts of some of these are included here.

13. The recording is slowed down by about a whole tone to account for what are probably differences in tape recorder speeds. I adjusted the recording so that the notated pitch G corresponded to the Western, equal-tempered standard. Then I isolated microsecond excerpts using Cooledit Pro (a computer program), analyzed their frequencies using various methods of fast Fourier transform, and when this did not work (most of the time), I compared the result to tones produced on a keyboard.
14. I.e., they, like *dāks*, are of different sizes. After completing the transcription, I played the temple opening tune for Duryodhana on the *pulāng* and showed him how I divided up the first few sections; he concurred that these, in Kota terms, constitute *dāks* or *meṭs*. In some cases, musicians have denoted my analytic units by such terms to one another in contexts that were independent of my analyses. Along with the letters assigned to melodic units, a prime sign indicates a variation and multiple prime signs indicate different variations of a core idea. A subscript indicates that a motive sounds like it is derived from the larger idea denoted by the letter to which it is attached. A superscript denotes transposition up (+) or down (–) by numbered scale degress. Section C has a stable variation labeled C2; this has its own variants and derivative motives.
15. I thank James Kippen for drawing my attention to the comparison.
16. See second anchor of Measures 3 and 17 and first beat of Measure 15 respectively.
17. Emeneau recorded a variant of this verb as *gagc-*, "to make first tentative unmusical notes on clarinet when starting to play," relating it etymologically to other Dravidian verbs of sound production—especially "emotion" sounds, crying, lamenting, bellowing, and animal sounds, neighing, and cawing (DEDR 1291). If Emeneau's etymology is correct, then the solfa-like status of the *gag* syllable and the verb relating to its production are results of convergent evolution. Usually the addition of [c] to a Kota verb makes it causative. Here, [c] is added to the onomatopoeia itself, conveying the meaning "to cause [the] *gag* [sound]."
18. Compare, for example, Sections C with C′ and E with E′. The primed sections illustrate "tonal envelope."
19. *Kob* players will also issue blasts intermittently during processions and dancing. Since these do not anchor the flow of activities very significantly, they are not represented here.
20. As in Emeneau's published text, the subscript numeral one indicates reported speech. (See Emeneau 1944–6, I: 65–9.)
21. Emeneau records the name Kitūrpayk, which must surely be a variant of the

name of the culture hero Koṭērvaykīṇ: "iṇ" means "father;" "p" frequently becomes "v" in compound words (although not always after "r"). For consistency within this chapter, I retain Koṭērvaykīṇ here.

Chapter 6

1. Throughout this chapter I draw on aspects of what Nancy Munn calls an "intersubjective spacetime," a "multidimensional, symbolic order and process" that consists of and is formed through acts and practices between persons living in different places—in her work, those living on Gawa and other islands of Papua New Guinea. This process is described in terms of such relational parameters as "distance, location . . . and directionality; duration or continuance, succession, [and] timing (including temporal coordination and relative speed of activities)" (1986, 10).
2. Sulli described the complex events surrounding this move. The village headman, *mundkānōn* and *tērkārn* consulted the *pēnpacōḷ*, the female spirit medium for souls of the dead "who becomes possessed by the music of the *bugīr*" (Mandelbaum, May 19, 1937, p. 1). She advised against using latrines, arguing that when Kotas defecate in the open at a distance from the village, the "air god," "sun god," and "rain god" break down the waste and prevent the smell from reaching gods in the temples. This is not possible with latrines in the village. In a meeting of all seven Kota villages, it was decided that Porgāṛ people should not use the latrines. They relocated.
3. See Emeneau (DEDR 4446).
4. Mandelbaum provided the following description of this part of the funeral: "Pretty soon two [*koḷs*] and several drums struck up on the veranda of the deceased's house and the kids crowded 'round to listen. When a village group arrived, they usually brought a couple of sacks of rice with them and this was loaded on a pony (the same one each time) and led around the corpse while the band played a certain tune, then unloaded and taken into the deceased's house" (Mandelbaum, August 11, 1937, p. 3).
5. Here too, DEDR 4446 is a sensible etymology.
6. If the deceased is male, female participants in this ritual would have been born to families outside the *kēr* of the deceased. If the deceased is female, however, the female participants in this ritual could be from the deceased's own family.
7. I thank Nancy Munn for suggesting this possibility to me.
8. See also discussion and photograph of this funeral in Wolf (2001).
9. For expression of the mourner's feelings, see the phrase "I have become a lone woman" in the *āṭḷ* "Kavdayo" in Chapter 2 (CD 20); regarding the power of the ancestors, see "Stone field, thorn field, Kanm father" in Chapter 3

(CD 23); as for positive memories of the deceased, see "En aṇ caḷo" in Chapter 4 (CD 27).

10. See also Herzfeld (1981, 49 and *passim*) who writes of analogies and oppositions between Greek weddings and funerals and the performance genres associated with them, both in terms of affect and "actual content."
11. See also Kivy (1989, 135–6 and *passim*).
12. See Bergson (2001 [1913], 132) on the relationship between words and such "fugitive impressions."
13. The concepts of "emotional contour" and "texture" are developed in Wolf (2001); portions of that discussion are paraphrased here.
14. See location of *nelāgōṛ* on Map 4.
15. On such "dicent" signs, see Peirce (1955, 115) and Turino (1999, 237–40). On iconic and indexical aspects of performance style of laments, see Feld and Fox (1994, 40); on "icons of crying" see Urban (1988, 389ff.)
16. I use this analogy because "redness" is a classic example of Peirce's "qualisign," a quality as a sign. In an extended sense, emotionality is a qualisign with respect to certain kinds of Kota music, for Kotas.
17. See Herzfeld (1997, 27) who writes, "Iconicity seems natural and is therefore an effective way of creating self-evidence. But it is in fact culturally constituted in the sense that the ability to recognize resemblance depends to a large degree on both prior aesthetic criteria and the politics of the situation."
18. In this sense they differ from the musical quality, or what Feld terms "style," of Kaluli "lift up over sounding"—an indigenous aesthetic category that covers music-making, speaking, the sound of waterfalls, and a variety of other phenomena (Feld 1994). When Feld explicates what Kaluli mean by this concept, outsiders (such as myself and my students) who listen to example recordings can hear "lift up over sounding" as a quality of the sounds. Not so with Kota music.
19. This ambiguity maps well onto discourses about the affective status of dry-funeral instrumental tunes (*varldāv koḷs*): are they primarily sad/funerary or happy/godly, or both? It is not surprising, given this ambiguity, that the *koḷ* for each *eṛ vecd* ritual is almost exactly the same in Kolmēl village. Now that Puccan has died, I am not sure the distinction will still be maintained at all. This example of "a posteriori iconism" rests on the idea that the *eṛ vecd* tune has its own melodic character which is inflected according to the larger ceremonial context in which it appears.
20. See Östör (1991, 179); Zimmer (1951, 400); Stutley and Stutley (1984 *s.v. tamas*). *Sattva*, one of the three essential "qualities" or "dispositions" (*guṇa*) of human beings associated with Brahmanical Hinduism, arises out of the Sāṃkhya philosophical school beginning in about the fourth century (Flood 1996, 234). The three terms, *sattva*, *rajas*, and *tamas*, have been applied in

many ways with differing degrees of abstraction by Hindus in their writings historically, in their discourses about their practices today, and by scholars attempting to explain Hinduism through indigenous categories (see Marriott 1989). It would be a mistake to rely on any one fixed representation of what should fit into these three categories because they are now applied with considerable flexibility both to describe and justify existing practice and to provide a basis for guiding future practice. Kotas do not consciously employ the concept of *sattva*, although some will be familiar with it through casual knowledge of Hindu philosophy.

21. See Stutley and Stutley 1984 (*s.v. tamas* and *rajas*); Östör (1991,178–9); Zimmer (1951, 400).
22. When I presented this last bit of explanation (about heaviness keeping god in the house) to Duryodhana shortly before sending this book to press, he greeted it with welcome laughter. My reasoning seemed plausible to him. Duryodhana asked, "OK, then during *devr* does the fact that we serve millet and salt stew [i.e. lighter food] mean that god should just eat and then leave immediately?" I responded, "Fair enough. But then could you expect god to survive for twelve days on fried sweets alone? Besides, the god ceremony is filled with activities that keep god's attention fixed on the Kotas and the *guṛyvāl*." Duryodhana accepted this response. After a few minutes of discussion and argument along these lines, Duryodhana thought that I should include my interpretation in the book. With his permission, I have included a footnote describing our discussion. Neither of us expects all Kotas to subscribe to this explanation. For the benefit of those many Kotas who do reflect upon their rituals, I include this as possible food for their further thought.
23. See Jagadisa Ayyar, who explains that the wife is purified by the "magnetism" of her husband's meditative practices (1985, 59).
24. If they can. In villages without *tĕrkārns* or *mundkānōns*, Kotas cannot perform the god ceremony; nor will some villages perform the ceremony without performing a *varldāv* first.

Chapter 7

1. See photograph of a nineteenth-century Kota temple reproduced in Wolf (2001).
2. The ball is made of cow dung, *nakarg* grass (*Andropogon foulkesii*), ash from the *doḍtic*, gold, copper, iron, brass, and silver.
3. They use gum benzoin ignited from the new bonfire.
4. The *vatm* consumed by ordinary people is par-boiled, dried in the sun, and pounded to remove the chaff before cooking. That consumed by the *mundkānōns* must be more painstakingly prepared by threshing the dried millet without par-boiling it.

5. For the story associated with this *koḷ*, see Wolf 1997b.
6. As of 2001, performers knew fewer of these tunes and did not maintain a consistent order.
7. The number of feasts is one or three probably because even numbers are unlucky. The feasts in general stand for a much longer series of feasts in days past, over the course of which the villagers would complete the entire temple-rethatching.
8. See further analysis of the god ceremony in Wolf (1997a; 1997b; 2001).
9. Some rituals of the god ceremony are performative in the Austinian sense in which saying constitutes doing—as in exchanging marriage vows, apologizing, or naming ships (Austin 1989, 235). The men's verbal assent in response to the question of whether everyone has "joined" is such an example. But the physical acts of unity that constitute "illocution" in god ceremonial rituals, unlike like Baptizing or naming, do not endure beyond the ceremonial time frame—unity is fleeting, lying in the actions themselves. Kotas hope these acts of coming together will have positive perlocutionary consequences (see Tambiah 1981, 128)—if not continuing to stimulate moral behavior, at least these acts may attract god's kind glance.
10. Mandelbaum (1954) provides an analysis of the diverse meanings of the dry funeral as it was performed and interpreted by Kotas of Kolmēl in the 1930s and 1940s. The following summaries of the two funerals draw from Wolf (1997a), which contains an outline of the *varldāv* and a detailed description of the Kota green funeral in historical and comparative perspectives.
11. Kotas deploy a proverb to sting those who defer helping a friend in need: *ān tatōnām vāyk kaj aṭlkm valārī*? "Would you also not come to pour barley broth in my mouth when I am dying?"
12. This combination of this grass and dung is used in a number of contexts and seems in each case to ward off the evil eye.
13. A Kota woman was impregnated by a man of the Gollan caste and, at first, outcasted. Later the new family was incorporated into the village but spatially segregated in this new middle *kēr*.
14. This mirrors the *devr* fires, in which the "great" divine fire is small while the less sacred but physically larger fire is used for warming instruments and dancing.
15. Note again the god ceremonial parallel, in which the temple pillar is rubbed with clarified butter after the coin offerings are removed.
16. The morpheme *gūc* in this tune name means "to join or come together"; it is the same term included in the name for the first dance, the "leg joining dance" (*kāl gūc āṭ*) and it is also cognate with *kūṭm*, the village council.
17. Literally, "saying *gaṛum gaṛum gaṛum*"; see photo section.
18. "Breast clutching" probably refers to beating the chest in sorrow; the boys are analogous to the *tic pac mog* ("fire-grasping boy").

19. See Wolf (1997b, 266–7; 287) for a discussion of a dispute over where the body of a young girl who had died should be cremated, and the *ātḷ* S. Raman's father Tūj composed about it. The story concerns both changing attitudes toward cow sacrifice and the ways in which *kēr* identity is articulated in locational relationships during the funeral.
20. In former times, the jewelry was actually melted in the green-funeral fire. These remnants, plus whatever the widow began wearing after that time, were merely exposed to this *varldāv* fire. The action is called *kaṇycd*, grammatically a causative of the verb "to see" but used, as far as I know, only in this context.
21. The ritualists' food remains separate, but is cooked in the same general vicinity, and then returned to the ritualists.
22. The quote is an excerpt from Michael Herzfeld's criticism of anthropologists who rightly rejected the "timeless perfections of structuralism," while failing to take account of the "very similar . . . models entertained and used by social actors in many societies" (1990, 305).
23. Even though the dry funeral is a moral bridge through which the village moves from "death" to "god," it and the green funeral are both nominally kinds of *tāv* and in that sense belong to the same category.
24. See discussion of "human pasts" associated with remembrances of the dead in Wolf (2000/2001).

Chapter 8

1. See also Stubley, who describes the "experience of self" in certain kinds of musical activities as an "identity in the making" (1998, 98).
2. See also Christopher Crocker's elucidation of Bororo culture through two indigenous concepts: a principle of timeless identity (*aroe*) and a principle of mutability (*bope*) (Crocker 1977).
3. Like Bourdieu's *habitus*, such models could be regarded as a set of "transposable dispositions" which function as "structuring structures" (1989, 72).
4. The spatiotemporal form is labeled "(ideationally centripetal)" because these performers index the spatial constructs that are central to them, but they do not (necessarily) physically move towards the village or the forest while playing at festivals or public displays.
5. I should emphasize, though, that Bergson viewed *duration* as inner experience and *representation* of time as space; hence the successive strokes of a bell could be experienced durationally in the manner of a qualitative whole; such strokes were not for him essentially spatial unless they were "stripped of their qualities" and counted in terms of the homogeneous intervals they marked (Bergson 2001 [1913], 86–7; see also 108–9; and on strokes of the clock, 127).

6. Schutz wrote, for instance, that the listener "participates with quasi simultaneity" in the composer's "stream of consciousness by performing with him step by step the ongoing articulation of his musical thought" (1977, 114).
7. See also Gell (1992), who argues strongly against the notion that different kinds of time exist.
8. "Retention," a term from Husserlian phenomenology (Husserl 1964), refers to holding a previously occurring event in one's consciousness. See Berger for an excellent application of the concept to a musical case study (1997, 470 ff.).
9. I quote Harris Berger, who attempts to get at more refined, individual levels of perception. He shows how the study of musical perception as "practice" can reveal insight into musical structure (1997, 466–7).
10. "[If] Ziats [a Heavy Metal drummer] . . . wanted to get into the smooth grooving feeling of the part . . . he would focus on the flow of sixteenth notes . . .; however, if the band was not tightly coordinated with the drums or his time was especially poor, he would focus on the quarter notes . . .; if the band was well coordinated and he wanted to connect with the audience, he could focus on the beats that they heard most strongly—two and four" (1997, 476).
11. I borrow here from Michael Herzfeld's concept of "social poetics" (1997, 143; 1985).
12. The German philosopher Edmund Husserl (1859–1938) used perception of melody to discuss distinctions in levels of time-consciousness: a melody exhibits its own succession; when we perceive this succession, our mind follows the movement of the melody in the manner of a "flow of consciousness." At the same time, at a deeper level, we are aware that our consciousness is flowing (Husserl 1964, 23). For Husserl, the data of phenomenological investigation should not be what he called "world-time," but rather how time and duration appear to be real to the perceiver. His argument that this "*immanent* time of the flow of consciousness" exists rests on the idea of a still deeper consciousness "that permits even our mental acts to be experienced as temporal" (Sokolowski 1995, 350).
13. I regard the former not as "kinds of time," but as musical patterns and the latter as categories through which Sufi thinkers have proposed differences in human experience. But terminology notwithstanding, Qureshi provides an innovative suggestion as to how these layers of temporal process/representation are related in the South Asian Sufi context.
14. Compare with Catherine Ellis's description of Pitjantjatjara music, whose most important structural feature "is its capacity for expansion and contraction of formal units within established boundaries" (Ellis 1985, 84).
15. Words spoken by the diviner during possession and certain formulaic words of prayer invoking god are both called by the same term, *vākm*, perhaps instantiating the ideal merging of god and human at those moments.

16. Sulli explained the phrase in terms of generational boundaries: men and women of different generations (determined by classification, not age) are proscribed from engaging in sex with one another (Emeneau 1944–6, 4: 288–9).
17. I use the term "root metaphor" in Ortner's sense (1973, 1340 ff.) as a type of "elaborating symbol." The term was introduced by Stephen Pepper (1942).
18. The name Bacava relates it to the 12th century founder of the Lingayat, Śiva-worshipping Hindu creed in Karnataka.

References

Asad, Talal. 1993. *Genealogies of religion: Discipline and reasons of power in Christianity and Islam.* Baltimore: The John Hopkins University Press.

Austin, J.L. 1989. *Philosophical papers.* Edited by J.O. Urmson and G.J. Warnock. 3rd edition. Oxford: Oxford University Press.

Babb, Lawrence A. 1981. Glancing: Visual interaction in Hinduism. *Journal of Anthropological Research* 37(4): 387–401.

Babiracki, Carol. 1991. Musical and cultural interaction in tribal India: The "karam" repertory of the Mundas of Chotanagpur. Ph.D. dissertation, School of Music, University of Illinois at Urbana-Champaign.

———. 2000/2001. 'Saved by dance': The movement for autonomy in Jharkhand. *Asian Music* 32(1): 35–58.

Bakan, Michael B. 1999. *Music of death and new creation: Experiences in the world of Balinese gamelan beleganjur.* Chicago: University of Chicago Press.

Bakker, Hans, editor. 1990. *The history of sacred places in India as reflected in traditional literature.* Papers on pilgrimage in South Asia. Vol. III, Panels of the VIIth World Sanskrit Conference. Leiden: E.J. Brill.

Barthes, Roland. 1977. The grain of the voice. In *Image, music, text,* 170–89, translated by Stephen Heath. New York: Hill and Wang.

Becker, Judith and Alton. 1981. A musical icon: Power and meaning in Javanese gamelan music. In *The sign in music and literature*, 203–15, edited by W. Steiner. Austin: University of Texas Press.

Berger, Harris M. 1997. The practice of perception: Multi-functionality and time in the musical experiences of a heavy metal drummer. *Ethnomusicology* 41(5): 464–88.

Bergson, Henri. 1965. *Duration and simultaneity, with reference to Einstein's theory*, translated by Leon Jacobson. Indianapolis: the Bobbs-Merril Company, Inc. (originally published as *Durée et simultanéité* in 1922).

———. 2001 [1913]. *Time and free will.* Reprint of 3rd edition. Mineola, New York: Dover Publications, Inc.

Bharucha, Jamshed J. 1996. Melodic anchoring. *Music Perception* 13(3): 383–400.

Bird-David, Nurit. 1997. The Nilgiri tribal system: A view from below. In *Blue mountains revisited: Cultural studies on the Nilgiris*, 5–22, edited by Paul Hockings. Delhi: Oxford University Press.

Blasco, Françoise and G. Thanikaimoni. 1974. Late quaternary vegetational history of southern region. In *Aspects and appraisal of Indian paleobotany*, 632–43, edited by Krishna Rajarat Surange, Rajendra Nath Lakhanpal, and D.C. Bhardwaj. Lucknow: Birbal Sahni Institute. (Cited in Lergerke and Blasco 1989, 62)

Blum, Stephen. 1996. Musical questions and answers in Iranian Xorāsān. *EM: Annuario degli Archivi di etnomusicologia dell'Accademia di Santa Cecilia* 4: 145–63.

———. 2004. L'acte musical: éléments d'analyse. *L'Homme: Review Française d'Anthropologie* no. 171–2: 231–48.

Bourdieu, Pierre. 1989. *Outline of a theory of practice.* Translated by Richard Nice. Reprint. Cambridge: Cambridge University Press.

———. 1990. *The logic of practice.* Translated by Richard Nice. Stanford: Stanford University Press.

Brăiloiu, Constantin. 1984. *Problems of ethnomusicology.* Cambridge: Cambridge University Press.

Buckley, Thomas and Alma Gottlieb. 1988. A critical appraisal of theories of menstrual symbolism. In *Blood magic: The anthropology of menstruation*, 3–50, edited by Thomas Buckley and Alma Gottlieb. Berkeley: University of California Press.

Burrow, T. and M.B. Emeneau. 1984. *A Dravidian etymological dictionary* [DEDR]. 2nd edition. Oxford: Clarendon Press.

Carter, Paul. 1987. *The road to botany bay: An essay in spatial history.* London: Faber and Faber (cited in Hirsch 1995.)

Casey, Edward S. 1996. How to get from space to place in a fairly short stretch of time: Phenomenological prolegomena. In *Senses of place*,

13–52, edited by Steven Feld and Keith H. Basso. Santa Fe: School for American Research Press.

Certeau, Michel de. 1984. *The practice of everyday life*. Translated by Steven Rendall. Berkeley: University of California Press.

Clayton, Martin. 2000. *Time in Indian music*. Oxford: Oxford University Press.

Cohen, Judah M. 2002. Becoming a Reform Jewish cantor: A study in cultural investment. Ph. D. Dissertation, Department of Music, Harvard University.

Cohn, Bernard S. 1987a. African models and Indian histories. In *An anthropologist among the historians and other essays*, 200–23, by Bernard S. Cohn. New York: Oxford University Press.

———. 1987b. The census, social structure and objectification in south Asia. In *An anthropologist among the historians and other essays*, 224–54, by Bernard S. Cohn. New York: Oxford University Press.

Crocker, J. Christopher. 1977. The mirrored self: Identity and ritual inversion among the Eastern Bororo. *Ethnology: An international journal of cultural and social anthropology* 16(2): 129–45.

Csikszentmihalyi, Mihaly. 1991. *Flow: The psychology of optimal experience*. New York: Harper Perennial.

Daniel, E. Valentine. 1984. *Fluid signs: Being a person the Tamil way*. Berkeley: University of California Press.

DEDR (see Burrow and Emeneau 1984)

Douglas, Mary. 1970. *Natural symbols: Explorations in cosmology*. London: Barrie and Rockliff, the Cresset Press.

———. 1999. Self-evidence. In *Implicit meanings: Selected essays in anthropology*, 252–83. 2nd edition. London: Routledge.

Dournon, Genevieve. 1980. *Inde Musique Tribale du Bastar*. Le Chant du Monde LDX 74736.

Duncan, David Ewing. 1998. *Calendar: Humanity's epic struggle to determine a true and accurate year*. New York: Avon Books, Inc.

Durkheim, Emile. 1915. *The elementary forms of the religious life*. Translated by J. Swain. New York: The Free Press.

———. 1933. *The division of labor in society*. Translated by G. Simpson. New York: Free Press.

Eichinger Ferro-Luzzi, Gabriella. 1987. *The self-milking cow and the bleeding liṅgam: Criss-cross of motifs in Indian temple legends*. Wiesbaden: Harrassowitz.

Eck, Diana L. 1998. *Darśan: Seeing the divine image in India*. 3rd edition. New York: Columbia University Press.

Ekeh, Peter P. 1990. Social anthropology and two contrasting uses of tribalism in Africa. *Comparative Studies in Society and History* 32(4): 660–700.

Ellis, Catherine. 1985. The pitjantjara musical system. In *Aboriginal music: Education for living*. Queensland: University of Queensland Press.

Emeneau, Murray B. 1937–8. Ritual games of the Kotas. *Bulletin of the Sri Rama Varma Research Institute* 5:114–22; 6:1–6.

———. 1944–6. *Kota texts*. 4 Volumes. Berkeley: University of California Press.

———. 1967. The South Dravidian languages. *Journal of the American Oriental Society* 67(4): 365–412.

———. 1971. *Toda songs*. Oxford: Clarendon Press.

———. 1987. The right hand is the "eating hand": An Indian areal linguistic inquiry. In *Dimensions of social life: Essays in honor of David G. Mandelbaum*, 263–73, edited by Paul Hockings. Berlin: Mouton de Gruyter.

———. 1989. The languages of the Nilgiris. In *Blue mountains: The ethnography and biogeography of a south Indian region*, 133–43, edited by Paul Hockings. Delhi: Oxford University Press.

———. n.d. Unpublished Kota vocabulary notes from 1936–8 fieldwork. [EVS]. Photocopy.

———, and Thomas Burrow. 1962. *Dravidian borrowings from Indo-Aryan*. [DBIA]. University of California publications in linguistics 26. Berkeley: University of California Press.

EVS. See Emeneau n.d.

Falk, N. 1973. Wilderness and kingship in ancient south Asia. *History of Religions* 13(1): 1–15. (Cited in Thapar 2001, 6n. 18)

Feld, Steven. 1994. Aesthetics as iconicity of style (uptown title); or (downtown title) "Lift-up-over sounding:" Getting into the Kaluli groove. In *Music grooves: Essays and dialogues*, 109–50, by Charles Keil and Steven Feld. Chicago: University of Chicago Press.

———. 1996. Waterfalls of song: An acoustemology of place resounding in Bosavi, Papua New Guinea. In *Senses of place*, 91–135, edited by S. Feld and K. Basso. Santa Fe: School of American Research Press.

Feld, Steven and Aaron Fox. 1994. Music and language. *Annual Review of Anthropology* 23:25–53.

Feld, Steven and Keith H. Basso, editors. 1996. *Senses of place*. Santa Fe: School of American Research Press.

Feldhaus, Anne. 1990. The image of the forest in the *Māhātmya*s of the rivers of the Deccan. In *The history of sacred places in India as reflected in traditional literature*. Papers on pilgrimage in South Asia, edited by Hans Bakker. Vol. III, Panels of the VIIth World Sanskrit Conference. Leiden: E.J. Brill

———. 1995. *Water and womanhood: Religious meanings of rivers in Maharashtra*. New York: Oxford University Press, 1995.

Fenicio, Giacomo. 1906 [1603]. Letters on the "Mission of Todamala," translated by A. d'Alberti. In *The Todas*, 719–30, by W.H.R. Rivers. London: Macmillan.

Fernandez, James. 1966. Unbelievably subtle words: Representation and integration in the sermons of an African reformative cult. *History of Religions* 6(1): 43–69.

———. 1986a. The mission of metaphor in expressive culture. In *Persuasions and performances: The play of tropes in culture*, 28–70. Bloomington: Indiana University Press.

———. 1986b. *Persuasions and performances: The play of tropes in culture*. Bloomington: Indiana University Press.

Flood, Gavin. 1996. *An introduction to Hinduism*. Cambridge: Cambridge University Press.

Francis, W. 1908. *The Nilgiris*. [Gazetteer of the Nilgiri District]. Madras district gazetteer. Madras: Printed by the Superintendent Government Press.

Friedson, Steven. 1996. *Dancing prophets: Musical experience in Tumbuku healing*. Chicago: University of Chicago Press.

Fuller, Christopher J. 1989. Misconceiving the grain heap: A critique of the concept of the Indian jajmani system. In *Money and the morality of exchange*, 33–63, edited by J. Parry and M. Bloch. Cambridge: Cambridge University Press.

Gell, Alfred. 1979. The Umeda language poem. *Canberra Anthropology* 2(1): 44–62. Cited in Gell 1995.

———. 1992. *The anthropology of time: Cultural constructions of temporal maps and images*. Oxford: Berg.

———. 1995. The language of the forest: Landscape and phonological iconism in Umeda. In *The anthropology of landscape: Perspectives on place and space,* 232–54, edited by Eric Hirsch and Michael O'Hanlon. Oxford: Clarendon Press.

Gottlieb, Alma. 1992. *Under the Kapok tree: Identity and difference in Beng thought.* Bloomington: Indiana University Press.

Hallowell, Alfred Irving. 1955 [1937]. Temporal orientation in Western civilization and in a pre-literate society. In *Culture and experience,* 216–35. Philadelphia: University of Pennsylvania Press.

Hanks, William F. 1990. *Referential practice: Language and lived space among the Maya.* Chicago: University of Chicago Press.

Harkness, Henry. 1832. A description of a singular aboriginal race inhabiting the summit of the Neilgherry Hills, or Blue Mountains of Coimbatoor, in the southern peninsula of India. London: Smith, Elder, and Co.

Herzfeld, Michael. 1981. Performative categories and symbols of passage in rural Greece. *Journal of American Folklore* 94(371): 44–57.

———. 1985. *The poetics of manhood: Contest and identity in a Cretan mountain village.* Princeton: Princeton University Press.

———. 1990. Pride and perjury: Time and the oath in the mountain villages of Crete. *Man,* new series 25(2): 305–22.

———. 1991. *A place in history: Social and monumental time in a Cretan town.* Princeton: Princeton University Press.

———. 1996. In defiance of destiny. In *Things as they are: New directions in phenomenological anthropology,* 149–68, edited by Michael Jackson. Bloomington: Indiana University Press.

———. 1997. *Cultural intimacy: Social poetics in the nation-state.* New York: Routledge.

Hirsch, Eric. 1995. Introduction. In *The anthropology of landscape: Perspectives on place and space,* 1–30, edited by Eric Hirsch and Michael O'Hanlon. Oxford: Clarendon Press.

Hockings, Paul E. 1997. Introduction. *Blue Mountains revisited: Cultural studies on the Nilgiris,* 1–4, edited by Paul Hockings. Delhi: Oxford University Press.

———. 2001. Mortuary ritual of the Badagas of southern India. *Fieldiana, Anthropology,* new series 32: vii–72. Chicago: Field Museum of Natural History

Hoskins, Janet. 1993. *The play of time: Kodi perspectives on calendars, history, and exchange*. Berkeley: University of California Press.

Hubert, Henri. 1905. Étude sommaire de la représentation du temps dans la religion et la magie. *École Pratique des hautes Études, section des sciences religieuses,* 1–39. Paris: Imprimerie.

———. 1999. Essay on time: A brief study of the representation of time in religion and magic. Edited by Robert Parkin and translated by Robert Parkin and Jacqueline Redding. Oxford: Durkheim Press.

Humphrey, Caroline. 1995. Chiefly and shamanist landscapes in Mongolia. In *The anthropology of landscape: Perspectives on place and space,* 135–62, edited by Eric Hirsch and Michael O'Hanlon. Oxford: Clarendon Press.

Hunter, William Wilson. 1886. *Imperial Gazetteer of India*. 2nd edition. 14 volumes. London: Trübner & Co.

Husserl, Edmund. 1964. *The phenomenology of internal time-consciousness*, edited by M. Heidegger, and translated by J.S. Churchill. Bloomington: Indiana University Press.

Jackson, Michael. 1996. Introduction: Phenomenology, radical empiricism, and anthropological critique. In *Things as they are: New directions in phenomenological anthropology*, edited by Michael Jackson. Bloomington: Indiana University Press.

Jagadisa Ayyar, P. V. 1985. *South Indian customs*. Reprint. (Originally published, 1925.) New Delhi: Asian Educational Services.

Jagor, Fedor. 1914. Aus Fedor Jagor's Nachlass, mit Unterstützung der Jagor-Stiftung, herausgegeben von der Berliner Gesellschaft für Anthropologie, Ethnologie und Urgeschichte unter Leitung von Albert Grüwedel. Berlin: Dietrich Reimer (Ernst Vohsen)

Keil, Charles and Steven Feld. 1994. *Music grooves: Essays and dialogues*. Chicago: University of Chicago Press.

Kivy, Peter. 1989. *Sound sentiment: An essay on the musical emotions, including the complete text of* The Corded Shell. Philadelphia: Temple University Press.

Knight, Roderic. 1983. *Tribal music of India: The Muria and Maria Gonds of Madhya Pradesh.* Folkways FE 4028.

———. 1993. *Baiga dances*. Video and notes. Original Music OMV007.

Kuper, Adam. 1988. *The invention of primitive society: Transformations of an illusion*. London: Routledge.

Lengerke, Hans J. von and Françoise Blasco. 1989. The Nilgiri environment. In *Blue mountains: The ethnography and biogeography of a South Indian region*, 20–78, edited by Paul Hockings. Delhi: Oxford University Press.

Mahias, Marie-Claude. 1997. The construction of the Nilgiris as a "tribal sanctuary." In *Blue mountains revisited: Cultural studies on the Nilgiris*, 316–34, edited by Paul Hockings. Delhi: Oxford University Press.

Mandelbaum, David G. 1937–8 (and *passim*) Series 8. The David G. Mandelbaum Papers. BANC MSS 89/129 cz, The Bancroft Library, University of California, Berkeley.

———. 1938. *India, Kota and Toda, 1938, sound recording*. 80 cylinders : 125 rpm, coarse groove; 2 1/8 in. x 4 1/4 in. + documentation. Archives of Traditional Music, Indiana University, Bloomington.

———. 1939a. Agricultural ceremonies among three tribes of Travancore. *Ethnos* 4:114–28.

———. 1939b. The Jewish way of life in Cochin. *Jewish Social Studies* 1:423–60.

———. 1954. Form, variation, and meaning of a ceremony. In *Method and perspective in anthropology: Papers in honor of Wilson D. Wallis*, 60–102, edited by Robert F. Spencer. Minneapolis: The University of Minnesota Press.

———. 1960. A reformer of his people. In *In the company of man: Twenty portraits by anthropologists*, 274–308, edited by J. Casagrande. New York: Harper.

———. 1970–2. *Society in India*. 2 volumes. Berkeley: University of California Press.

Marriott, McKim. 1989. Constructing an Indian ethnosociology. *Contributions to Indian Sociology*, new series 23(1): 1–39.

McLennan, J. M. 1865. *Primitive marriage: An inquiry into the origin of the form of capture in marriage ceremonies*. Edinburgh: Black. (Cited in Kuper 1988.)

Mehta, Piarey Lal. 1991. *Constitutional protection to scheduled tribes in India: In retrospect and prospects*. Delhi: H.K. Publishers and Distributors.

Mines, Diane Paull. 1995. Making and remaking the village: The pragmatics of social life in rural Tamilnadu. Ph. D. dissertation, department of Anthropology, University of Chicago.

Monier-Williams, Monier. 1990. *A Sanskrit-English Dictionary*. Reprint. Delhi: Motilal Banarsidass Publishers.

Morphy, Howard. 1995. Landscape and the reproduction of the ancestral past. In *The anthropology of landscape: Perspectives on place and space,* 184–209, edited by Eric Hirsch and Michael O'Hanlon. Oxford: Clarendon Press.

Munn, Nancy D. 1974. Symbolism in a ritual context: Aspects of symbolic action. In *Handbook of social and cultural anthropology*, 579–612, edited by J. J. Honigman. New York: Rand McNally.

———. 1986. *The fame of Gawa: A symbolic study of value transformation in a Massim (Papua New Guinea) society.* Durham: Duke University Press.

———. 1992. The cultural anthropology of time: A critical essay. *Annual Review of Anthropology* 21:93–123.

Needham, Rodney. 1975. Polythetic classification: Convergence and consequences. *Man*, new series 10:349–69.

OED. Oxford English Dictionary. Online edition.

O'Flaherty, Wendy Doniger, editor. 1983. *Karma and rebirth in classical Indian traditions*. Indian edition. New Delhi: Motilal Banarsidass.

Ortner, Sherry B. 1973. On key symbols. *American Anthropologist* 75(5): 1338–46.

Östör, Ákos. 1991. Cyclical time: Durgāpūjā in Bengal. In *Religion in India*, 176–98, edited by T. N. Madan. Delhi: Oxford University Press.

Panikkar, T. K. Gopal. 1983 [1900]. *Malabar and its folk*. Reprint. New Delhi: Asian Educational Services.

Peirce, Charles Sanders. 1955. Logic as semiotic: The theory of signs. In *Philosophical writings of Peirce*, 98–119, edited by Justus Buchler. New York: Dover.

———. 1960. *Collected papers of Charles Sanders Peirce*. 2 volumes. Cambridge, MA.: Harvard University Press.

Pepper, Stephen. 1942. *World hypotheses: A study in evidence*. Berkeley, Los Angeles: University of California Press (cited in Ortner 1973).

Pollock, Sheldon. 1989. The idea of *śāstra* in traditional India. In *Shastric traditions in Indian arts,* 17–26, edited by A.L. Dallapiccola and S. Zingel-Avé Lallemant. Wiesbaden: Steiner. Beiträge zur Südasien-forschung.

Powers, Harold. 1980. India, subcontinent of, I, II. In *The New Grove dictionary of music and musicians*, edited by Stanley Sadie. London: Macmillan.

———. 1986. Rhythm. *The new Harvard dictionary of music*, edited by Don M. Randel. Cambridge: The Belknap Press of Harvard University Press.

Price, John Frederick, Sir. 1908. *Ootacamund: A history*. Madras: The Superintendent, Government Press.

Qureshi, Regula. 1994. Exploring time cross-culturally: Ideology and performance of time in the Sufi *Qawwālī*. *The Journal of Musicology* 12(4): 491–528.

Raheja, Gloria Goodwin. 1988. *The poison in the gift: Ritual, prestation, and the dominant caste in a north Indian village*. Chicago: University of Chicago Press.

Ram, Kalpana. 1991. *Mukkuvar women: Gender, hegemony and capitalist transformation in a south Indian fishing community*. Asian Studies Association of Australia, women in Asia publication series. London: Zed.

Ramanujan, A.K., translator. 1967. *The interior landscape: Love poems from a classical Tamil anthology*. Bloomington: Indiana University Press.

———. 1985. Afterword. In *Poems of love and war from the Eight Anthologies and the Ten Long Poems of classical Tamil*, tr. A.K. Ramanujan. New York: Columbia University Press/UNESCO.

Reddy, William M. 2001. *The navigation of feeling: A framework for the history of the emotions*. Cambridge: Cambridge University Press.

Rice, Timothy. 1984. *May it fill your soul: Experiencing Bulgarian music*. Chicago: University of Chicago Press.

Rivers,William Halse Rivers. 1906. *The Todas*. London: Macmillan.

Robertson, Carol E. 1979. "Pulling the ancestors": Performance practice and praxis in Mapuche ordering. *Ethnomusicology* 23(3): 395–416

Rowell, Lewis. 1981. The creation of audible time. In *The study of time*, 198–210. Edited by J.T. Fraser, N. Lawrence, and D. Park. New York: Springer-Verlag.

———. 1982. Abhinavagupta, Augustine, time and music. *Journal of the Indian Musicological Society* 13(2): 18–36.

Sahlins, Marshall. 1985. *Islands of history*. Chicago: University of Chicago Press.

Schutz, Alfred. 1977. Making music together: A study in social relationship. In *Symbolic anthropology: A reader in the study of symbols and meanings*, 106–19, edited by J. Dolgin, D. Kemnitzer, and D. Schneider. New York: Columbia University Press.

Smith, Barbara Herrnstein. 1968. *Poetic closure: A study of how poems end.* Chicago: The University of Chicago Press.

Sokolowski, Robert. 1995. Husserl, Edmund. In *The Cambridge dictionary of philosophy,* 347–50, edited by Robert Audi. Cambridge: Cambridge University Press.

Stubley, Eleanor V. 1998. Being in the body, being in the sound: A tale of modulating identities and lost potential. *Journal of Aesthetic Education* 32(4): 93–105.

Stutley, Margaret and James Stutley. 1984. *Harper's dictionary of Hinduism: Its mythology, folklore, philosophy, literature, and history.* San Francisco: Harper and Row, Publishers.

Tambiah, Stanley. 1981. A performative approach to ritual. *Proceedings of the British Academy* 65: 113–69.

——— 1985a. On flying witches and flying canoes: The coding of male and female values. In *Culture, thought, and social action: An anthropological perspective*, 287–315. Cambridge, MA: Harvard University Press.

——— 1985b. From varna to caste through mixed unions. In *Culture, thought, and social action: An anthropological perspective*, 212–51. Cambridge, MA: Harvard University Press.

Tamil Lexicon. [TL]. 1982. 6 volumes and supplement. Madras: University of Madras.

Thani Nayagam, Xavier S. 1966. *Landscape and poetry: A study of nature in classical Tamil poetry*. London: Asia Publishing House.

Thapar, Romila. 2001. Perceiving the forest: Early India. *Studies in History,* new series 17(1): 1–16. New Delhi: Sage Publications.

Thurston, Edgar. 1912. Omens and superstitions of southern India. London: T. Fisher Unwin.

Thurston, Edgar and K. Rangachari. 1909. *Castes and tribes of Southern India*. Madras: Government Press.

Toren, Christina. 1995. Seeing the ancestral sites: Transformations in Fijian notions of the land. In *The anthropology of landscape: Perspectives on place and space,* 163–83, edited by Eric Hirsch and Michael O'Hanlon. Oxford: Clarendon Press.

Turino, Thomas. 1999. Signs of imagination, identity, and experience: A Peircian semiotic theory for music. *Ethnomusicology* 43(2): 221–55.

Tylor, Edward Burnett. 1866. The religion of savages. *The Fortnightly Review* 6: 71–86. (Cited in Kuper 1988.)

Urban, Greg. 1988. Ritual wailing in Amerindian Brazil. *American Anthropologist,* new series 90(2): 385–400.

Verghese, Isaac. 1974. The Kota (reprint). Bulletin of the Anthropological Survey of India 18(2): 103–82.

Wade, Bonnie C. 1980. India, subcontinent of, section VI. In *The New Grove dictionary of music and musicians*, edited by Stanley Sadie. London: Macmillan.

———. 2000. Visual sources. In *The Garland encyclopedia of world music, Volume 5, South Asia: The Indian subcontinent*, 298–318, edited by Alison Arnold. New York: Garland Publishing, Inc.

Williams, Raymond. 1973. *The country and the city.* London: Chatto and Windus. (Cited in Hirsch 1995.)

Wolf, Richard K. 1997a. Of god and death: Music and ritual in everyday life. A musical ethnography of the Kotas of south India. Ph. D. dissertation, School of Music, University of Illinois at Urbana-Champaign.

———. 1997b. Rain, god, and unity among the Kotas. In *Blue mountains revisited: Cultural studies on the Nilgiri hills*, 231–92, edited by Paul Hockings. Delhi: Oxford University Press.

———. 2000/2001a. Three perspectives on music and the idea of tribe in India. *Asian Music* 32(1): 5–34.

———. 2000/2001b. Mourning songs and human pasts among the Kotas of south India. *Asian Music* 32(1): 141–83.

———. 2001. Emotional dimensions of ritual music among the Kotas, a south Indian tribe. *Ethnomusicology* 45(3): 379–422.

———. *ca.* 2006. Music and performance. In *Encyclopedia of the Nilgiri Hills*, edited by Paul Hockings. New Delhi: Manohar Books; Walnut Creek, Cal.: AltaMira Press.

Zimmer, Heinrich. 1951. *Philosophies of India*, edited by Joseph Campbell. Princeton: Princeton University Press.

Zvelebil, Kamil. 1979–82. *The Irula (Erla) language*. 3 parts. Wiesbaden: Otto Harrassowitz.

Main Index

(Italics denote map, figure, and illustration. IMDE denotes Index of Music and Dance Entries. NI denotes Name Index)

action
  constituting world through, 245n. 9 (24)
  "ideas" *versus*, 79, *79*
  models pertaining to, 4, 20, *75*, *79*, 221
    categories correlated with music/dance, *222–3*, 225
  organization of, 2, 3, 4, 24, 221
  "physical actions," *75*, 76, 78, *79*
    movement of musicians, 21
  place and, 73, 74, 78, 94, 95, 135, 162
  "space" and, 78
ādivāsī. *See* tribe
affect. *See* emotion
age
  affecting song rendition, 63, 66
  children officiate at death ceremonies, 91
  factor in participation, 170, 192, 193, 194
agriculture, spatiotemporal factors related to, 107, 139
aksak (Turkish "limping" rhythms), 49, 50
ancestors. *See* spirit (*āyv*)
anchoring. *See* anchor points
anchor points. *See also* reference points; *see also* IMDE
  action and movement
    arrivals, as, 5, 6, 21, 65, 68
    anticipation, 7, 138, 150, 160
    attraction to a spot, 138
    direction of orientation, 72, 133–5
    milking, 65
    playing ritual games, 182
    ritual preparation, 7, 160
  ceremonies, in, 142–54, 196, *222–3*
  definition of, 4, 5, 134, 136
  identity/subjectivity and, 4, 5, 135, *222–3*
    Kota domain, of, 137
    tribals in the nation state, 15
  kinds of
    cow's footprint, 72, 232
    eclipse, 161
    fire, 99, 206
    houses, 135–6
    natural, 139
    places as, 79, 135, 138
    ships' anchors and captains, 134
    temple, 72, 94, 191, 192
  lack of, 139
  metaphorical aspects, 5, 134–42
  necessity of, 22, 141
    resolving joined, flexible structures, 139

Index of Music and Dance Entries

MI = main index

Name Index

Musical Examples on CD

All recordings by Richard K. Wolf
unless otherwise noted

(1) *Guṛy terdd koḷ* (temple-opening tune) as rendered by Kaṇṇan and one other man for the "cane and bamboo ritual" in Kolmēl, Jan., 2001. Exhibits relatively flexible points of melodic return compared with recordings of K. Puccan, especially from the 1970s. (see 2, 47, 129, 143, 193)

(2) "Lamp, lamp, where are you?" Women singing at god ceremony, Kolmēl, Jan. 12, 2001. (see 7, 52, 87)

(3) High-pitch tremolo, excerpt, K. Puccan and Veḷn rendering the *guṛy terdd koḷ,* 1970s. (see 8, 194)

(4) "Bier lighting tune" (*tic iṭ koḷ*), Feb. 4, 1992. (see 9, 175)

(5) *Nāṛ gūc koḷ* (*veyḷ mīn koḷ,* morning star tune), rendered on *koḷ* by S. Raman, dry funeral, Mēnāṛ, Jan. 24, 1992. (see 9, 208)

(6) *Vatm iṭ koḷ* (millet pouring tune), demonstrated by K. Puccan on the *koḷ*, Dec. 31, 1991. (see 9, 179, 209)

(7) "En aṇṇe aṇṇe" (my older brother), an *āṭḷ* rendered by V. Mathi, May 27, 1992. (see 52)

(8) *Guṛy terdd koḷ* (temple opening tune) as rendered by K. Puccan and Veḷn. Recorded by Dr P. Varadharajan, 1970s. See Fig. 10. (see 143)

(9) "En aṇ caḷo," rendered on *bugīr* by K. Mundan, June 8, 1992. See Fig. 8. (see 22, 51, 116, *118*)

(10) *Guṛy terdd koḷ* (temple opening tune) as rendered vocally by K. Puccan, Dec. 23, 1991. (see 22, 113, 143)

(11) *Koḷ* solo: *Kāl gūc āṭ* (leg joining dance). Fancy version played only

on the *pacāl*, demonstrated by K. Puccan, Dec. 23, 1991. (see 23, 71)

(12) Beṭṭa Kurumba instrumental music, with percussion equivalent of Kota *cādā dāk*. Madan, *koḷaḷ* (shawm); *tambaṭe* (frame drum), *davil* (cylinder drum). Recorded in Gudulur town, Nov. 1, 1992. Demo courtesy ACCORD (Action for Community Organisation, Rehabilitation and Development). (see 39)

(13) *Tiruganāṭ dāk*—a percussion pattern, presented here in conjunction with women's dance melody, god ceremony, Kolmēl, Jan. 8, 2001. See Fig. 3. (see 41, 43, 45, 47)

(14) *Koḷāḷ dāk*—a percussion pattern for non-Kota deities, performed here by Kurgōj musicians for goddess Sikkamman, Ooty, Aug. 12, 1991. (see 49)

(15) *Guṛy terdd koḷ* (temple opening tune) demonstrated by S. Raman, *koḷ, Kuy tēl* (forest), Oct. 31, 1992. (see 143, 247n. 11 (51))

(16) *Guṛy terdd koḷ* demonstrated by S. Raman, *pulāng* solo, Kolmēl, April 25, 1991. (see 143, 247n. 11 (51))

(17) *Pījl* (bamboo jew's harp) demonstrated by S. Cindamani, Jan. 15, 2001. (see 51)

(18) "Father, older brother, younger brother, listen!" God song composed and sung by S. Raman, Kolmēl, Aug. 8, 1992. (see 52, 54)

(19) "You, daughters of Kotas, stop crying!" Composed by A.K. Rangan, sung by P. Kamatn, Kolmēl, May, 1992. (see 57)

(20) "Kavdayō," *aṭḷ* rendered by R. Mathi, Kolmēl, May 1992. (see 52, 59–63, 255n. 9 (174))

(21) "They shot the hunting bow," god song sung by Pa. Mathi, Kolmēl, Dec. 28, 1991. (see 52)

(22) *Kalgūc āṭ koḷ* ("leg joining dance tune"). Ordinary version, with drummed accompaniment in *cādā dāk*, Kolmēl, Jan. 10, 1992. (see 71)

(23) "Stone field, thorn field, Kanm father," *āṭḷ* rendered by Pa. Mathi, Feb. 11, 1992. (see 52, 85–6, 256n. 9 (174))

(24) Sounds from the Kuytēl, a forest near Kolmēl, Oct. 31, 1992. (see 89)

(25) Duryodhana (R. Kamaṭn) doing bird and animal imitations and storytelling: (1) karvaky bird; (2a) crow (ill omen sound); (2b) ordinary sound; (3) owl, inauspicious sound (4) pemaṇḍvaky (bird,

auspicious sound); (4a) story of hunter and pemaṇḍvaky; (5a) dog bark (good sign); (5b) dog howl (bad sign), Jan. 2001. (see 89)

(26) "18 god-calling tune" (*padneṭ devr ātd koḷ*), in *tiruganāṭ dāk*, rendered on *koḷ* by K. Puccan and S. Raman, god ceremony, Kolmēl, Jan. 12, 1992. Note melodic similarity to "Little father god tune" (CD 39). (see 111, 179)

(27) "En aṉ caḷo," *āṭḷ* rendered by S. Cindamani, June 7, 1992. See Fig. 7. (see 52, 116, *117*, *121*, 122, 256n. 9 (174))

(28) Dr P. Varadharajan vocalizing drum sounds, Jan. 13, 2001. (see 126)

(29) *Guṛy terdd koḷ* rendered by Kaṇṇan and one other man, god ceremony, Kolmēl, Jan. 9, 2001. (see 129, 143)

(30) *Guṛy terdd koḷ* rendered by K. Puccan and S. Raman, god ceremony, Kolmēl, Jan. 12, 1992. (see 143)

(31) "āḷ āṛāde arvangāṛe," *āṭḷ* rendered by Māgāḷi, *mundkānōḷ* of Kināṛ village, May 3, 1991. (see 52)

(32) *Aṇviṛcd koḷ* (channel-clearing tune) recorded on wax cylinder by David G. Mandelbaum, May 1938 (Mandelbaum 1938). Note similarity to temple opening tune. (see 142, 143)

(33) The "hunting god tune" (*vēṭkār cōym koḷ)* rendered by K. Puccan and S. Raman, god ceremony, Kolmēl, Jan. 12, 1992. (see 151)

(34) A god tune from Kurgōj village, recorded by Nazir A. Jairazbhoy, April 14, 1975. (see 151)

(35) Transitions between tunes for first three men's dances on the *pacāl* during the god ceremony, Kolmēl, Jan. 13, 1992: *kālgūc āṭ*, *tiruganāṭ*, *cāda āṭ* (length of each tune shortened to highlight transitions). Note use of *kob* at the beginning. (see 152)

(36) Ragi harvest song in Badaga language sung and played instrumentally by Kotas. First played on *koḷ* by P. Kamaṭn as example of Kota women's dance tune in Ticgāṛ village; then words sung by P. Kamaṭn and Bēṛy Mathi. Laughing at the end due to Kamaṭn's choice of (possibly improvised) words, June, 1991.

(37) "Bacāna Bacavanīlo," one of the most common god songs, sung by women during the god ceremony, Kolmēl, Jan. 12, 2001. (see 52, 232)

(38) "Sixty cubit buffalo pen," *āṭḷ* rendered by Bēṛy Mathi, Aug. 10, 1991. (see *169*, 169–70)

(39) "Little father god tune" (*kunayṇōr koḷ*), in *cādā dāk*, rendered by K. Puccan and S. Raman, god ceremony, Kolmēl, Jan. 12, 1992. Note melodic similarity to "18 god-calling tune" (CD 26). (see 179)